FOCUS ON THE CHILD

Libraries, literacy and learning

**Writen and edited by
Judith Elkin and Ray Lonsdale**

**Library Association Publishing
London**

Published by
Library Association Publishing
7 Ridgmount Street
London WC1E 7AE

First published 1996

British Library Cataloguing in Publication Data
A catalogue record for this book is available from the British Library

ISBN 1-85604-109-3

Typeset from authors' disks in 11/13pt Elegant Garamond and Futura Extra Black by Library Association Publishing
Printed and made in Great Britain by Bookcraft (Bath) Ltd, Midsomer Norton, Avon

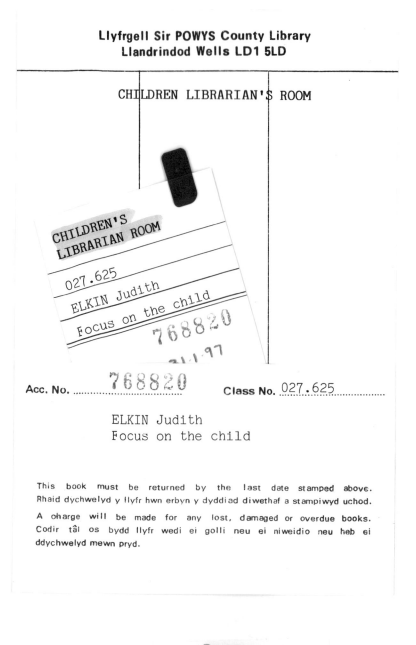

FOCUS ON THE CHILD

Libraries, literacy and learning

Dedicated to the memory of

Judith's mother,
Cicely May Atkin (1912–1996)

and Ray's father,
Ted Lonsdale (1914–1996)

Contents

List of contributors

Professor Judith Elkin is the Head of the School of Information Studies, University of Central England in Birmingham. She was previously Head of Library Services to Children and Young People, Birmingham Public Libraries. Judith is a member of the Library and Information Commission. She serves on The Library Association Council and is Secretary of BAILER Heads of Departments and Schools Committee. She has written and edited a number of children's books, including *The new golden land anthology*, *The Puffin book of twentieth century children's stories* and two anthologies of black and Asian poetry for children. She has also written the text for a number of children's picture books, including the award-winning *Nowhere to play* and *The Hiroshima story*. She was awarded the Eleanor Farjeon award by the Children's Book Circle of the Publishers Association in 1986 for 'contributions to the children's book world'.

Ray Lonsdale is a Senior Lecturer in the Department of Information and Library Studies at the University of Wales Aberystwyth, having previously been Assistant Principal Librarian for Education and Youth Services in Knowsley Metropolitan Library Service. Formerly Associate Editor of the *International review of children's literature and librarianship*, he currently edits *Youth library review*, has written extensively on children's libraries and is an officer on the national committee of the Youth Libraries Group of The Library Association. For the past 20 years, Ray has acted as an overseas consultant for the British Council, The World Bank, the Overseas Development Administration and various national governments in Europe, Africa, the Middle East and South East Asia. He has also run many training programmes in children's and school librarianship in the UK. He is co-organizer of the Arts Council/W. H. Smith Children's Literature Summer School.

Keith Barker is a librarian at Westhill College, Birmingham. Review Editor of *The school librarian* and former Chair of the Youth Libraries Group of The Library Association; he is co-organizer of the Arts Council Children's Literature Summer School. He is author of *In the realms of gold* and of monographs on Gillian Cross and Dick King-Smith, as well as editor of *Graphic account* and *Bridging the gap*. A contributor to *Twentieth century children's writers* and *International encyclopedia of children's literature*, he is also author of numerous articles and reviews.

Gayner Eyre is a chartered librarian currently working as the Administration/ Liaison Officer for the Department of Information and Library Studies, University of Wales Aberystwyth, where she was previously research assistant. She still teaches the school libraries and services to young people options. Previously Principal Librarian for Library Service to Young People at Sheffield Libraries and Information Services, she is currently completing a PhD with Sheffield University. In 1985 Gayner began a five year period as a committee member on the YLG National Committee and in 1991 was National Chair. From 1986 to 1991 she was Adviser on services to schools and young people to to the Association of Metropolitan District Chief Librarians.

Margaret Kinnell (Evans) is Professor of Information Studies and Head of the Department of Information and Library Studies at Loughborough University. Before becoming a university teacher she worked as a public librarian with Nottinghamshire County Libraries and has also run a bookselling business. She is currently engaged in projects on Internet provision for schools and the promotion of adult reading in public libraries. Recent titles for Library Association Publishing include editorship of *Managing library resources for schools* and of *Learning resources in schools*, the LA guidelines for school libraries.

Introduction

It is over 20 years since Janet Hill's *Children are people* was published. This is the only British book to have attempted an exploration of the broad conceptual and philosophical issues underlying the provision of library services to children and young people in the United Kingdom. Important though the work was, the intervening years have witnessed significant developments in the nature of library services to the young, developments which have had to accommodate new and powerful changes in education, technology and politics as well as the general social and cultural fabric of Britain. The concept of literacy, too, has broadened: the term now embraces dimensions such as visual, oral, aural and computer literacy – areas not previously considered in the context of library services to the young.

The purpose of this book is to provide a critical analysis of library services to young people in the UK, assessing the degree to which they are responding to the contemporary needs of the child and the forces of change presented by society. The book offers a broad conceptual framework and philosophical approach for students and practitioners alike.

The starting point for this approach is the child and the child's needs in the way of books and other materials to support literacy and learning.

Children are complex individuals growing up in a rapidly changing world. If books and literacy are so important for early development and lifelong learning, even in today's technological age, then access to the materials that bring that wealth of learning are critical. Early access to stories and to books is an essential part of the child's pre-reading experience and needs reinforcing as they become sophisticated readers, learners and thinkers. The role of libraries is paramount in supporting the child's reading and access to information and ensuring equitable access to all, regardless of age, gender, race, wealth, physical or intellectual ability or geographical location. Yet libraries of all kinds exist within the structure of their society: political, economic and social issues influence society and the way libraries can operate within it.

In addition to working with books, librarians need to be responding to the challenges brought about by the 'information age'. Media and technology impact hugely on the development of the child and have had a significant impact on publishing for children. Provision of multimedia, audiovisual and computer technology, in addition to the printed word, are the prerequisites for developing library services to children of the 21st century. Children's libraries now and in the future must have a remit to respond to established media and the emergence of new technologies both through its collections and its services

The book starts by looking at the child growing up in the UK today. Inevitably there is considerable complexity and diversity: children live and grow up in many different environments, cultures and family surroundings; their abilities, physical and intellectual, differ significantly as well as their personal likes and dislikes, pleasures and despairs. The premise is taken that reading and books play an important part in the child's personal development and education. Thus access to books through libraries and the role of libraries in supporting the child's learning and early literacy are seen as helpful in preparing children for life in an uncertain and ever-changing world.

Chapter 2 explores the critical role that the media play in shaping the social, emotional and intellectual development of the child as well as making an important contribution to the child's recreational needs.

Chapter 3 looks at the genesis of library services to children and places them in the context of the political, professional and education framework within which they developed and now operate. It looks at recent legislation which has affected children's library provision and introduces current guidelines and reports.

Chapter 4 takes this further by looking in some detail at the role of children's and school libraries and schools library services. It then explores the role of the professional librarian in these contexts. It studies the ways in which individual library authorities have responded to the influential report, *Investing in children* (Department of National Heritage, 1995). It also focuses on the success of a number of recent campaigns which have been launched to draw attention to the demise of libraries, as a result of local and central government cutbacks in expenditure and the deleterious effect this can have on provision for the individual child.

The political, educational and social framework discussed earlier similarly affects children's book publishing, bookselling and library supply. A study of children's book publishing over the last 25 years and the crisis publishing, bookselling and library supply are facing today is analysed in Chapter 5.

This is followed by three detailed chapters which look at three different aspects of library provision for children: collection development, marketing library services to children and young people and promoting libraries and literature. All three analyse the literature and offer a framework for delivery of services.

Chapter 9 brings all of these together through a survey of current practice in childrens libraries, looking at recent developments of charters, mission statements, policies, activities and events and some recent new service initiatives.

There follows a chapter on professional library and information studies education, training and research with specific reference to children's and school librarianship.

Chapter 11 summarizes the current context of library provision for children and takes a tentative look towards the future, asking the question whether public libraries will exist into the next century. The book concludes with a postscript which discusses the contribution of professional and non-professional bodies to children's librarianship.

The book concentrates on the UK but believes that there is a universality of childhood experience which makes many of the lessons learnt in the UK relevant to children growing up anywhere in the world. It is hoped that many of the messages about reading, literacy and the role of libraries and librarians in shaping the future for the young in society are applicable everywhere.

Some of the legislation, reports and guidelines discussed in some detail are specific to the UK or, at times, to specific parts of the UK, as legislation is not necessarily uniform in England, Scotland, Wales and Northern Ireland. We believe that this does not detract from the book's usefulness in applying these concepts elsewhere.

The two editors have long discussed the possibility of compiling a book such as this. Both are lecturers of considerable experience, who have specialized, as a result of their early careers in libraries, in work with children through school and public libraries and in literature for children. Both have a national and international reputation in this field and have sought to invest in the book the fruits of their experience together with the findings of the extensive research they have conducted into children's librarianship. Similarly, both have been frustrated over the years in having no textbook or inspirational book to offer to aspiring young students or practitioners. It is hoped that this book meets this need and will be a source of inspiration and succour to librarianship and information students and experienced practitioners alike. There is also much here for students of education and social sciences, as well as to teachers, parents and others in the children's book world.

Professor Judith Elkin
Ray Lonsdale

REFERENCE

The Department of National Heritage (1995), *Investing in children: the future of library services for children and young people*. London, Library and Information Services Council (England), Working Party on Services to Children and Young People. London, HMSO.

1

The child

Judith Elkin and Ray Lonsdale

Childhood is the world of miracle and wonder: as if creation rose, bathed in light, out of darkness, utterly new and fresh and astonishing. The end of childhood is when things cease to astonish us. When the world seems familiar, when one has got used to its existence, one has become an adult. (Ionesco, 1990)

The most turbulent, the most restless child, has, in the midst of all his faults, something true, ingenuous, and natural, which is of infinite value, and merits every respect. (Dupanloup, F.A., *The child*)

INTRODUCTION

This chapter begins by seeking a profile of today's child. The United Kingdom has a population of some 56 million people, of whom about 20% are under the age of 16. Some two-thirds live in large cities, particularly in London, the industrialized Midlands, the North of England, Scotland and Northern Ireland. The remainder live in largely rural areas of England, Wales, Scotland and Northern Ireland.

If we look at the child growing up in the UK today, we see considerable diversity and complexity. Much of this diversity is applicable to children growing up anywhere in the world, but influenced by local politics and cultures. Similarly, the increasing globalization of the world, with reductions in distance and differences between nations, brought about by the communications revolution, is common to children everywhere. The chapter continues with an exploration of 'literacy' and a look at the influence of reading and books in children's personal development and education and at how access to books through libraries and the role of libraries in supporting children's learning and early literacy can help to prepare them for life in an uncertain world.

THE CHILD

Can we get a picture of the UK child? Is he or she:

- a child of the city; a child of the country?
- wealthy; poverty-stricken?

- living within a warm family environment, perhaps with a large extended family and lots of siblings; a child with a single parent, step parents, grand-parents, adoptive parents, a gay couple?
- a secure, loved child; an insecure, abused child?
- able-bodied; singly or multiply-handicapped; a child with sensory impairment; a child in hospital?
- a young person who is homeless, a child of a homeless family?
- a child who appears to have suffered or is likely to suffer significant harm; whose emotional development has been impaired?
- a child in care?
- a child of a travelling family?

The child may be any of these and in addition:

- live in very varied geographical areas, rural or urban, flat or mountainous, in England, Ireland, Scotland or Wales, with very different local or national traditions, cultures and languages;
- be part of the 'North-South' divide, which separates the more privileged south from the traditionally less privileged rest of the UK.

A further dimension is added by the broadening nature of the UK population, with immigration over recent decades from every part of the world, but particularly from the English-speaking Commonwealth countries. Thus the UK child:

- may originate from cultures very different from traditional UK cultures, from Africa, the Caribbean, the Indian sub-continent, the Middle East, the Far East;
- may belong to any of a variety of religions, e.g. Anglican, Buddhist, Catholic, Hindu, Jewish, Muslim, Sikh;
- may speak languages other than English as his or her mother tongue or community language, particularly Urdu, Punjabi, Bengali, Vietnamese, Mandarin, or European languages, e.g. French, Spanish, Greek, Italian.

It is a mix of all of these that make up the child living in the UK in the 1990s. In reality, though, none of the above recognizes the child as an individual, as the child of today's electronic age. So, in addition, we have the child:

- as thinker;
- as carer, concerned at what is going on in the world and often politically aware;
- as campaigner: for animal rights; feminist issues; gay rights; anti-nuclear issues; for peace and conservation;
- coping with growing up: with sibling rivalry; adolescence; broken home; child abuse; drugs; unemployment and an uncertain future;

- handling insecurity at home, at school, in society at large;
- living in a society where the role of the child is unclear and the environment insecure, threatened by the increasing violence on the streets, as well as in rural areas;
- meeting new emotions, new relationships, coping with the realities of life, of survival and death;
- growing up in a world increasingly dominated by technology, influenced by radio, television, video and multimedia and increasingly able to access the uncharted and largely uncontrolled wastes of the information superhighway, through the Internet.

The UK is a multicultural, multilingual, multi-faith society, increasingly part of a Europe with a growing sense of identity and part of a shrinking world. The general profile is of an ageing community, as people live longer and the birthrate declines. The proportion of children from black and ethnic minority groups is much higher than for the population as a whole. Unless children are to develop an inward-looking insular perspective, educating them for the future implies educating them to live in and play a positive role in a society where cultural diversity and equal opportunity are recognized and respected and a global perspective assumed. Young people need to be prepared for a world where many of the barriers between groups, between cultures and between nations have been broken down and where respect for, and understanding of, others, can be assumed.

In today's Western society, children face enormous negativity and are generally seen as trivial by decision-makers. One city in Scotland recognized that children need to be given a mainstream place in the life of the city: Edinburgh was the first city in the UK to become a 'child-friendly' city: 'Edinburgh is a beautiful but masculine, hard and craggy city . . . The grown-ups are moving over to make time and space for children', to create a city where children are valued as customers and citizens. Children are the citizens of the future: 'Let's not look at work with children as educational, as putting something right that is wrong, as remedial; give children opportunities' (Willshaw, 1992).

The child's development

It is impossible here to undertake a full study of child development but it is important to acknowledge the early years as critical in any child's development. An understanding of child development is immensely valuable to parents and all those working with children, and vital for the children's librarian, who is so closely involved with the child's emotional and intellectual development. The most accessible guides to child development that this author uses regularly with students and recommends to practitioners are *Understanding child development: psychological perspectives in an interdisciplinary field of enquiry* by Sara Meadows

(1986); *The developing child* by Helen Bee (1989); *From birth to five years: children's developmental progress* by Mary D. Sheridan (1992). All three, in different ways, emphasize in their studies of the child and analyses of research in the field, how children are the same, how they change and how they differ from one another. They give some feel for the fact that all children are individuals and need to be perceived as such and helped to reach their full potential, whatever that may be.

There has always been controversy, in child development circles, about the internal and external influences on the child. This is a core theoretical issue within developmental psychology. Are the changes we see in children due to internal influences, such as heredity or other biological differences, or external influences such as environmental variations (the nature/nurture or the heredity/environment controversy)? The view which appears to dominate at present is that the child's development results from complex interactions of the effects of internal *and* external influences:

> In common with all other living creatures man is subject from the moment of his conception to the compelling, inseparable influences of heredity and environment . . . Heredity determines the limits of each individual child's capacity to achieve optimal structural and functional maturity; environment determines the extent to which each individual can fulfil his potential capacity . . . It is in the nature of the developing body to be continually active, of the developing mind to be intensely curious and of the developing personality to seek good relationships with other people. (Sheridan, 1992, p.13)

For the very young child, it is the family which is all important. With very rare exceptions, children grow up in families, even if the family is one adult and one child. As Bee says:

> Over the course of just the first few years of a child's life, the child and the parents have literally millions of conversations or encounters – feeding, changing, dressing, undressing, providing names for objects, answering questions, rescuing the child from danger . . . In the midst of this richness and diversity, psychologists have identified several major dimensions on which families differ that seem to be significant for the child: the emotional tone of the family, the manner in which control is exercised, the quality and amount of communication, and the quality and quantity of cognitive enrichment provided. (Bee, 1989, p.471)

The major socializing influences on the child are the home, school, peer culture, the media and social institutions, of which the library is one part. This book is particularly concerned with reading and literacy in relation to the individual child's development, as a stimulus to helping that child reach its full potential and discover a road to learning for life. The stance adopted is that it is only through wide access to books and other learning materials that every child is empowered to achieve its potential, and the library is the most significant point of access.

Reading

The study of the reading process itself is still unclear. Frith (1980) calls reading and spelling 'complex and astonishing accomplishments'. There is still no full understanding of what people do when they read. As Meadows says:

> Researchers agree that very many linguistic, perceptual, attentional, memory and cognitive skills are involved, but they vary considerably in which they emphasize . . . It is clear that 'reading' includes many different activities at different perceptual, linguistic and cognitive levels, which no doubt interact in changing ways as the reader becomes more skilled, or when the reader is faced with different sorts of reading tasks or texts . . . Children, as they begin to learn to read probably have, then, most of the perceptual capacities – eye movements, pattern recognition and discrimination, attention – which they need. They are also very well used to dealing with the language that they hear. (Meadows, 1986, p.77)

The above deals with the mechanics of reading but research shows that children need access to a wide range of meaningful and stimulating reading materials to move beyond the mechanics to the joys of wider reading. Babies and the very young need stimulating language, rhyme and story to give them a firm foundation for their own later reading. This is explored later in this chapter.

The teaching of reading and writing remains a contentious issue in Britain (and in many other countries) at present. The media, politicians and educationalists engage in perpetual debates about falling reading standards and the need to re-evaluate teaching and learning methods in schools. Periodically, concern surfaces about the incidence of adult illiteracy and new bodies or campaigns are established such as the National Literacy Association, formerly the 99 × 99 Campaign (see Chapter 12). In short, it is possible to believe that there is an ongoing crisis in education with reading at its centre. However, rarely is literacy carefully defined or elucidated by those involved. For many, literacy is synonymous with reading and writing. Later in this book the role which libraries play in supporting literacy will be discussed but first an exploration of the concepts of literacy and reading is required to set the discussion in context.

LITERACY

In one of the most stimulating contemporary studies of literacy, David Barton sets out a fundamental problem which we should address at the outset of our search for what 'literacy' means, namely that there is no single adequate definition:

> All sorts of people talk about literacy and make assumptions about it, both in education and beyond it. The business manager bemoans the lack of literacy skills in the work force. The politician wants to eradicate the scourge of illiteracy. The radical edu-

cator attempts to empower and liberate people. The literary critic sorts the good writers from the bad writers. The teacher diagnoses reading difficulties and prescribes a programme to solve them. All these people have powerful definitions of what literacy is. They have different theories of literacy, different ideas of 'the problem' and what should be done about it . . . Part of this current conflict resolves around what is meant by literacy, and to some extent the disputes can be viewed as struggles between different definitions. (Barton, 1994, p.2)

As long ago as 1975, the famous and hugely influential Bullock Report *A language for life* (Department of Education and Science, 1975) had identified this problem: 'An immediate difficulty is in arriving at a universally acceptable definition of the terms "literacy", "semi-literacy" and "illiteracy", for the uncertainty surrounding them makes objective discussion far from simple'. Today there is a consensus within the literature that no single definition exists but that different definitions can be ascribed to the term 'literacy' (McGarry, 1994).

Literacy, an interdisciplinary study

Literacy is not simply the preserve of educationalists. There is a large and growing field which is designated 'literacy studies' bringing together individuals from a range of disciplines, as McGarry suggests. Any consideration of literacy and education must take account of the social, psychological, ecological, linguistic and political dimensions. The historical perspective of literacy development is also important in an understanding of the concept and the realization of what literacy contributes to individuals and society.

Literacy, the acquisition of reading skills

'Literacy . . . depends on the availability of writing technology, however crude' (McGarry, 1994, p.5). This is a central tenet in McGarry's thesis, and is reflected in many other writers' analyses. It suggests a mastery of the skills required to decode and interpret symbols, i.e. reading. Traditionally these constituted the printed word as in books. However, this interpretation of literacy as the acquisition of skills to manipulate symbols has been extended beyond books to include the media and new technologies such as television and computers. The notion of 'reading' can be applied to visual material (text or non-text) relayed by the new technologies, hence the introduction into the literature of the terms 'computer literacy', 'visual literacy', 'media literacy'. Wray, et al. (1989), Meek (1991) and Barton (1994) suggest that the process of 'reading' is basically the same whatever the medium. What changes are the skills needed to access those processes. With the advent of the new technologies the concept of 'literacy' has not changed but widened: 'Literacy is the ability and willingness to exercize mastery over the processes used in contemporary society to encode, decode and evaluate meanings conveyed by printed symbols' (Wray, et al. 1989, p.169).

Literacy and writing

There is some debate as to whether literacy includes the skill of writing (again interpreting the term 'writing' in the broader context of the new technologies), although literacy studies do reveal a strongly held assertion that writing should not be excluded. Indeed, a term 'literacy events' has been coined (Anderson, 1984), and is used widely in the literature to refer to 'any action sequence involving one or more persons, in which the production and/or comprehension of print plays a role' (Jackson, 1993, p.59). Two types of event can be discerned, reading events (comprehending graphically encoded messages), and writing events, whereby the individual produces those graphic signs encoding spoken language.

Literacy and language

There is a body of opinion that believes this definition of literacy is still too restricted, and that it should be expanded to embrace the ability to decode and interpret oral language. Barton makes the point that it is virtually impossible to distinguish between 'literacy events' and other events where the purpose is learning about literacy, i.e. where language is a critical intermediary and impacts upon reading or writing (Barton, 1994, p.186). He offers the examples of primary school children undertaking a cooking lesson where there is considerable verbal interaction between themselves and with their teacher, and then being asked to write up the session. Is not that verbal exchange an equally significant element of the acquisition of literacy?

Several other writers support this view, notably G. Wells who suggests that literacy is concerned with learning new forms of spoken language and 'all those uses of language in which its symbolic potential is deliberately exploited as a tool for thinking' (Wells, 1989, p.252). Langer too believes that literacy involves uses of language, and that these and the resultant cognitive behaviours which they evoke need not be encoded in print (Langer, 1986).

Thus, the definition of literacy moves beyond reading and writing and encompasses ways of thinking and speaking.

Functional literacy

> The phenomenon of literacy or the state of being literate has a broader connotation than just being able to read and write, in the sense of possessing the necessary skills. (Jackson, 1993, p.2)

Margaret Jackson's assertion raises the question of the contributions which literacy presents to the individual and to society. The earliest uses of literacy suggested that the ability to read and write enabled individuals to become familiar with the great canon of literature and through that to engage with the cultural heritage of their country. Literacy was the privilege of the élite and indicated standing in society: a situation not unfamiliar in the UK up to the mid-nineteenth century. With the advent of mass education, literacy was gradually viewed as a skill which enabled people to operate within society and which contributed to the economic infrastructure. 'Functional literacy' emerged and this implied 'measurability, adaptability to a given cultural context, and the possibility of a return on human capital investment' (McGarry, 1994, p.5). In the 1950s definitions of literacy were simplistic and vague: 'an ability to read and write for practical purposes of daily life' is how the Bullock report put it (Department of Education, 1975, p.11). However, UNESCO (1982) offered more sophisticated definitions indicating that the knowledge and skills of reading and writing should equip a person to function effectively within his/her own group and community, and global functional literacy campaigns began to develop.

Jackson, Meek and other observers share McGarry's reservations about the inherent limitations of functional literacy since it does not take into account the role of literacy as an agent of change and can be synonymous with 'literacy for work'. By teaching so much literacy but no more than will suffice to make individuals functional members of a modern state, and by emphasizing instrumental skills, individuals may be deprived of the opportunity of critical and creative thought and chance of betterment. Such literacy has been used by some countries as a form of social control.

Today, UNESCO has revized its original definition of literacy in keeping with a more commonly held view that literacy should be synonymous with control: 'Fully literate children have the potential to control themselves and their environment through access to information, ideas, opinions: such is the power of literacy that teaching it could be defined as "empowerment" ' (Jackson, 1993).

John Willinsky (1990), among others, maintains that proponents of what he terms 'the new literacy' have 'failed to live up to the social and political implications of this way of thinking'. The new literacy requires not just a new approach to teaching but 'a new way of thinking'. Here is Margaret Jackson again:

> On 10 November 1991 the leader of the *Mail on Sunday* launched an attack on 'progressive' teaching methods. Applauding the proposal to introduce the teaching of grammar and 'formal teaching methods' in English, the article said that children would now receive, 'an education where they are taught the basics; an education which equips them for the adult world; an education which tests and challenges them'. The contrast between this and the view expressed by Willinsky is interesting. On the one hand there is a view of literacy as giving learners the power to create their own meanings, in which 'response becomes connection' within a community of readers; literacy is seen as a way of enabling and empowering people. On the other hand, the teaching of basic skills, using the methods of several decades ago, where literacy is

seen as a value-free skill, is considered the way forward. The political implications of this are enormous. (Jackson, 1993, pp.4–5)

The cultural context

Implicit in this exploration of literacy is the understanding that literacy requires a cultural context, and this raises some critical questions about *whose* culture? Several issues can be identified and these relate to language, multicultural societies, and the potential conflict between print-based culture and the dominant mass media and new technologies. Another important issue concerns the conflict between societal literacy and school literacy. Unquestionably, children's understanding of literacy is conditioned by the literacy which has been created in their home and local environment. Thus they will have very different expectations of, and ways of approaching, literate behaviour in the school. There is a belief that literacy can only be understood in the context of the social practices in which it is acquired and used: 'Literacy is not simply knowing how to read and write a particular script but applying this knowledge for specific purposes in specific contexts of use' (Barton, 1994, p.24).

Barton raises another contentious issue: 'Schooling is not the rationale for, or the end point of, literacy. Schooling is part of the picture, but literacy is not an end in itself: rather, in everyday life literacy serves other aims' (Barton, 1994, p.177). At the heart of this statement is the degree to which school literacy should dominate. Schools are traditionally associated with the teaching and learning of reading and writing, and for those who hold literacy to be no more than the acquisition of the technical skills, school literacy is of primary importance. However, a school is a society in its own right having its own physical characteristics, organizational structure, divisions of time, modes of learning and teaching, rules and regulations. Within this environment (and this will differ between schools), reading and writing are taught reflecting a 'schooled view' of literacy, using textbooks and mediated by teachers. Reading and writing will have specific and definable ends (usually formal and educational), and literacy is sometimes interpreted as a psychological variable which can be measured and assessed. Skills are seen as things which people possess, some are transferable, some are not. As a school-based definition of literacy, this view is very persuasive. Other, non-formal forms of literacy will, however, also be present, e.g. graffiti and illicit materials, but these will be largely invisible or be dismissed. The fundamental questions are whether this particular view of literacy should predominate, and to what extent does the school take cognisance of the literacies which the child has encountered within the home or locale? The latter is at the heart of many (often controversial) issues concerning:

- learning and teaching methods in primary and secondary education;

- children's existing knowledge is not recognized and their experience seems to be in conflict with the expectations of the classroom.

These questions are exercising educationalists, and there is a belief that the literacy practised beyond the school should be acknowledged and not undervalued. Teachers should explore these literacies critically, and facilitate a full two-way exchange between home and school. In specific terms, the social purposes of reading and writing need to be acknowledged, focusing on reading and writing for 'real purposes'. Children should be encouraged to write and read their own writing. Parents and teachers need to collaborate in the teaching of literacy. Greater cognisance should be made of the impact of the new technologies on literacy.

There are many dimensions to the concept of literacy, and the varied interpretations which have been explored will doubtless change in time. Revaluation is a continuing process. Inevitably, institutions and authorities will establish their own working definitions of literacy and librarians need to be aware of these (possibly to influence them), in order to tailor library services accordingly. A good example is the growing recognition in public libraries that there is a responsibility to support literacies associated with multimedia and computer technologies (an issue explored in the next chapter). In this respect, it is important to remember what Kevin McGarry (1994) says about cooperation. He maintains that librarians need to work with those other professions who have an integral role to play in fostering literacy.

ROLE OF BOOKS IN A CHILD'S DEVELOPMENT

Story

Stories are part of one's consciousness and this was never more clear to this author than during a conference in Moscow at the time of the 1991 coup. There were tanks on the streets, the Kremlin was sealed off and there was a complete news blackout. The only source of information for the first 24 hours was hearsay and rumour. We lived on stories: from colleagues, from people on the streets. Stories helped me to make sense of what was one of the most emotional weeks of my life. Stories helped me to reflect on my experiences. Stories helped me to share my understanding with other colleagues, with family and friends (Elkin, 1992).

In *Story at home and school*, Barrie Wade explored the use children make of story in the learning process:

> . . . narrative form is one of the important ways in which thoughts and feelings are organized by learners . . . Young children and adults use story to organise their experiences and to communicate them to other people. The only difference is that while

adults may also have other ways of organising and communicating at their disposal, children may rely on narrative alone. (Wade, 1984, p.8)

His research supported the crucial importance of narrative in helping children to organize their understanding of the world and the main mode in which they articulate their ideas. He emphasized that the role of narrative in the child's thinking and development and thus in teaching and learning should not be underestimated. The research demonstrated the power of parental involvement in this process and shows that 'opportunity, encouragement and practice have considerable influence'.

Children need access to stories from an early age to help them to understand their lives and the wider society. In many developing societies the oral tradition still dominates at all levels, often reinforcing the social strata. The freedom which literacy can bring is vital to allow people the freedom to escape their surroundings, to help people to think and to reflect. In developed Western societies, literacy again brings freedom, and early access to books remains vital, to encourage wide, diverse reading and to help children to understand the enormous pleasure and excitement to be gained from reading and learning.

Books open new worlds, as an old Chinese proverb sums up nicely: 'A book is like a garden that can be carried in the pocket.' The personal pleasure to be gained from reading and its value throughout life is fundamental to much of Margaret Meek's writing:

Reading can give people access to more experience than anyone can encompass in a single lifetime . . . a book is a place where children can try on all the lives they haven't got.

Learning to read and write stands out as something very important because literacy is the condition of belonging in our society. Everyone has to be literate on leaving school to lead a full life. We simply cannot imagine our children growing up unable to make sense of the print that surrounds them, or unable to read not only books and newspapers, but anything else they want to.

Reading is challenged in all advanced technological societies where children grow up fascinated by the magic of electronic media [but] not all the electronic media in the world will replace what happens when a reader meets a writer. Reading is far more than the retrieval of information from a collection of printed records – it is the active encounter of one mind and one imagination with another. (Meek, 1982, p.10)

Michel Landsberg, writing about her own childhood, confirms some of these sentiments:

Books were far more than amusement in my childhood: they were my other lives . . . The spell was never broken; all through my adult life, children's literature has given me unabated pleasure. It's like those huge gob stoppers we used to buy: the longer you rolled one around inside your cheek, the more splendid and various were the colours revealed. As my own children grew, the books I had loved and the books I discovered through and for them took on ever-new colours and shades of meaning, and confirmed my belief that a child's life without books read for pleasure is a child's life deprived . . . The books I read as a child transformed me, gave meaning and perspective to my experiences, and helped to mould whatever imaginative, intellectual or creative strengths I can lay claim to now. (Landsberg, 1988, p.3)

Sharing

Jim Trelease also reinforces this in *The read aloud handbook*, promoting the pleasure and value of parents reading aloud to their children:

> I can promise that once you begin the daily experience of reading aloud to children, it will become one of the best parts of your day and the children's day, minutes and hours that will be treasured for years to come. My children and I have sat in a one-room schoolhouse with Carol Ryrie Brink's *Caddie Woodlawn*, chased monsters with Maurice Sendak and Mercer Mayer . . . We have searched for wayward brothers and sisters, evaded wolves, lost friends, and learned how to make new ones. We have laughed, cried, shaken with fright, and shivered with delight. And, best of all, we did it together. Along the way, we discovered something about the universality of human experience – that we, too, have many of the hopes and fears of the people we read about. (Trelease, 1982, p.21)

> The cost of such a wondrous experience is well within your means as a parent or teacher. It costs you time and interest. If you are willing to invest both, you can pick up a book, turn to a child, and begin today. I promise you, you will never want the experience to end. (Trelease, 1982, p.22)

Dorothy Butler, in her excellent *Babies need books*, advocates the importance of sharing stories and books with the very young, from their earliest days:

> I believe that books should play a prominent part in children's lives from babyhood; that access to books, through parents and other adults, greatly increases a child's chances of becoming a happy and involved human being. (Butler, 1995, p.xi)

> It is my belief that there is no parent's aid which can compare with the book in its capacity to establish and maintain a relationship with a child . . . Its effects extend far beyond the covers of the actual book and invade every aspect of life . . . Parents and children who share books come to share the same frame of reference . . . Incidents in everyday life constantly remind one or the other of a situation, a character, an action, from a jointly shared book – with all the generation of warmth and well-being that is attendant upon such sharing. (Butler, 1980, p.10)

> For relationships, minds have to engage. Ideas are essential, and books constitute a superlative source of ideas. Books can be bridges between children and parents and children and the world. (Butler, 1995, p.243)

Tony Bradman also promotes the value of books and sharing of stories in *Will you read me a story?*:

Of all the options open to them I believe that books represent the best value . . . Books can entertain, inform, instruct; they can teach you about other people and yourself. They can stimulate the imagination and help you learn about living. Books can actually help your child in that most difficult of tasks, growing up. (Bradman, 1986, p.18)

New horizons

Twenty-five years ago, Gladys Williams in *Children and their books*, recognized that:

Books open to a child a range of communication far greater than that of conversation within his own family . . . for books and the written word are still the primary means by which knowledge is passed from mind to mind, between people who have never met and never likely to meet, between people of different countries, and of different epochs. A child who learns to read and understand has his own independent road to every kind of knowledge. (Williams, 1970, p.24)

In the same year, Richard Hoggart, in an essay exploring the value of literature, made a number of salutary points:

I value literature because of the way – the peculiar way – in which it explores, re-creates and seeks for the meanings in human experience; because it explores the diversity, complexity and strangeness of that experience (of individual men or of men in groups or of men in relation to the natural world); because it re-creates the texture of that experience, and because it pursues its explorations with a disinterested passion (not wooing nor apologizing nor bullying). I value literature because in it men look at life with all the vulnerability, honesty, and penetration they can command . . . and dramatize their insights by means of a unique relationship with language and form. (Hoggart, 1970, p.11)

Aidan Chambers related the above to the needs of children:

Hoggart's key phrase, 'explores, re-creates and seeks for meanings' brings us at once into an understanding of the value of literature for children. You would have to go a long way to find a better description of the essential vocation of childhood than it is a time when people explore, re-create and seek for meanings in human experience with a greater intensity than at any other period in their lives . . . Clearly, any form of human expression which has at its heart this same purpose, and helps people to continue in it beyond their childhood years, must be brought into the center not only of school education but of everyone's life outside and beyond school. (Chambers, 1983, p.16)

In many ways this echoed the UNESCO London Declaration, when writers, translators, publishers, printers, booksellers, librarians, educationalists, from 88 nations declared their continued support for the principles and objectives established ten years previously during International Book Year 1972:

Books . . . retain their pre-eminence as the carriers of knowledge, education and cultural values in human society. They serve both national development and the enrichment of individual human life. They foster better understanding between peoples and strengthen the desire for peace in the minds of men, to which UNESCO is dedicated. The Charter of the book, agreed upon in 1972, embodies ten principles: everyone has the right to read; books are essential to education; society has a special obligation to enable writers to exercise their creative role; book manufacturing facilities and sound publishing industry are vital to national development; booksellers and libraries provide necessary services to publishers and the reading public; free flow of books between countries is of fundamental importance; books serve and promote international understanding and peaceful cooperation. (UNESCO, 1982)

Cultural awareness and identity

Whatever the child's race, gender, or circumstances, books are the medium through which they can come to terms with their own existence and become their own being. Children of all ages have the right to a body of literature which reflects naturally the varied experiences and rich cultural diversity of the people who together make up our society. In particular, in a multicultural society, books have the power to involve children in previously alien backgrounds, cultures and religions, and give the child a sense of pride in his/her own cultural and religious heritage. Books can foster racial and cultural understanding and offer children positive role models, in stories where children of different ethnic groups can be seen participating as equals and cooperating together in realistic ways. Through books, curiosity among children in their own country of origin, the culture and language of their parents and grandparents can be encouraged, thus strengthening a sense of belonging.

Similarly, children with a disability have the right to see themselves represented in books. By experiencing a wide range of books, all children should be able to identify themselves, to see their lives in perspective and as having some significance in society. Books can help children to a deeper understanding of themselves and others and help them to mature into ripe, balanced personalities.

The concept of books as bridges to international understanding is clearly relevant today but was seen as fundamental in the immediate postwar period: Jella Lepman, founding the International Youth Library in Munich said: 'The earlier in life we lay the foundation for international understanding and tolerance the sounder the bridges built later and the more ready for peaceful traffic and exchange back and forth' (Lepman, 1969, p.36).

Education

Successive government reports (e.g. DES, 1989) have proposed that the purpose of learning in primary and secondary schools should be to help pupils to:

- develop lively, enquiring minds;
- question and argue rationally and apply themselves to tasks and physical skills;
- acquire knowledge and skills relevant to adult life and employment in a fast-changing world;
- use language and number effectively;
- respect religious and moral values, and develop tolerance of other races, religions and ways of life;
- understand the world in which they live, and the interdependence of individuals, groups and nations;
- appreciate human achievements and aspirations.

These are still widely accepted and reflected in the educational aims drawn up by many local authorities. In the context of this framework, reading and books and access to information are paramount.

Research shows that the earlier and better children read, the higher their educational aspirations and achievements. The best prediction of 16-plus success is reading scores at 11; in turn, the best prediction of reading scores at 11 is reading skills on entering nursery school (Tizard et al, 1988). Success in examinations at 16 and in later higher qualifications is virtually denied to the student who cannot use books. This is reinforced by Margaret Meek, who, as a long-time teacher of reading to children and adults has been concerned about the distress caused by children not learning to read early and without stress:

> Some children learn to read before they go to school; some never need a single reading lesson; others progress slowly; some isolated people remain illiterate all their lives. The individual differences of children are both perplexing and intriguing . . . Before a child goes to school he doesn't really know he can fail. Parents rarely fail to teach their child what they want them to learn. Their parents have already taught them all the things that make them human – to smile, to walk, to talk and to take part in conversations, to meet people, and to feed and wash themselves. At first, reading seems another natural activity. Then, as school approaches, it suddenly becomes strange, something to be learned in a different way, in a different place . . . The victim of all this anxiety is, of course, the child. (Meek, 1982, p.7)

Aidan Chambers, in his seminal book, *Introducing books to children*, highlighted the need to encourage wide reading:

> Every teacher, and every librarian, parent, anyone who cares about children and literature, can and should play a part in encouraging the young to read voraciously . . . there is a marked relationship between the children who quickly and permanently grow into avid literary readers and a home-and-school environment where books are thought important, are frequently used, often discussed, and are everywhere in evidence . . . any child who comes to school at five years old without certain kinds of lit-

erary experience is a deprived child in whose growth there are deficiencies already difficult to make good. (Chambers, 1983, Preface)

Trevor Dickinson, former inspector of schools, argued that children and the adults they become need to be able constantly to ask the right questions about life and its living. They need the best language in which to frame these questions and in which to understand the answers:

> Some things stay the same because they are rooted in the deepest fabric of our human being. One of these constancies is the need for story, story told and, more recently, for story read . . . They need to be surrounded by rich print worlds – which places special obligations upon school and public libraries. They share a particular responsibility to demonstrate, through their book provision, that the adult world deeply cherishes its children. That essential demonstration pays dividends, I believe, in helping the growing of children into adults who, touched from their earliest years by the sad and joyful magic of books, have been given the chance to be creative, imaginative beings, more fully conscious of, and more sensitive to, the needs of the many living worlds about them . . . in presenting our children with the best, most considered of language in the best of books, teachers and librarians are enabling them all to possess a music of speech, giving them all an improved chance of something to say and the means by which to say it for themselves. (Dickinson, 1990, pp.4–5)

Yet, surveys in the UK by the Adult Literacy and Basic Skills Unit (now the Basic Skills Unit) show that: one-third of 14-year-olds have a reading age of 11 or less; 6.5 million, or one in eight of over 16s, have serious difficulties in reading, writing, understanding or speaking English; 40% of 16 to 19-year-olds in further education lack basic literacy and numeracy skills (ALBSU, 1993). Why are these figures so high, when these are children who have studied for a minimum of eleven years of compulsory schooling in the UK? Why has the wider literacy apparently been denied them? Where were books and libraries in their early development?

CONCLUSION

Children are complex individuals growing up in a rapidly changing world. If books and literacy are so important for early development and lifelong learning, even in today's technological age, then access to the materials that bring that wealth of learning are critical. Early access to stories and books is an essential part of the child's pre-reading experience and needs reinforcing as they become more sophisticated readers, learners and thinkers. The role of libraries is paramount in supporting the child's reading and access to information and ensuring equitable access to all, regardless of age, gender, race, wealth, physical or intellectual ability or geographical location and in promoting reading and connecting the right book to the right child. These issues are explored in considerable detail in later chapters, beginning with a study of the new literacies required to fully appreciate and accommodate the new media as we move to the next century.

REFERENCES

ALBSU (1993), *Annual report*, 1992/1993. London, ALBSU.

Anderson, R. et al (1984), *Becoming a nation of readers: the report of the commission on reading*. Illinois, the Centre for the Study of Reading.

Barton, D. (1994), *Literacy: an introduction to the ecology of written language*. Oxford, Blackwell Publishers.

Beard, R. (1993), *Teaching literacy: balancing perspectives*. London, Hodder & Stoughton.

Bee, H. (1989), *The developing child*. 5th edn. New York, Harper & Row.

Bradman, A. (1986), *Will you read me a story? the parent's guide to children's books*. London, Thorsons Publishing Group.

Butler, D. (1980), *Babies need books*. London, The Bodley Head.

Butler, D. (1995), *Babies need books*. 3rd edn. London, Penguin Books.

Chambers, A. (1983), *Introducing books to children*. 2nd edn revised and expanded. London, Heinemann.

Department of Education and Science (1975), *A language for life*. (The Bullock Report). London, HMSO.

Department of Education and Science and the Welsh Office (1985), *Better schools*. London, HMSO 1985.

Department of Education and Science (1989), *The curriculum from 5 to 16*. 2nd edn. Curriculum Matters 2. London, HMSO.

Department of Education and Science (1989), *Better libraries: good practice in schools*: a survey by HM Inspectorate. London, HMSO.

Dickinson, T. (1990), 'The need for story', *Books for keeps*, no. 64, 1990, 4–5.

Elkin, J. (1992), 'Moscow: August 1991', *Books for keeps*, no. 72, January 1992.

Frith, U. (1980), 'Reading and spelling skills' in *Scientific foundations of developmental psychiatry*, ed. M. Rutter. London, Heinemann.

Hoggart, R. (1970), 'Why I value literature', *About literature*, vol.2 of *Speaking to each other*. London, Chatto and Windus.

IFLA (International Federation of Library Associations) (1995), *UNESCO public library manifesto*.

Ionesco, E. (1990), *Fragments of a journal*. New York, Paragon House. Translated by Jean Stewart from *Journal en miettes*.

Jackson, M. (1993), *Literacy*. London: David Fulton.

Landsberg, M. (1988), *The world of children's books: a guide to choosing the best*. London, Simon & Schuster.

Langer, J. (1986), *Language, literacy and culture: issues of society and schooling*. Norwood, Ablex.

Lepman, J. (1969), *A bridge of children's books*. Translated from the German by Edith McCormick. London, Leicester, Brockhampton Press.

McGarry, K. (1994), 'Definitions and meanings of literacy' in Barker, K. and Lonsdale, R., *Skills for life? The meaning and value of literacy*. London, Taylor Graham.

Meadows, S. (1986), *Understanding child development: psychological perspectives in an interdisciplinary field of enquiry*. London, Hutchinson.

Meek, M. (1982), *Learning to read*. London, The Bodley Head.

Meek, M. (1991), *On being literate*. London, The Bodley Head.

Sheridan, M. D. (1992), *From birth to five years: children's developmental progress*. London, Routledge.

Tizard, B. et al (1988), *Young children at school in the inner city*. Erlbaum Lawrence.

Trelease, J. (1982), *The read aloud handbook*. London, Penguin Books.

UNESCO (1982), UNESCO London Declaration. *Library Association record*, 84 (6), June 1982, 213.

Wade, B. (1984), 'Story at home and school', *Educational review* (occasional publication).

Wells, G. (1989), 'Language in the classroom: literacy and collaborative talk', *Language and education*, 3, 252–73.

Williams, G. (1970), *Children and their books*. London, Duckworth.

Willinsky, J. (1990), *The new literacy: redefining reading and writing in schools*. London, Routledge.

Willshaw, I. (1992), 'Working for a child-friendly city': paper presented by Isabel Willshaw, Director, Edinburgh Vision at *The Child in the City conference*, 1992 Birmingham Child Care Conference, International Convention Centre, Birmingham, 21 October 1992, unpublished.

Wray, D. et al (1989), *Literacy in action*. London, the Falmer Press, 1989.

2

....

Media and the child

Ray Lonsdale

INTRODUCTION

In Chapter 1, our consideration of the new literacies served to underline the significance of television, films, video, and computer software in the world of young
people. Unquestionably, the media do play a critical role in shaping the social,
emotional and intellectual development of the child as well as making an important contribution to the child's recreational needs. In 1984, the North American
academic, Adele Fasick, wrote what is now seen as a seminal article on the media
and children's librarianship (Fasick, 1984). She suggested that children's librarians had, more than ever before, a special obligation to respond to the emergence
of the new technologies both in the collections they were developing and in the
services offered. Also implicit in her thesis is the need for children's libraries to
consider their remit to support the new literacies. If we are to undertake this task
effectively, she argued, then librarians need to be fully conversant with the broad
range of influences exerted by the media, and the interrelationship between the
media and book publishing, issues to be addressed in this chapter.

'Media' is an imprecise term and many different connotations may be attached
to it. For our purpose, 'media' is used to embrace a range of audiovisual, computer and multimedia formats as well as the broadcast mass media such as television and radio.

THE INFLUENCE OF TELEVISION, COMPUTER
AND MULTIMEDIA TECHNOLOGY

In exploring the influence which the media have on the child, easy generalizations are difficult to make for two reasons. First, although there is evidence to
show that the media can directly influence social behaviour and educational performance, they are not the only teachers of values, norms and attitudes. Other
socialization and educational agents such as parents, siblings, peers and teachers
interact and compete. The media are perhaps best viewed as a default mechanism
in that their influence will prevail when the issues involved do not receive much
attention from these other primary agents.

Second, generalizations are difficult due to the inadequacies of research.
Certain media have received greater attention than others most notably televi-

sion, and there is also uneven consideration of issues, with topics such as reading, violence or stereotyping dominating. Furthermore, there is sometimes disagreement about the validity and interpretation of presented evidence. Wherever discrepancies occur in the findings they will be outlined, and the array of evidence presented. Care must be taken, however, when reading the literature, since discrepancies are not always identified.

The primary focus is upon the influence of television since it is the most pervasive and researched medium. However, there is a growing literature on video, computer and multimedia technology and these formats will be given due consideration. While the constraints of space make our examination cursory, there is a large and rich literature which may be explored at leisure.

TELEVISION

Pervasiveness

We will begin by looking at the most pervasive medium, television – the 'Electronic Pied Piper' or the 'Third Parent' as it is variously called. It is difficult to be precise about its pervasiveness since statistics vary according to country, age and social grouping, as well as gender. In North America, for example, it is estimated that 98% of homes have at least one television set and in Australia c.96%. The current figure for the UK is 97%.

Pervasiveness is also reflected in the number of viewing hours. The Broadcasters' Audience Research Board (BARB) is the body to which both the BBC and ITV subscribe for the information it collects from the Audits of Great Britain (AGB) about the viewing habits of audiences in Britain. In 1987 it provided the following statistics to the Central Statistical Office's publication *Social trends* about the average hours of viewing by young people:

Children aged 4 to 7   22 hours per week
Children aged 8 to 15 24 hours per week

Average: 23 hours (compared with an adult average of 29 hours)

Since then, BARB analyses suggest a decline in the weekly viewing of broadcast television by children and adults. In 1990, the weekly average for children aged 4 to 15 was 18.5 hours, a drop of 4.5 hours, and in 1994, the last year for which data is available, the average has declined to 18 hours (Central Statistical Office, 1996). This is probably a conservative estimate since it does not take account of other viewing patterns such as the viewing of off-air and commercial video recording which has increased dramatically in recent years. With Britain having one of the largest penetrations of video recorders in the world (about 77%) there is a suspicion that children possibly watch as much as 30 hours per week on average.

For some years now it has been a cause for concern in the USA that, by the age of 16, children have spent more time watching television than going to school, a statistic which we are approaching in Britain. The importance of these figures will become clear when the influence of the medium is discussed, since there is a belief that television displaces other forms of activity such as reading and play.

Patterns of viewing

Patterns of viewing are also important although comprehensive up-to-date data is not easy to obtain. In 1983/4 the BBC carried out a major survey of children's viewing preferences (BBC Broadcasting Department, 1984) and this was complemented by an IBC survey in 1986 (Wober, 1986), and the 1994 BARB study mentioned above. The findings of these investigations are revealing and confirm anecdotal evidence about viewing habits.

The heaviest viewers were the 7–9 year olds, socio-economic groups D and E watched most television, and children between the ages of 4 and 12 watched an average of five programmes a day. The highest concentration of viewing occurred in the winter months with peak viewing between 1600 hours and 1800 hours. There was a noticeable decline in weekend viewing although the emergence of early morning programmes on Saturdays and Sundays has had a significant influence on viewing figures. These programmes are now attracting huge audiences, as indeed, are the breakfast shows scheduled during the school holidays. Roland Rat, a notorious children's television character has the dubious reputation of doubling audience figures overnight for ITV's failing early morning television programme, and ever since his appearance in the mid 1980s he has been a major political issue. There was much acrimony when he was 'stolen' from ITV by the BBC in an attempt to boost Aunty's ratings. One interesting fact to emerge about early morning television was the concern of children's producers to ensure that programmes contained sufficient educational content to allow parents to 'sleep in' without a conscience.

In recent years there have been several other aspects of the viewing habits of children which have given rise to concern. One major concern is the increase in the viewing, by children, of adult programmes with astute scheduling, such as the soaps 'EastEnders', 'Neighbours', 'Heartbreak High', and established programmes like 'DEF II' and 'Top of the Pops'. It is estimated that the last-named is watched by 25% of *all* children between the ages of 4 and 15 years – quite a sobering statistic. Consternation about the viewing of late evening adult programmes such as 'Eurotrash' has been voiced in many quarters in the UK especially as children as young as 6 and 7 years watch television alone in their bedrooms after 9pm (Sheppard, 1992). The significance of this will become clear when we explore the socializing influence of television on children.

Another issue is the advent of cable and satellite television and the availability of children's channels, which are broadcast throughout the day and evening. Spending on pay cable and satellite channels is the fastest growth sector – £262m in 1991 compared with £18m in 1986. This is corroborated by viewing figures which indicate a rise from 5.4 million in 1991 to 9.7 million in 1994, and there will be a fifth channel in existence in 1997. There is concern, too, that satellite television will not only increase the incidence of viewing but will detrimentally influence the content of children's programmes. A diet of cartoons, quiz shows and other light entertainment is likely to prevail, and there is consternation that, with the deregulation of British television, many of the important documentary and drama programmes will disappear. ITV programming, it seems, is destined to focus upon imported shows similar to those found on satellite television. Recently, the importation of pornographic television programmes such as 'Red Hot Dutch' from Holland and other European countries has given rise to new worries. Such is the concern, that a pressure group was formed to submit evidence to Parliament recommending regulatory powers which would prevent the disbandment of established children's programmes. They have won some concessions but there remains a genuine fear that children's broadcasting will suffer an irrevocable change for the worse.

Children's viewing habits have implications for librarians working with young people. Two major issues can be identified. First, the fact that some librarians feel that the children's collection and activities should reflect the topics, personalities and programming of television. This is a contentious point and one to which we will return but it does imply that librarians should be au fait with children's viewing habits.

The second implication concerns the timing of the library's promotional activities. There is one camp of opinion which holds that these should be scheduled to avoid conflicting with prime television viewing and another that suggests the opposite since they believe that library activities can help to wean children from watching.

Cognitive development and visual literacy

To appreciate the ways television may influence the child we need to consider briefly how children perceive the visual images and information which are broadcast. A child's understanding is likely to be conditioned by his/her age, level of cognitive development and also by the degree to which he/she has acquired certain visual literacy skills. Maire Messenger Davies (1989) and Patricia Greenfield (1984) provide substantial accounts of these factors but a brief comment is apposite here.

With respect to cognitive development, there is particular concern about what happens during the egocentric period in a child's life (from about 2-6 years). Due to the limited ability of children at this stage to interpret and undertake abstraction fully, they frequently cannot distinguish between reality or fantasy on the screen. Television may be equated with reality and what is revealed is taken as an accurate reflection of life. Research has shown that children do make concrete assumptions, e.g. bad people have guns, and assertions made in commercials for products *must* be correct. It is not until children reach the age of 7 or 8 years that they can make sense out of film plots, and frequently they grasp interpersonal relationships only in a limited way. This is particularly true for television drama, although there is evidence that these limitations also apply to cartoons. A recent survey of primary school children in Leeds revealed that children had no difficulty rating their heroes (Turtles) and villain (Shredder) in the 'Teenage Mutant Hero Turtles' cartoon but when asked about motives and plot the majority of 6 and 7 year olds got it wrong (Sheppard, 1992).

During the egocentric period, children also identify with, and imitate, characters in programmes. Research has shown that the more a character is rewarded for his actions the greater is the imitation. Naturally, there is consternation as to who constitutes the hero in children's programmes, be they drama, cartoons or quiz shows – what sort of role models do they represent for the child?

The degree to which a child has acquired visual literacy also dictates his/her perception and understanding of the information being transmitted. There has been scant research into this area as yet, but we do know that information is presented in short visual bursts, the pacing of which is often too quick for the young child to absorb. The use of camera angles, cutting devices, panning shots and other film editing techniques can disorientate the child's perception of what he/she sees. It is not uncommon, for example, for children as old as eight or nine to experience difficulty in understanding the interrelationships between images and shots. Even when the scene changes dramatically from one continent to another the young child may not perceive the shift in geographical context.
Media studies in schools are helping children to develop a greater understanding of film techniques which in turn influence their ability to comprehend and interpret what they watch on the screen.

The effects of television on the social and intellectual development of the child

Acquisition of adult norms

Neil Postman in his challenging book *The disappearance of childhood* (1985), expressed his concern about the way children increasingly acquire adult norms at an early age. He develops a hypothesis linking this with an increase in juvenile delinquency and social misdemeanours. His thesis (admittedly idiosyncratic) suggests that the primary influence is television which fails to differentiate between the child and the adult audience. Unquestionably, children's programmes have acquired a greater sophistication and are oriented to the child of the 21st century. Many television dramas such as 'Grange Hill' have been deliberately conceived as vehicles for promoting an increased awareness among the young about social issues which 15 years ago would not have been permitted in children's programming. Increasingly, children are treated and portrayed as mini adults in terms of their behaviour and dress, possessing a sub-culture of their own. The advertising world has deliberately sought to reinforce these images; witness two small children cuddling and kissing over a chocolate bar. Whether we should countenance this or not, whether we agree with Postman that increasing social disorder is a direct consequence, are issues under current debate.

Consumerism

There is a recognized body of research which points to a causal relationship between television viewing and increased materialism in children. Even when there is no advertising, television tends to reinforce consumerism through a visual emphasis on lifestyle and objects, be it the backdrop to a drama, the middle-class trendy settings for children's television specials or the lucrative prizes offered in quizzes. But it is the impact of commercials which constitutes the most significant influence. In the USA, a body of pressure groups has emerged to campaign for a more honest and less materialistic approach on the part of advertisers. Given the vulnerability of young children during the egocentric phase of development, one can appreciate the misgivings of those who believe that children under the age of about eight years are at the mercy of the powerful commercial sector. There are implications for the parents and carers of young children who need to act as mediators.

Stereotyping

Sex role conditioning derives from a number of socializing influences, with expectations being conditioned by the family, school and peer groups as well as by the personality and physical make up of the child. It would appear that in the UK society, at least, television sex role stereotypes are broadly consistent with these general social influences. Sex role portrayals on the television are biased, i.e. females are under-represented and males usually enjoy high prestigious positions. Television commercials are especially guilty of reinforcing stereotypes and studies reveal that girls and women are still seen in traditional roles within the home while boys tend to be depicted in conventional 'male' occupations.

Research suggests that television can play a significant part in helping children to acquire these prejudiced and narrow perceptions of the appropriate roles for males and females, although as Kevin Durkin indicates, there is no real evidence to show that 'viewing traditional sex stereotyped material has led to the establishment of these attitudes in the first place' (Durkin 1985). Television, it would appear, serves to reinforce rather than to initiate.

The studies which Durkin has undertaken also suggest that television may have a positive influence when counter-stereotyping is purposely integrated into a programme. Children have been seen to change their perceptions of sex role attitudes but again, much depends upon the strength of the other, competing, social influences.

Racial stereotyping and cultural identity are issues which have received some attention from the researchers. While there has been an increase in the representation of ethnic groups in British television, studies indicate that they are still under-represented and stereotyping persists. Little work has been undertaken in the UK on the racist content of programmes but research in the USA suggests that there is a high degree of institutional racism associated with television broadcasting.

Violence

During the past 20 years the single most researched aspect of the influence of television has been violence. Today the debate still rages, based upon diverse and frequently conflicting evidence. The North American experience suggests a correlation between television violence and unusually aggressive behaviour in young people. For an excellent summary of the research on this highly complex issue see Marie Messenger Davies' work (1989) and Gunter and McAleen (1990).

Passivity

There is no evidence to link television viewing with increased passivity in children. Emotionally disturbed children, especially those who are experiencing relationship problems within the family or at school do, however, tend to use television as a form of escapism. Studies have revealed that there is a greater incidence of viewing by these children, who also display a higher degree of retention of programme content.

Acquisition of knowledge, attitudes and reading

Turning to the influence which television has upon the 'intellectual' development of the child, we are confronted with a large and diverse range of research. Does television increase the child's reservoir of knowledge? Investigations are relatively few, but evidence points to a high degree of correlation between viewing and the child's acquisition of factual information (largely of an ephemeral nature) about the entertainment world. Studies into television as a more formal educational influence have focused largely on the subjective responses of parents and children, and suggest that children do derive much general knowledge from programmes. Certainly, British television offers young people highly sophisticated news programmes and documentaries such as 'Newsround' and 'Blue Peter' which match the coverage provided by the adult schedules. Children's drama producers have also used plays and series as vehicles to debate current social issues, 'Grange Hill' being a prime example. The small number of scientific investigations into this subject are discussed by Maire Messenger Davies (1989), and suggest that acquisition of factual knowledge is to some extent dependent upon the degree of visual literacy.

The influence of television on reading development has attracted more investigations than any other aspect of intellectual development. The field is vast, and comprehensively documented by Davies (1989), Buckingham (1987) and Singer and Singer (1981) who identify and discuss the complex array of findings. Before approaching these works, it is useful to have a cursory overview of the major theories which underpin current thinking.

The findings of early research suggested the existence of a displacement effect, i.e. that television replaces reading in terms of time and incentive, particularly among young children. The effect appears to be a temporary one with some studies showing children reverting to pre-viewing reading habits after approximately three years. Certain kinds of reading material are displaced more than others, comics being the prime victim.

In recent years, research began to focus on a new theory which postulated that television may have a deleterious effect on the development of reading skills for physiological reasons. Neurological studies have revealed that the activities of reading and viewing involve different functions of the brain, the right-hand side of the brain processing visual data and the left-hand side interpreting printed information. Concern has been expressed that television viewing may enhance the right-hand side of the brain thus making the child more reliant on visual representation. The resultant demise of reading skills is also seen by some psychologists as a threat to the imaginative development of the child (Singer and Singer, 1981).

Until recently, the overwhelming body of research suggested that television viewing had a negative influence on the reading development of the child. Investigations undertaken in the mid and late 1980s produced results which were contrary to prevailing hypotheses. In North America, S. B. Neuman discovered no evidence of displacement, indeed, there was the suggestion that television may have a positive influence on reading (Neuman, 1986). Two years later a study undertaken at the University of Exeter reported an unexpected correlation between heavy viewing and increased reading (Hincks and Balding, 1988).

The relationship between television viewing and library use and book loans has not been investigated in any scientific way in the UK. Local surveys and anecdotal evidence from school and public libraries does, however, point towards an increase in the loan of books which have been dramatized on television or which are based on television programmes.

VIDEO, COMPUTER AND MULTIMEDIA TECHNOLOGIES

Unlike television, research into the influence of computer and video technology on children is still in its infancy. Much of the work being undertaken in these fields emanates from North America, Europe or Australasia, although there is evidence that studies will be underway in the UK in the near future. This does appear somewhat ironic given the emphasis placed on developing computer literacy in education and the massive demand for software games noted by the publishing industry. A recent study shows that the British people are now spending £1.42bn on video recording equipment and with 77% of households having recorders, it is estimated that £100m worth of games were imported into Britain in 1992, up 264% on 1991. The figures for home computers are currently at about 25%. However, the past two years has witnessed an explosion in multimedia provision which is destined to continue.

Perhaps the most explosive development has been in the acquisition of multimedia pcs. It is estimated that in 1996, 50% of CD-ROM multimedia hardware sales will be to the domestic market, a statistic matched by a 150% increase in CD-ROM software sales (Agnew, 1995 p.32). Recent educational initiatives to introduce multimedia technology into primary and secondary education, and into the teacher training sector, has contributed to an expanding British market.

Attraction of formats

The incidence of home computers and videos suggests that these media hold special attractions for children, a subject which has been investigated by psychologists. Greenfield (1984) offers an excellent summary of the elements responsible. She maintains that a number of elements combine to entice the child: the dynamic visual imagery of games, the ability to explore and participate, the opportunity to interact with the subject of the programme, the existence of a goal, an objective which can be sought and achieved by the child, and the sound effects and musical content. More recent research into the use of interactive multimedia adds other dimensions including the amalgamation of video clips.

Displacement

Given the ability of computers and video technology to seduce children away from a dominant medium like the television, there has been concern over the possible displacement effect of these media. No research has yet been conducted in the UK into the relationship between reading and computer and video technology, although anecdotal evidence does point to a displacement of reading in terms of time and incentive. The evidence from the USA and France is patchy, revealing that while children do not become addicted there is displacement of television, but not necessarily of reading. We will see later that book publishers have developed a close rapport with these technologies and that software producers have linked games to the use of the book.

Physical effects and unsocial behaviour

Adverse effects of excessive playing of video and computer games, (i.e. more than 1½ hours at a time sustained over a period) include physical and visual fatigue and headaches. Although adults have been seen to suffer a degree of nervous tension as a result of handling the succession of very fast events on the screen, children do not show any kind of nervous tension or stress.

Physical isolation can occur when the video game is the only alternative between school and free time. However, recently Dr Bonnafont, Director of Communications Studies at the University of Dijon, and a leading researcher in the field of video technology in France, dismissed the criticism that video games per se lead to social isolation. He maintains that it is not the game itself that makes the child solitary, rather it causes a rupture in the communication between the child and his or her parents. Indeed, games create a great conviviality among children: playing together, exchanging software and information and setting up clubs.

Violence

Many video and some computer games have a violent content which has created an unease among adults. As yet, research into this field is in an embryonic state, and it will be some time before we see the fruits of research into the possible correlation between violent games and unusually aggressive behaviour in children.

Positive influences

Are computer and video games simply mindless technologies? There is a body of opinion which fervently believes that important skills are inculcated through interaction with these technologies. One example is the development of sensory motor and spatial skills – the latter being the ability to handle three-dimensional objects presented in a two-dimensional way. Some computer games create an attitude to learning which differs from that attained by children educated entirely through print-based media. Frequently, these games offer an achievable goal and provide very positive encouragement to the child in pursuit of that goal. Instead of marking a child's work wrong or giving him/her negative feedback on failing a task, the computer prompt is usually most encouraging, persuading the child to try again and offering supportive clues. When a child completes a given task the final words of praise from the computer are usually effusive – how often does this happen in the classroom or in the home?

Moderate use of video and computer games can develop intelligence and speed of thought in certain children, and they can help improve observation, attention and precision of response. To play games effectively requires a good memory and continuous attention, traits that may be developed through exposure to play.

Consternation has been expressed by educationalists and parents that these formats, like television, may have an adverse effect on the development of the imaginative faculties of the child. Yet, increasingly, games are being developed where the child interacts with the storyline, creating characters and incidents and generally employing the imagination.

This has been of necessity a cursory overview due to a dearth of studies. Undoubtedly, we will see much more research on the influence of these formats in the next five years and also of new technology, most notably the Internet and Virtual Reality which are becoming increasingly accessible to young people.

OTHER MEDIA

Other media such as the music industry, cinema and radio are also socializing agents, and although there is not the same degree of documentation available for these media they do merit a brief comment. British radio, in particular, is a fascinating field. From the 1920s to the 1960s its influence on children was almost unsurpassed, with 'Children's Hour' prominent in the lives of many young people and promoting children's literature. The advent of television wiped away this legacy, and yet the appearance of discreet programmes for children on BBC Radio 4 and Radio 5 could provide a rich resource. We know that children listen to the radio for about 3.5 hours per week, half of which is centred on the music of Radio 1. There has been a small but receptive audience to Radio 5, but we know little about the way children perceive this medium and the contribution it could make to the development of auditory skills. This is perhaps a field for future investigation.

The music trade too should not go unnoticed by librarians concerned to offer materials that are 'important' to children. One statistic is revealing – 15% of all pop singles are purchased by children between the ages 8-13 years. Do (should) children's libraries accommodate this need?

THE MEDIA AND BOOKS FOR CHILDREN AND YOUNG PEOPLE

For years the argument has raged about the vulnerability of the book in the face of the information technology 'onslaught'. Yet, children's book publishing in the West, and in Britain in particular, appears as healthy as ever (Fisher, 1994). There is ample evidence to refute the accusation that the 'book is dead' or that books and technology should necessarily be perceived as 'foes' (Fasick, 1984; Meek, 1991, McGarry, 1994). Indeed, quite the contrary. Much of the evidence suggests an amiable coexistence. More intriguing is the question of how book publishing for young people is being influenced by the mass media and new forms of computer technology, and it is to this complex subject that we turn.

Since the early years of radio and cinema, children's publishing has been influenced and shaped by the media. With the advent of television and the newer computer and multimedia technologies, that influence has been extended. Children's books have responded to many of the techniques and devices of the media, absorbing and using them for literary ends. Changes in the physical format of the book, content and themes, the emergence of new genres, the increase in the popularity of old genres, new narrative structures and writing styles, and innovatory illustration are all manifestations of this influence (Fasick, 1984).

Tie-ins

One of the oldest links between literature and the media are tie-ins. Traditionally, children's literature has always offered fertile ground for film makers and producers of radio drama who have sought to adapt a novel to the screen or radio. Film versions of classic novels such as *Alice in wonderland* and Charles Dickens' *A Christmas carol* were amongst the earliest translations to the cinema screen. It was during the 1950s that the history of filmed adaptations for children's books in North America effectively began with the Disney studios adapting some of the more famous American children's books. A convention was established which has persisted until today.

In Britain, 'Children's Hour', from its inception in 1923, sought to adapt some of the finest and most popular of children's novels for radio drama, a trend that continued until the 1960s and the demise of the programme. In recent years, BBC Radio 4 and Radio 5 resurrected the tradition with fine productions of dramatizations of historical and contemporary children's books.

The tie-in was given an unprecedented impetus with the arrival of television. The long line of dramatizations which ensued have, admittedly, varied considerably in quality, but, at best, they have resulted in some of the finest television productions.

There is ample evidence to suggest that tie-ins offer great financial rewards for publishers, and the importance with which some publishers view the possibility of a television production of old or new titles is reflected in the number who have established departments which specialize in film or television tie-ins.

This form of tie-in has done much to revive interest in books which have lain dormant for many years. One of the most spectacular examples was the re-issue of John Masefield's *The box of delights* in paperback following the British television production in the mid 1980s. The production used some of the most advanced forms of television technology to capture the fantastic flights of imagination depicted in the novel, and was acclaimed by the critics. More recently a production of Mary Norton's *The borrowers* received equal acclaim and sales of the book soared.

The translation of literature to screen or radio has raised a number of issues. These concern the belief that adaptations can never do justice to the original text, that the media can blunt the imaginative faculties of the child, and that television or film can have a detrimental influence on reading. It is important to be aware of these issues and to explore the pros and cons of the adaptation and screening of children's books.

Little scientific research has been undertaken in the UK into the relationship between the screening of a children's book on television or in the cinema and book loans in libraries. Small-scale local surveys within library authorities and anecdotal evidence suggest that there is an increased demand for tie-ins commensurate to the increase in book sales.

Novelizations

In recent years a different form of tie-in has emerged, known as the novelization. This is a book which is based on the storyline of a film, computer or video game or even a toy. Realizing the powerful role that the media play in the success of the tie-in, many successful television, video and computer game programmes, commercial films and toys have been translated into novelizations. Novelizations can be a high-risk venture for the publisher, but the rewards can be enormous. The publishers of the *Star wars* books sold one million copies in Britain and the Commonwealth countries alone.

Much of this form of literature has been produced by hack writers, and although the books may contain attractive visuals from the production, the quality of the writing frequently leaves much to be desired (the Sindy stories are a prime example). Characterization is usually minimal and narrative description frequently terse and clichéd. However, not all titles can be condemned and one area of particular interest concerns novelizations which have been written by established children's writers. 'Grange Hill' was among the first television programmes to attract writers of the calibre of Robert Leeson and Jan Needle, who sought to develop novels based on the characters of Phil Redmond's popular series. In many senses these writers extended the storylines and characterizations, creating original forms of literature. Leeson acknowledges that he was 'looking for a way of writing a book alongside a television series which would make the two media partners in the best sense of the word' (Leeson, 1984, pp.8–9). He views novelizations as more than simply 'spin-offs', they 'should be original novels' which introduce new characters and take the stories into areas which the television could not reach. Embedded in this statement is his belief that there is a need for contemporary children's writers to reach the audience 'over the top of the literary-critical tradition' (Leeson, 1984, p.8). Novelizations are an ideal way of achieving this end. In his book *Reading and righting*, the thesis is expounded in some depth and deserves attention (Leeson, 1985).

Examples of the kind of books which Leeson, Westall and Needle, among others, have produced are indicative of a growing trend in publishing of novelizations. They are more than a literal translation of the stories on the screen or in the computer game, and as such can be seen as edifying works of literature which combine the attractiveness of the media with quality writing.

Choose-your-own-stories

Perhaps the most obvious example of the influence of the media on children's book publishing is found in the do-it-yourself or choose-your-own-stories. The American writer, Edward Packard, who is acknowledged to be the originator of this form of fiction, created his first series in the late 1960s. Several American publishers, including Bantam, published 'reader participation' stories in the late 1970s, but the sub-genre did not begin to flourish in the UK until the early 1980s with the appearance of the *Fighting fantasy* series by Steve Jackson and Ian Livingstone which were published by Puffin. Over three million copies of the first series were sold, and the international success of this series is reflected in the fact that it has been translated into over 13 languages. Indeed, a new series for younger readers was subsequently launched and is enjoying equal success.

The technique employed by these books is derived from educational programmed learning, computer programming and video games. The reader is confronted by a number of alternative ways of fulfilling a goal. The story branches into multiple plots and themes, and the player is able to control his/her destination and can enjoy determining the outcome of the story. Unquestionably, the sense of participation and feedback are two of the primary factors which attract children to this type of story. Another attraction is the fantasy theme, influenced largely by the series of board games of Dungeons and Dragons.

The narrative of these books is characteristically short – each adventure may be no more than 500 words in length – and terse and pithy. They make little demand on the concentration of the child and this is perhaps the key to their undoubted attraction.

Fantasy series written for the older child continue to be published and there has been controversy about the increasingly salacious nature of these, especially some of the titles emanating from the USA. Even the *Fighting fantasy* series has come under attack. An early title, *Hall of Hell*, caused great consternation when it appeared owing to its exploration of devil worshipping, and other titles in this series have been the subject of legal proceedings under the Children's and Young People's Harmful Publications Act.

Another criticism of this literature is sex role stereotyping, which abounds. In the fantasy series, the hero is usually a valiant macho warrior and his opponents are typically male and engage in macho power struggles. Female characters are similarly drawn, even in books which are specifically written for girls.

These criticisms have important implications for librarians, and calls for censorship have led some libraries to incorporate special statements about this type of fiction in their collection policies.

Recent years have witnessed changes in this field of publishing. Children of all ages have been targeted, even the under-fives, an age group which is surely ill-equipped to perceive and appreciate the changes in plot and point of view and the necessity of choice. Marcia Leonard's *Little mouse makes a mess* (Bantam) is a good example of the type of publications appearing for the pre-school child. Themes are also changing, and there are series which explore domestic themes. Indeed, some publishers are bringing out choose your own versions of familiar titles such as Hodder and Stoughton's series on the *Famous five*. Several publishers are attempting to produce series of a higher standard. Cambridge University Press, for example, created *Storytrails* where there are fewer permutations and where decisions are based on real knowledge of character, plot and setting. The publishers even organized a competition inviting readers to formulate their own story trails.

Whatever the shortcomings, choose-your-own-stories have been hugely successful and have captivated children world-wide. Furthermore, they are seen by some publishers and writers alike to be a way of enticing the reluctant child and young adult reader to reading. Ian Livingstone has collected many comments from parents who testify to this. He also maintains that his series has weaned children from the grip of television. These books may have a legitimate educational contribution to make in the classroom according to educationalist and author David Hill. He believes that they can be successfully used to develop skills associated with planning, collecting information, note-taking, developing empathy, problem-solving and decision-making (Hill, 1984).

There is a suggestion that children can also be brought into contact with myths, legends and folk literature, and perhaps ultimately to the mainstream literature of high fantasy and authors such as Tolkien and Le Guin. Pat Thomson has stated that 'the great and growing enthusiasm for fantasy games suggests that we have needs at deeper levels which require an acceptable framework for their release' (Thomson, 1984, p.11). Ironically, the choose-your-own-stories may provide the ideal 'acceptable framework' for many children.

Abridgments

Abridgments of novels for children have been a common and popular feature since the last century. There is a view that this form of publishing has been stimulated because of the tendency of the media age to emphasize the importance of easy and direct communication. Writing in *The Bookseller*, Peter Opie puts forward a thesis held in certain quarters, namely: 'that as the means of communication have become more easy so has the feeling grown that the material communicated should be easy to understand; indeed, that any idea not being communicated is itself at fault if comprehension is not immediate' (Opie, 1977, p.2812).

Although there is scant research into how and why children select books, there is evidence that they frequently opt for fast-moving dialogue and informal oral language. The work of Adele Fasick suggests that children find some books boring because of the 'higher incidence of description, the inverted sentences, the leisurely pace of narration' (Fasick, 1985, p.22), which is in total contrast to the fast action, dialogue and informal style offered by television and films.

A more direct influence of media upon the publishers' wish to produce abridgments is seen in the numerous tie-ins which have appeared following the film or broadcast of a dramatization of the novel (John Masefield's *Box of delights* discussed earlier was published in a new, abridged version which had little in common with the original work).

A variation of this is found in the form of a bastardized abridgment based not on one novel but on several, which have been gutted and reprocessed to form a film or television drama. *Return to Oz* is one of many examples of books which have a new text, frequently far removed in style and content from the authors' original works, and which rely on the lavish visuals made up of stills from the film. We must not overlook the fact that similar bastardized forms also appear as productions on audio cassette.

Simultaneous publications

Simultaneous publications, the presentation of information in more than one medium at the same time, is based on the assumption that learning and retention are improved when print, visual and oral approaches are combined. Publishers have not been slow to develop simultaneous publications linking books with audio cassettes, film formats and more recently computer and video software.

Aside from the obvious importance of a multimedia approach for children with special needs (dyslexic children are particularly attracted to audio recordings which can help them to cope with the printed word), a multi-format publication can induce the reluctant reader or the early reader to read. Series such as Cover to Cover, Ladybird, Hippo, MacDonald, as well as individual titles, vary in quality and approach, and it is incumbent on the librarian or teacher to explore the nature of each. One development has been the linking of books to video and computer games. Terry Jones' saga of *Eric the Viking* was the first of a series of packages designed to ensure that the child read and understood the book in conjunction with the game.

Media scripts

The concept of publishing the scripts of children's favourite television programmes developed in the early 1960s in North America. Originally designed to engage young people in reading, the idea of reading scripts alongside the programme is common in North America. There is some evidence to show a correlation between the use of scripts and an increase in reading interest and ability, and school libraries have reported a high level of borrowing of scripts by young people. Today, television scripts are seen as a bridge to 'real' books and a major means of promoting reading and creative writing.

For some years, a select range of scripts of British adult radio and television programmes such as 'The Morecambe and Wise Show' and 'Monty Python' have been published. However, it is only recently that publishing has been extended to children's programmes. There is now a small but important corpus developing of scripts of children's television programmes, usually based on original plays or serials, such as Bernard Ashley's *Break in the sun* and *Country boy*, or Jan Needle's *A game of soldiers*. These contain not only the dialogue but production directions and can be used for individualized reading or performance.

The appearance of this kind of publication was met with enthusiasm by young people who derive pleasure from a swift-moving dialogue and the possibility of re-creating, albeit mentally, the scenes and characters from a television programme which they have enjoyed.

The popularity of media scripts prompts the question, should we perhaps reconsider the place of their older and seemingly discredited relatives, play texts, as important yet discarded sources of reading. Little attention has been paid in the history of children's literature to dramatic writings for young people, and not a great deal more has been said about the contribution which these natural extensions to storytelling have to make to the development of reading skills. Many librarians and teachers view play texts as only in the context of performance, and yet they could be conceived as reading materials in their own right. In media and play texts, the author frequently uses all his/her skill to set scenes, atmosphere and characterization by weaving deftly chosen language into action dialogue without indulging in lengthy passages of descriptive narrative. Anecdotal evidence suggests that some children respond to media and play scripts more positively than to other forms of fiction for this very reason. Given the stimulus of media scripts, perhaps it is time to reassess the place of media and play texts as sources of reading in our library collections.

Novelty books

Novelty books and mechanized books have a long and glorious history in British children's literature. The profusion of publishing of these books during the past two decades has been seen by many as the result of two influences, dramatic improvements in paper engineering and the power of television. Admittedly, the link with television is tenuous but the child's perennial fascination with animation may well be transferred to the 'movable' book. Heinemann, the publishers of Graham Tarrant's pop-up book *Frogs* maintain that they can present concepts such as the evolution of the tadpole and the leap of the frog in a more realistic way, one which is akin to television. Certainly, the arrival of the microchip sound books reveals a more direct influence of the media.

Electronic books

We have seen how choose-your-own-stories have been influenced by computer technology, and we have explored the new forms of simultaneous publications which link books with software. During the mid 1980s a rapidly developing and more intimate relationship between computer technology and books emerged in the guise of the 'computer' book. This constitutes computer software containing the text of published fiction enhanced by computer graphics and extended to permit interaction between the 'reader' and the text. A direct descendant of the videogame, this new genre of interactive computer fiction has adapted many popular young people's classics such as *Swiss family Robinson*, *The hobbit*, *Hitchhiker's guide to the galaxy* and converted them into electronic novels in which the child is the hero ordering the narrative information. Laurene Brown elucidates:

> Choosing the hero's next steps becomes a job shared between player and programme designer. By commanding their character to perform certain actions and seeing what each decision brings, children try to forge a safe, successful path through an adventure. They accumulate information about characters, settings and events, piecing together a story terrain much as they would a puzzle . . . One constructs a version of a tale, rather than witnessing it take a single predetermined path. (Brown, 1986, p.124)

The electronic novel is not without its critics, and yet it does demand that the child makes judgments as to the direction of the story and the nature of characters as well as translating language into mental pictures – an exercise in problem-solving as well as creative thought. In 1984, Tolkien's *The hobbit* had already sold 100,000 copies in computer form and sales are still increasing. C. S. Lewis is among the names of a number of best-selling authors today whose literary estates are being approached by software publishers hoping to produce electronic versions.

Several variations now exist. For example, there is a programme which permits the child the opportunity of writing a story using prescribed vocabulary at the base of the screen and the story is acted out on the top half of the screen. Another innovation (although not a computer software format), is the personalized book which originates from North America. Conceived for an individual child or family, the book uses the name of the child and family members (including pets) as characters in the story. Place names in the child's neighbourhood are also included and this information is woven into preconceived storylines. The child or parent can order the book from bookshops where the relevant details are submitted.

Personalized books have been successful in the USA and are becoming popular in Britain, and there are claims that they can aid reading retention and reading comprehension and that they stimulate children to read. Computer software programmes are now being developed by the manufacturers of electronic books to allow children to both personalize and interact with their own fiction.

With the advent of CD-ROM multimedia technology, exciting new forms of electronic publishing are developing for children of all age groups. Many of these new manifestations have been discussed in an excellent paper by Ann Clyde (Clyde, 1993). Since that review was published, several British publishers including Penguin, have recently established electronic publishing sections promoting interactive multimedia fiction and non-fiction titles, and the computer world giant IBM have now entered the world of multimedia publishing for children. Interactive CD-ROM magazines such as the British publication *Unzip* (IPC) and the US *Blender* (Dennis Publishing) have appeared, offering video clips of new films and soundbites from new CD releases, bringing more excitement to the teenage magazine.

We are on the threshold of even more innovatory publishing developments in the form of virtual reality fiction and non-fiction. The novels of Agatha Christie and Conan Doyle are already available, and the young people's author, Chris Westwood, is working on a virtual reality fantasy for teenagers influenced by Broderbund's *Myst*. The Internet, too offers new opportunities for publishing initiatives both nationally and internationally for children's writers.

The impact of media on literary style

Margaret Meek, in a fascinating address on the role of the story, maintains that 'while stories and storying remain, the way of telling changes . . . because each new generation demands a new narrative identity' (Meek, 1983, p.12). Today that new narrative identity appears to be influenced largely by television and video technology. Many contemporary children's authors have acknowledged the influence of television on their work. This has come about either as a result of working for television or because writers believe that they face direct competition from that medium. Listen to Robert Leeson on the subject:

> What cannot be disputed is that the rivalry and cooperation with television has affected the writing style of every author writing for young people, giving dialogue greater importance, trimming down 'purple' descriptive passages . . . This change

affects writers whether or not they have had direct contact with television. (Leeson, 1984, p.187)

James Watson is another author who points to the necessity of competing with the media:

> In competition with the clamour of mass communication the writer's is still a small voice . . . daily the competition gets tougher: how does the storyteller with only words on the printed page compete against conquistadors of the airwaves? (Watson, 1986, p.70)

To summarize the observations of a host of commentators on this matter, the answer appears to suggest that successful books will have fast action, easy dialogue of everyday speech, sophisticated reproduction of visual and moving images in colour, the ability to manipulate time and to present different or even conflicting perspectives easily and economically. Aidan Chambers is one of several authors who see even more complex relationships emerging between the author and the media. He explored film techniques such as cutting, zooming, panning, slow motion, action relay and stop frame and reproduced them as media metaphors in his work. These techniques, so integral to the medium of television, have provided inspiration to other writers and illustrators in structuring the language of fiction and illustration. The advent of the electronic book will inevitably alter the relationship between author and reader and, the nature of fiction. How this will be manifested is a matter for conjecture.

CONCLUSION

Implicit in the introduction to this chapter is the suggestion that librarians should be responding to the challenges brought about by the 'information age', to use Adele Fasick's phrase. We have seen how the media can impact upon the development of the child, and we have explored the influences of the media on children's book publishing. These are the prerequisites for developing library services to children of the 21st century. However, does the public library service to children and young people have a remit to respond to established media and the emergence of the new technologies both through its collections and services? If it does, to what extent are libraries facing up to the challenges of the media? These questions will be addressed in later chapters.

REFERENCES

Agnew, K. (1995), 'Captivating the kids', *The Bookseller*, 26 May, 31–3.

BBC Broadcasting Department (1984), *Daily life in the 1980s: a study by BBC broadcasting research into how UK people spend their time during summer and winter 1983/1984*. London, BBC Data.

Brown, L. K. (1986), *Taking advantage of the media: a manual for parents and teachers*. Routledge and Kegan Paul.

Buckingham, D. (1987), *Children and television: an overview of research*. London, British Film Institute.

Central Statistical Office (1996), *Social trends 26*. London, HMSO.

Clyde, L. A. (1993), 'Computer-based resources for young people: an overview', *International review of children's literature and librarianship*, 8 (1), 1–21.

Davies, M. M. (1989), *Television is good for your kids*. London, Hilary Shipman.

Durkin, K. (1985), *Television, sex roles and children: a developmental social psychological account*. Milton Keynes, Open University Press.

Fasick, A. M. (1984), 'Moving into the future without losing the past: children's services in the information age'. *Top of the news*, 40 (4). 405–13.

Fasick, A. M. (1985), 'How much do we know about what children are reading?', *Emergency librarian*, 12 (3), January/February, 17–24.

Fisher, C. (1994), 'Publishing and bookselling – an overview', in Barker, K. and Lonsdale, R. (eds.), *Skills for life: the meaning and value of literacy*. London, Taylor Graham.

Greenfield, P. M. (1984), *Mind and the media*. London, Fontana.

Gunter, B. and McAleen, J. L. (1990), *Children and television: the one-eyed monster?* London, Routledge and Kegan Paul.

Hill, D. (1984), 'Fighting fantasy rules: Orcs in the classroom', *Books for keeps*, 27, July, 10.

Hincks, T. and Balding, J. W. (1988), 'On the relationship between television viewing time and book reading for pleasure: the self reported behaviour of 11- to 16-year olds', *Reading*, 22 (1), 40–50.

Leeson, R. (1984), 'Novelisation', *Books for keeps*, 19, Autumn/Winter, 8–9.

Leeson, R. (1985), *Reading and righting*. London, Collins.

McGarry, K. (1994), 'Definitions and meanings of literacy', in Barker, K. and Lonsdale, R. (eds.), *Skills for life: the meaning and value of literacy*. London, Taylor Graham.

Meek, M. (1983), 'The role of the story', in *Story in the child's changing world: papers and proceedings of the 18th Congress on the International Board of Books for Young People held at Churchill College Cambridge from 6th to 10th September 1982*. International Board of Books for Young People, 5–14.

Meek, M. (1991), *On being literate*. London, The Bodley Head.

Neuman, S. B. (1986) *Television and reading: a research synthesis*. Paper given to the International Television Studies Conference, London.

Opie, P. (1977), 'The future of children's books lies in the past', *The Bookseller*, 12 November, 2812.

Postman, N. (1985), *The disappearance of childhood*. London, Comet.

Sheppard, A. (1992), *Children, television and morality*. London, Broadcasting Standards Council.

Singer, J. L. and Singer, D. G. (1981), 'Television and reading in the development of imagination', *Children's literature*, 9, 126–36.

Thomson, P. (1984), 'Light at the end of the dungeon', *Books for keeps*, 27, July, 11.

Watson, J. (1986), 'Challenging assumptions: ideology and teenage fiction in today's global village', *International review of children's literature and librarianship*, 1 (3), 65–71.

Wober, J. M. (1986), *Children and how much they view: a discussion paper*. London, IBA.

3

The political, professional and educational framework

Judith Elkin and Ray Lonsdale

Here are the children all among us, and yet we often talk to one another, as if nobody under twenty had anything to do with the great things which are of such unspeakable importance after we have come of age. (Brook, Phillips, *Visions and tasks*)

We can't give our children the future, strive though we may to make it secure. But we can give them the present. (Norris)

Children are born optimists, and we slowly educate them out of their heresy. (Guiney, L. I., *Goose-quill papers*)

INTRODUCTION

Chapter 1 outlined the place of books and literacy in the child's learning development and highlighted the essential role of libraries and access to books in that process. It suggested that this will remain vital for the foreseeable future, regardless of ever-more sophisticated technology: the ability to read and to read widely is crucial for the survival of the individual. Chapter 2 explored other media and its influence. This chapter looks at the genesis of children's libraries and recent guidelines and reports which, in the absence of legislation, in many ways strive to create a climate for a legislative framework. The chapter also considers, in brief, recent legislation concerned with children, education and local government reform which have had a significant impact on library provision for children and children's access to reading and learning opportunities.

THE GENESIS OF CHILDREN'S LIBRARIES IN THE UK

To appreciate fully the nature of contemporary library provision for young people, one needs to know how the children's library movement in the UK emerged. Here is a summary of the genesis of this movement.

1850–1919

Until the passing of the 1850 Public Libraries Act, library provision for children in the UK was sparse, and comprised collections in a small number of day schools, Sunday schools and in the Mechanics Institutes – voluntary bodies which had been established to provide education to mechanics and working men.

It was with the passing of the Public Libraries Acts of 1850 and 1855 that the public library service to children was created. The earliest known provision was a reading department for boys in Manchester Public Library in 1862, and in the ensuing years of the 19th century children's collections were established in several other provincial towns, Birkenhead (1865), Birmingham (1869), Cambridge (1872) and Newcastle upon Tyne (1880). A further stimulus came with the 1870 Elementary Education Act. Nevertheless, as one library historian has observed, 'In 1898, however, only 108 out of more than 300 libraries in England and Wales had made provision for young people' (Ellis, 1971, p.14).

Development throughout the first two decades of the 20th century continued in an ad hoc fashion, not as a result of any national plan, but through the dedication and enthusiasm of individual librarians. Among the notable early pioneers were such indomitable figures as John Ballinger (Cardiff), Richard Hinton (Birkenhead), J. J. Ogle (Bootle), J. Potter Biscoe (Nottingham) and later, L. Stanley Jast (Croydon) and W. C. Berwick Sayers (Wallasey). Several of these librarians were cognisant of the innovative developments in children's library provision which were occurring at that time in North America and they endeavoured to emulate their counterparts.

Provision took a variety of forms, with many libraries establishing small sections of juvenile books within the main lending collection. Some created children's sections, and there were occasional examples of separate children's libraries. The most outstanding at that time was the Library for Boys and Girls in Nottingham, which was regarded as a pioneer in respect of its balanced collection of contemporary children's fiction, the accommodation, furnishings and general ethos (Kelly, 1977, p.79).

While there were rare examples of imaginative provision, many collections contained inappropriate stock and were available only on 'closed access'. It was not uncommon for children under the age of 12 to be denied access, and in a few instances segregation of the sexes was practised.

1919–44

A major impediment to development was a limitation on the amount of money which local authorities could spend on libraries and books. This was used by many authorities as an excuse for not providing a library service. Another factor responsible for the slow and restricted evolution of children's libraries was the fact that county councils, which controlled large rural areas of Great Britain, were not empowered to provide a public library service. The introduction of the 1919 Public Libraries Act went some way towards resolving these impediments, but even this legislation did not create a significant rise in the development of libraries. It was not until the 1930s that children's libraries began to break free of the constraints of former years, extending the eligibility of membership to younger children, introducing open access, and extending their services beyond the physical confines of the library to children in hospitals and youth clubs. Coincidentally, many authorities began to acknowledge the critical importance of appointing staff who had a specific remit for working with children and young people. Although specialist education for children's librarians was not to appear for another two decades, many of these protagonists were highly imaginative and innovative, and deeply dedicated to the needs of the young. The overwhelming majority of individuals responsible for children's services were women. This was something that was to characterize children's librarianship for half a century, and a factor which some believed to be detrimental to the development of this specialism.

During the late 1920s and 1930s many children's libraries began to recognize the need to reflect the growing corpus of children's publishing in their stock. Librarians also began to extend services beyond the provision of collections, and there was a significant expansion of the range of 'extension activities' which had been slowly emerging since the late 19th century. Film shows replaced lantern slides, and storytelling, reading circles, quizzes, talks by authors and other events slowly became popular. Extension activity work was given an unprecedented boost and a national focus with the establishment in 1925 of the National Book Council which instigated a national Boys' and Girls' Book Week during the 1930s. During the Book Week, children's librarians, parents and teachers came together and engaged in a range of activities, and later, similar events were held locally around the country.

Many librarians, including the legendary Eileen Colwell, were of the conviction that extension activities constituted an important corollary to book provision – a means of enriching the lives of children. This view was not shared by everyone, however. The Library Association expressed concern on several occasions about the lack of purpose of extension activity work and the danger that it would usurp the primary purpose of the library which was the provision of books (Ellis, 1971, p.100). Intriguingly, these were the seeds of an ideological conflict that was to reappear half a century later.

1944–59

With the end of the Second World War, we entered a period which saw a number of new and influential initiatives. The 1944 Education Act led to a marked improvement in educational standards and afforded a considerable stimulus for improved library services for children in schools and public libraries. The McColvin report (1942) *The public library system* . . . was a 'watershed in public library thinking', and drew the nation's attention to the importance of children's libraries. McColvin recognized the limitations of existing collections and reaffirmed the important of special qualifications for children's librarians and the need to possess appropriate personal qualities (Whiteman, 1986).

The professional status of children's librarianship was considerably enhanced during the 1940s with the creation of a specialist branch of the Library Association, The Youth Libraries Section, a group dedicated to supporting the professional interests of those individuals working with young people. This period also witnessed a growth in the output of professional and biographical literature about children's libraries which contributed to a much greater awareness of their value and importance.

The exciting developments witnessed in children's book publishing during the 1930s had been given a considerable jolt by the economic effects of the Second World War. The immediate post-war years saw a decline both in the quality and quantity of writing, and the physical production suffered too (Colwell, 1947). As the economy prospered during the 1950s, however, so children's publishing began to re-establish its earlier reputation. Exciting new authors were appearing, and children's fiction, with perhaps the exception of stories and picture books for the young child, began to flourish again. The growth of school and public libraries, combined with changes in educational practice, began to stimulate what had been the ailing non-fiction side of the children's book publishing industry. Children's collections began to reflect these new titles, helped by a greater awareness of the need for selection policies and the emergence of guides to children's literature published by the public library and school library professional associations. Alongside the new children's publishing imprints, the reviewing of children's literature prospered. *Junior bookshelf* had already established itself as a major reviewing journal, and the *Times literary supplement* began to include occasional sections on children's books, offering welcome guidance for librarians.

For all these significant developments, the children's library movement grew slowly. A survey undertaken by The Library Association in the late 1950s bemoaned a 'most depressing picture of service' emphasizing in particular the general paucity of designated posts for qualified and non-qualified staff – a picture which contrasted sharply with that of North America.

1960–89

Calls for more qualified staff continued but not until the 1964 Public Libraries and Museums Act were authorities in England and Wales obliged to encourage young people to make full use of the public library, and specialist posts began to be created. The influence of this legislation and of the 1962 Bourdillon Working Party (Ministry of Education, 1962) whose proposals for standards on space, stock, staffing and services were central to the requirements of the Act was not insignificant. As Alec Ellis observed: 'Whilst the standards were not by any means ideal, they did result in progress in many areas . . . Between 1964 and 1967 there was a 30 per cent increase in expenditure by public libraries in England and Wales, which was partly due to rising costs but also to the Act' (Ellis, 1971, p.119).

It is noteworthy that while the provision of a public library service by local authorities is enabled by the Act, the nature and extent of that service has not been prescribed. An authority is only required to provide a 'comprehensive and efficient' service. Whether or not the place of services for children and young people lies within the core of public library services has never been defined. As we shall see, the implications of this have led to contentious debate in recent years.

Scotland and Northern Ireland were served by their own committees (the Robertson Committee and the Hawnt Committee respectively), who published reports outlining standards as the basis for legislation (Scottish Education Department, 1969; Northern Ireland, 1966).

Throughout the mid to late 1960s considerable progress was made, especially in the county authorities. Many new libraries were built, often incorporating innovatory ideas in library planning and design (Dewe, 1995), which had the effect of stimulating provision to the young. Physical and regulatory restrictions, which had been imposed on many children, especially the younger age group, began to diminish with the relaxation of age restrictions in some authorities, and the integration of facilities for adults and children. The problem of provision in the rural areas also received attention with the growth of public library and schools mobile services.

Collections in children's libraries became more diverse, reflecting the exciting developments which were occurring within the publishing sector. The range of authors continued to grow as did the array of new children's book illustrators. New publishing imprints and series appeared, and the concept of the television tie-in began to make its presence felt with an increasing number of dramatizations of children's books by the BBC. Perhaps the most important phenomenum of this period was the spectacular rise of the paperback, which had an important influence especially on library provision to teenagers. Several new reviewing journals appeared, including Margery Fisher's *Growing point* and *Children's book news*.

Library provision to children in school received an important boost from the recommendations of the Bourdillon, Robertson and Hawnt reports and also from several seminal education reports which were published during the decade. The most influential were the Newsom Committee report, *Half our future* (Ministry of Education, 1963), whose survey of secondary modern schools alerted the profession to serious deficiencies in provision and the Plowden Committee who advocated greater provision within the primary sector (Department of Education and Science, 1967).

A decade of considerable change for British public library services opened in 1970. Perhaps the most significant event was the reorganization of local government in 1974. As a result of the these wide sweeping measures, many children's library departments were restructured and their services reappraised. New schools library services were created with the amalgamation of county and urban authorities. Despite the trauma of reorganization, for many in the profession this was a period of comparative optimism and tolerable resourcing. The publication of the Bourdillon Report had served to emphasize the importance of children's libraries and had lent weight to the case for specially qualified children's librarians which was now being realized nationally.

The concept of resource-based learning was being promulgated by figures such as Norman Beswick (Beswick, 1977) and this took hold in education. Public libraries and school libraries in particular began to give serious attention to the development of multimedia collections; libraries became 'resource centres' where material was not simply deposited but created and where teaching took place. Librarians working in education began to undertake new responsibilities, working in partnership with teachers, actively involved in curriculum development and frequently engaged in creating and teaching information skills programmes.

The publication of the Bullock Report (Department of Education and Science, 1975), which stressed the importance of children's reading and the potential contribution of the public and school libraries to supporting literacy, lent impetus to the children's library movement. As Jennifer Shepherd suggests, the report did 'more to clarify and support the role and objectives of librarians working with children than any previous document' (Shepherd, 1982, p.131).

During the late 1970s, children's book publishing continued to flourish partly in response to many of the new user groups which were attracting the attention of children's librarians. Multiculturalism, special needs provision, teenage libraries and services to the under-fives, dimensions of the service which were being acknowledged in the late 1960s, came under the spotlight and began to flourish during the mid to late 1970s, with some authorities establishing specialist posts to serve these users. A number of library authorities took advantage of the benefits of the urban aid programme established in 1969, which was designed to address the social problems of the inner city. This was most commonly manifested in the provision of mobile libraries (Book Buses) which visited an array of venues in the inner city areas, creating an important new dimension to the concept of outreach.

The 1980s heralded a decade of unprecedented change, politically and economically. Conservatism introduced new ideologies which were to pervade all segments of society, not least libraries, and which persist today. The effects of the encroaching recession had been felt as early as the mid 1970s, and in 1980 Virginia Berkeley warned of the dire consequences of financial cutbacks to public service and to children's librarianship in particular (Berkeley,1980). Against a backcloth of continuing financial constraint came radical changes in education, social services, and in the role and place of local government and the cultural demeanour of the UK, occasioned by the introduction of new and significant legislation discussed below. The 1980s also saw what has been described as a third revolution in communication – the Information Technology revolution. These forces were to alter the face of children's librarianship irrevocably, as later chapters will describe.

LEGISLATION

Education Reform Act 1988

The Education Reform Act 1988 was an enabling Act which set out to transform the education system, with reforms dedicated to reshaping the nature and management of education throughout the primary and secondary sectors. The 1985 White Paper, *Better schools* (Department for Education, 1985) had identified the importance of establishing national objectives for the school curriculum to ensure that every child had the opportunity to pursue a broad, balanced and relevant curriculum and this was carried through in the legislation. As stated in the White Paper, *Choice and diversity*, which later heralded a revision to the earlier legislation:

> Central to everything the Government has done since 1979 has been a search for higher quality for the nation's children in our schools. Five great themes run through the story of educational change in England and Wales since 1979: quality, diversity, increasing parental choice, greater autonomy for schools and greater accountability. (Department for Education, 1992, p.2)

Laudable sentiments, particularly the emphasis on improving quality, but the educational change heralded has caused huge disruption, realignment and restructuring in all areas affected by education in its broadest sense. The major changes which affected libraries, access to books and other resources and publishing, have been the introduction of a National Curriculum, the introduction of standard attainment targets and testing, and delegation of financial responsibility to schools and their governors (Local Management of Schools). The implications of these, with regard to libraries and publishing are discussed in more detail in later chapters.

The Education Reform Act 1988 required the curriculum of a school to provide for (among other things) the 'spiritual, moral, cultural, mental and physical development of pupils at the school' and to prepare pupils for the 'opportunities, responsibilities and experiences of adult life'. How to use books for intellectual and imaginative growth was, therefore, a basic, statutory aspect of a school curriculum. 'Cultural' was a new demand, added to the 1988 Act in the sentence which otherwise remained the same as in Section 7 of the Education Act 1944.

The National Curriculum, as defined by the Education Reform Act 1988, comprised core (English, Mathematics and Science, and Welsh in Welsh-speaking schools) and **foundation** subjects (history, geography, technology, music, art, physical education and a modern foreign language). The curriculum for each subject was set out in statutory Orders which specified:

- **attainment targets**: the knowledge, skills and understanding which pupils of different abilities and maturities are expected to have by the end of each **key stage**. In all subjects other than art, music and physical education, each attainment target is arranged hierarchically in ten levels of achievement, known as the **ten-level scale**. These define the academic progress the pupils can make between the ages of five and sixteen. Typically a pupil was expected to advance one level every two years, with only the most gifted expected to achieve level 10 by the age of sixteen;
- **programmes of study**: the matters, skills and processes which are required to be taught to pupils of different abilities and maturities during each **key stage**;
- **assessment arrangements**: the arrangement for assessing pupils at or near the end of each key stage for the purpose of ascertaining what they have achieved in relation to the attainment targets for that stage.
- **Key stages** were:
  Key Stage 1: pupils aged 5–7;
  Key Stage 2: pupils aged 7–11;
  Key Stage 3: pupils aged 11–14;
  Key Stage 4: students aged 14–16.

Apart from the breakneck speed with which the National Curriculum was introduced, one of the major difficulties in terms of implementation in the classroom was the enormous detail and ensuing restrictive nature of the published Orders for individual core and foundation subject areas, allied to problems caused by too many attainment targets and statements of achievement. A further controversial element was introduced in *Education into the next century* (Department for Education, 1992b) which summarized the White Paper entitled *Choice and diversity* (Department for Education, 1992a). It set out to explain to parents the government's proposals for education, including the introduction of a parent's charter which meant that all schools would have to publish their test and examination results (Department of Education and Science, 1991). The era of published league tables was with us and looks set to stay, despite enormous controversy.

The Dearing Review of the National Curriculum was asked to consider the scope for slimming down the curriculum; how the central administration of the National Curriculum and testing arrangements could be improved; how the testing arrangements might be simplified and the future of the ten-level scale for recognizing children's attainment. It sought to respond to many of the concerns from teachers and to give more scope to schools to respond to the needs and talents of their pupils by removing unwarranted complexity. The accent of the final Dearing Report (1993) was on reduction and simplification and the promise of stability and consolidation. It recognized that the National Curriculum remained fundamental to raising educational standards but suggested that urgent action was needed to reduce the statutorily required content of its programmes of study and make it less prescriptive and less complex. It recommended that a closely coordinated review of all the statutory curriculum Orders should immediately be put in hand, guided by the need to:

- reduce the volume of material required by law to be taught;
- simplify and clarify the programmes of study;
- reduce prescription so as to give more scope for professional judgment;
- ensure that the Orders are written in a way which offers maximum support to the classroom teacher. (Dearing, 1993)

The revised National Curriculum is still organized on the basis of four **key stages,** which are broadly as before: Key Stage 1: 5–7; Key Stage 2: 7–11; Key Stage 3: 11–14; Key Stage 4: 14–16. The following subjects are included in the National Curriculum at the key stages shown:

Key Stages 1 and 2 English, mathematics, science, technology (design and technology, and information technology), history, geography, art, music and physical education;

Key Stage 3 as at Key Stages 1 and 2, plus a modern foreign language;

Key Stage 4 English, mathematics and science; from August 1995, physical education; and, from August 1996, technology (as above) and a modern foreign language.

For each subject and for each key stage, programmes of study set out what pupils should be taught and attainment targets set out the expected standards of pupils' performance. At the end of Key Stages 1, 2 and 3, for all subjects except art, music and physical education, standards of pupils' performance are set out in eight **level descriptions** of increasing difficulty, with an additional description above level 8 to help teachers in differentiating exceptional performance. At Key Stage 4 public examinations are the main means of assessing attainment in the National Curriculum. New GCSE syllabuses which reflect the revised National Curriculum begin in September 1996.

The new Programmes of Study for English emphasize the need to develop pupils' abilities to communicate effectively in speech and writing and to listen with understanding. It encourages the development of enthusiastic, responsive and knowledgeable readers with extensive experience of children's literature. Pupils should read on their own, with others and to the teacher, from a range of genres that includes stories, poetry, plays and picture books. Under key skills it is stressed that pupils should be taught to read with fluency, accuracy, understanding and enjoyment.

In parallel, the government launched the National Targets for Education and Training (NETTs) in 1991, to encourage a vocational route towards skills achievement for young people. Four of the eight NETTs laid down by the government are foundation targets and are particularly relevant to schools. These entail pupils reaching (National Vocational Qualification) NVQ 2 and NVQ 3 or equivalent. The existence of effective libraries are specifically required for schools seeking accreditation to GNVQs (General National Vocational Qualifications) and BTEC (Business Technology and Educational Council) qualifications. While the overall importance of NETTs as part of the government's overall educational policy is recognized by OFSTED, the role of the school library and librarian is still insufficiently recognized.

The Children Act 1989

One other piece of legislation which has had significant effect on children, carers and, by implication, libraries is the Children Act 1989, implemented in October 1991. It covers all aspects of childcare law, combining public and private childcare arrangements and is based on the principle that the child's welfare must be the paramount consideration, in the light of the ascertainable wishes and feelings of the child concerned; the child's physical, emotional and educational needs; the likely effect of any change in circumstances, the child's age, sex, background, any harm the child may have suffered or is at risk of suffering and how capable the parents are in meeting the child's needs. It emphasizes that families must be free to bring up their children in a variety of ways (Children Act, 1991). The emphasis is on shifting power to the individual from the social services, by giving people sufficient information to allow them to exercise choice; by moving from doing things **for** people towards doing things **with** people. This moves social services departments from **providers** to **enablers** and **facilitators**.

The Children Act identifies access to information as an important part of the support for parents and carers. Citizens cannot exercise rights unless they get the right information, reliable, up-to-date, sensitive and understandable. The public library clearly has a key role as an information provider. Libraries need to look at how they can improve access to information for children, carers and others and improve the quality of information.

The Children Act requires local authorities to make provision for the social, cultural and recreational activities of children and young people. This also has very direct implications for public libraries and many authorities have already experienced increased demands for stock and services from local community groups in order to meet the requirements of the Act.

Birmingham Libraries, responding to the Children Act, accepted a key role as an information provider, in terms of information for parents and carers on the Act itself and also as being able to refer parents and carers to materials and other agencies which can help their needs. They identified the following groups as having specific information needs: children who have been deprived of opportunities because of where they live; children with disabilities; children with sensory impairment; children in hospital; young people who are homeless and children of homeless families; children who appear to have suffered or are likely to suffer significant harm; children in care; children with educational needs not met by mainstream service provision; children with religious and cultural needs not met by mainstream provision; children of travelling families; children whose emotional development has been impaired; children who are separated from one parent; children who have been deprived of opportunities because of poverty (Birmingham City Council, 1991).

Local government reform

In 1991, the government initiated a general review of local government, which looked in particular at finance, structure amd internal management. The general reasons for requiring a review were numerous, but included changes in responsibility, for example the loss of the polytechnics, further education colleges and grant-maintained schools from local authority control following the 1988 Education Reform Act, the unsatisfactory nature of two-tier systems, causing local confusion, lack of integration of services and the unpopularity of newer authorities, e.g. Avon, Cleveland, Humberside, the 'new' counties of 1974. Enormous controversy ensued with the introduction of the Council Tax to raise revenue locally and polarization of support of unitary versus two-tier authorities. This was followed by the Local Government Act in 1992, with the general theme of 'enabling' councils, i.e. councils no longer had to provide directly the services they are responsible for but could commission or contract out. Other buzz terms emerged such as 'value for money' and 'customer focus', and there was the beginning of customer charters, performance indicators, CCT (compulsory competitive tendering), and the setting up of the Local Government Commission. The Scottish and Welsh Local Government Bills were presented along similar lines in 1993/1994.

The Local Government Commission (England), set up in 1992, developed the following criteria to assess proposals for structural change: communities, their identity, accessibility, responsiveness and democracy; costs and benefits of change and cost-effective service delivery. It was anticipated that the English county authorities would be reviewed in five tranches lasting up to 1998. But in 1993 the review was speeded up, with all county authorities not included in the first tranche, to be reviewed by the end of 1994. In many cases the recommendations from the Commission supported the status quo. The sacking of the chairman and appointment of new commissioners led to the suggestion that the status quo was not acceptable to the government. The process through 1995 was swift, with the Isle of Wight being vested as a unitary authority, a second review of 21 districts, with 13 new unitary authorities vested in April 1996.

It would appear that by 1998, there will be 48 new library authorities (including the 14 already vested) in England, giving a total of 149. In Wales there will be 22 library authorities (compared with 13 previously). All authorities as part of the Act have to prepare service delivery plans showing how they will provide services. Research by the Welsh Library Association on Directorates of Libraries shows that they are spread across Education (14); Leisure (4) and others (4). In Scotland, there will be 32 library authorities (replacing the previous 41 districts). Under the Act each authority *must* prepare a decentralization plan, there is a stronger requirement for local authorities to maintain their archives, and there are permissory powers to obtain those of others. The Scottish Library Association has been successful in persuading new authorities to set up Cultural Services Departments, within which about 25 of the total of 32 library directorates now reside.

GUIDELINES AND REPORTS: PUBLIC LIBRARIES

The above legislative changes have significantly altered the profile of education, social services and local authority structures and clearly impact on local provision of library services to children and young people, through public or school libraries. The following guidelines and reports attempt to assess the implication of some of these areas of change and provide a framework for future planning and development.

Public Library Research Group

In the early 1970s, the Public Library Research Group (PLRG) published as a discussion document a statement of aims and objectives for public libraries. The response was disappointing to the group at the time: 'a silence which led the group to believe that the profession was not ready for such a document' (Brown, 1979). Eventually, it became clear that the original statement, far from having made no impact, was being widely adopted as a basis for new management systems by various authorities. Thus the group began work on a set of objectives, management targets, performance measures and decision options for each well-defined area of service. The first area of service to be completed, children's services excluding school libraries, was published in 1979. These were seen as providing useful performance indicators which many local authorities used as a model. But they were tools for management and did not stop the growing concern about the lack of attention being paid in government and educational circles to the role of libraries in the education and development of children, both through public libraries and school libraries (*Library Association record*, 1979).

Library Association guidelines: children's libraries

In 1991 the influential *Children and young people: Library Association guidelines on public library services* (Library Association, 1991) was published. This constituted a rare example of national guidance on the provision of services to children and young people, setting out service philosophy and offering pragmatic advice to librarians (Marshall, 1991). The guidelines focused attention on:

> the right of every child to have access to a service through its local public library. That all local authorities make provision for children cannot be denied. The level and scope of this provision, however, varies greatly . . . library work with children and young people should be seen in the context of the whole library, to ensure a continuum of service . . . The implications of this are all pervasive, affecting every aspect of service . . ..
> (Library Association, 1991, p.5)

> Whatever the age or ability of the child, the experience of literature (whether fiction or non-fiction) and other library materials is acknowledged by all who study and work with children to be of great benefit to child development. It plays a formative role which is unique to children, whose mental boundaries are not yet drawn. (Library Association, 1991, p.8)

While now somewhat out of date (revised edition due 1997), particularly with reference to more recent technological developments, these guidelines are eminently sound and recognized universally as such:

> The public library service, then, has much to offer children . . . it plays a vital role in providing for children's leisure and educational needs. It provides a uniquely objective source of information for young people, enabling them to discover and use the power of access that information skills can bring in the society of today and tomorrow. It plays a social role, too, bringing children together in activities and events, and developing relationships between the child and the librarian, who can do so much to guide those first reading journeys . . . well-developed services to children ultimately create habitual readers, and adults who retain a positive image of libraries throughout life. (Library Association, 1991, p.9)

The guidelines were significant in laying out an agreed framework for children's library services and it is noticeable that many authority's policies, statements of service, etc., rely quite heavily on the wording of these guidelines. But again, they are only guidelines, *not* a full investigation or statement about the current state of children's library services and how recent changes have affected the quality and delivery of services. Neither do they attempt any strategic vision for the future.

Public library review

In 1995 the Department of National Heritage (the governmental body responsible for public libraries) published the report of a study of public libraries in England and Wales, *Review of the public library service in England and Wales* (Aslib, 1995), the first major examination since the seminal McColvin Report (McColvin, 1942). As stated in the foreword:

> we have undertaken our research at a time of great social, technological, economic and demographic change. We face political changes relating to our relationship with Europe, technological opportunities, and debate and challenge in the fields of employment and education. It has been an interesting period in which to examine the current standing of a national institution and to suggest ways in which the public library service might develop in the next century ... Our research is the largest piece of research into public libraries ever undertaken in the world. (Aslib, 1995)

The research team from Aslib (The Association for Information Management) surveyed users, non-users, library staff, chief librarians, chief executives and leading local authority practitioners. The review concentrated on the adult population, over 16, rather than overlapping the work being done for *Investing in children* (Department of National Heritage, 1995a). Despite the lack of specific attention given to the library and information needs of children, the significance of libraries for children featured strongly in responses (Aslib, 1995). The review found that public libraries remained the most popular cultural institution in the country and that they made an immeasurable contribution to the quality of people's lives, enhancing the community, supporting literacy and numeracy and facilitating learning at all stages of life. Three-quarters of the sampled users and non-users of public libraries emphasized as a key function for the public library: enlightening the young, in particular encouraging them to read and develop a thirst for information. They valued the expertise professional librarians used to nurture young minds and to serve the interests of future generations. As John Myers, one of the research team said: 'It is a role which fits in well with the purpose many people see for the public library, that is, to serve the interests of future generations' (Myers, 1994, p.426).

The final report outlines 4 purposes for the public library and 13 core functions. Among these core functions are: 'Ways to enlighten children, by enabling and encouraging them to discover information and the advantages of reading.'

While the public library review has been welcomed for its wide-ranging market research which provides an invaluable picture of users, their attitudes, behaviour and preferences and the concepts behind the 13 core functions listed in the report, it has been criticized for 'using the right arguments but drawing the wrong conclusions' (Barnes, 1995). For example:

The final report, and its summary, really need a sharper focus and a more cogent summary of the strategic actions required by Government, including a clear funding plan, which would enable the public library service to develop into the 21st century . . . We need the cash to do the job properly . . . the investment in public libraries is an investment in a future well educated, well informed, economically active citizenry. (Hopkins, 1995)

Comedia report

There was also a general feeling that too narrow a view of the role libraries play in a democratic society had been adopted by the Public Library Review and that this had been better described in the Comedia report, *Borrowed time?: the future of public libraries in the UK* (1993), and the more closely argued follow-up, *Libraries in a world of cultural change* (Greenhalgh and Worpole, 1995), as enshrining 'the principle of the right to know – the right to literacy and the right to knowledge. This is not just an intellectual right but a social right as well' (Greenhalgh and Worpole, 1995, p.89).

The five elements of *Borrowed time?* are often seen as more appropriate and relevant to today and the needs of the future, starting as they do from where society is in its thinking and reactions:

- **education**: support for self-education and lifelong learning;
- **social policy**: acting as an entry point into the wider culture for many of Britain's ethnic minority communities;
- **information**: providing more and more information services in a society in which individual rights and the need to know are at a premium;
- **cultural enrichment**: providing a choice of books, recorded music, videos across a range of interests; acting as an entry point for children into literacy and 'the book of life', storytelling, after-school activities;
- **economic development**: the economic power of libraries is immense, representing a strategic buying power in publishing and media markets for products which would otherwise not exist (Comedia, 1993, Summary).

In a review of the Comedia report, Maurice Line suggested that no other institution does so many useful things all together than the public library, but herein lies its greatest weakness: 'It is by far the most popular and widely used cultural institution in contemporary society . . . but public libraries suffer from trying to be all things to everybody' (Line, 1993, p.35).

Working party on library services to children

In 1987, the Society of County Children's and Education Librarians (SOCCEL) and the Association of Metropolitan District Education and Children's Librarians (AMDECL) with the support of the Association of Metropolitan

District Chief Librarians (AMDCL), had expressed a growing concern about the deterioration in children's library services. They presented a paper to the Library and Information Services Council for England (LISC(E)), urging it to reappraise public library services to children and emphasizing the special needs of the client group:

> The impact of books and information on children's learning and development is recognized by an increasing amount of published documentation. The findings show: children's attitudes to one another and to society are significantly shaped by the reading experience; story and language experience particularly in the pre-school years is critical to children's development; parental involvement in children's reading is crucial; the need for children to acquire skills to cope with reading and information demands of adult life; the overall importance of reading and information skills in relation to education as increasingly recognized in new curriculum initiatives. (SOCCEL, 1987)

It also highlighted the threat to the specialism of children's librarianship:

> There is now a need for a clear re-assessment of the balance between responsibilities of all staff to be responsive to children as a client group and the establishment of specialist posts to lead development, to monitor services, and to provide specialist advice and support. (SOCCEL, 1987)

There was no immediate reaction from LISC(E) perhaps because of more pressing priorities, although they did commission the report *Public library services for children and young people: a statistical survey* (Edmonds and Miller, 1990). This was followed by annual surveys of library services to children by LISU (Library and Information Statistics Unit, 1992–4) at Loughborough University of Technology. Neither of these initiatives, however, while worthy, produced the much-needed, wide-ranging study and report on the needs of children and the ability of libraries to provide quality services to meet them.

The Edmonds and Miller study was a fact-finding statistical survey of library services for children and young people during 1987–88. It was quantitative not qualitative and showed no hard evidence of any of the suggested decline in children's library services and did not attempt to show the quality of work being undertaken or attempt to assess the changing demands being made on libraries: the gist of SOCCEL's concerns. At the LISC open meeting in 1989, the major topic of debate was concern about the increasing demand on public libraries from the recently introduced General Certificate of Secondary Education (GCSE). A wide cross-section of chief librarians called upon LISC to undertake a study of children's libraries. It took a further three years before any progress was made: at the launch of the LA guidelines in 1991, in the presence of the then Minister for Arts, Tim Renton, the LA President, Tom Featherstone called for a full investigation of the current state of public library services for children. LISC(E) was finally persuaded to take this seriously, although it took another 12 months to set up a working party, with the final report, *Investing in children* being published in 1995 (Department of National Heritage (1995a).

A national debate was held in October 1992 to allow leading practitioners to highlight areas of particular concern, before the LISC(E) working party began its work. The major issues raised were: the Education Reform Act of 1988 (National Curriculum, Local Management of Schools and Grant Maintained Schools); local government reorganization; the national and local economic situation causing cuts in services; the relationship between school and public libraries; decline of schools library services; libraries and literacy; the need for a national statement on the value of children's library services; decline of specialist posts; decline in specialisms in the departments of information studies; decline in training opportunities; lack of research demonstrating the role and importance of libraries in a child's learning; inequality of access to libraries; the future role of libraries in the 21st century; information technology; definition of a 'quality service' (Library Association, 1992). This was the broad agenda for the working party which over the next 18 months gathered evidence from local library authorities in England and Wales. The terms of reference were:

- to examine the library needs of children and young people and the extent to which they are being met by existing services and levels of staffing;
- to examine the way in which library services for children and young people are provided through the public library service, school and further education libraries, and the schools library service;
- to review recent research and development work into library services for children and young people, and assess its effectiveness and impact on services;
- to examine the effect of cultural change on the library needs of children and young people and on library services for them;
- to recommend improvements, and how to bring them about, in library services for children and young people (Department of National Heritage, 1995, p.2).

School library provision for children and young people was considered in the earlier LISC Report: *School libraries: the foundations of the curriculum* (Office of Arts and Libraries, 1984). The recommendations of this were revisited during the deliberations of the working party and the majority were found to be still valid in broad terms.

Investing in children

In the final report, *Investing in children* (Department of National Heritage, 1995a) the introduction from Stephen Dorrell, then Secretary of State for the

Department of National Heritage, is unequivocal about the role of public libraries:

> Our libraries are no longer concerned solely with books, but try to meet the literary needs of children, and their desire for information, in a variety of media from CD Rom to posters and prints. However, the fundamental need is still for children to learn to read, and research has shown that key factors in helping them to do so successfully are, on the one hand, being read to, and, on the other, access to, and the availability of a wide range of books and stories. In making available this wide range of material, the potential of the library as a force in encouraging reading and information literacy cannot be too strongly emphasized. (Department of National Heritage, 1995a, p.i)

The executive summary recognized the key problems as:

- Problems in public and education library services for children and young people are evident in inequality of access to facilities and services; wide disparities in standards of provision across the country; lack of integration of services; failure to accord proper priority to children and their needs; inadequate or no research into reading and information needs;
- The role, function and mission of library services for children and young people have to be seen in the round, with integration of the major channels of delivery – the public library service for children and young people, the schools library service, and libraries in individual schools – at strategic level;
- The potential of the public library service as a force in support of reading and information literacy cannot be too strongly emphasized.

Statement in the House

At the time of writing, the research and final report for the *Review of the public library service in England and Wales* (Aslib, 1995) and *Investing in children* (Department of National Heritage, 1995a) have had little obvious effect on government policies. The recent statement by Virginia Bottomley, Secretary of State for National Heritage, in which she defined what the government expected public libraries to deliver to their users, will not ease criticisms, largely because they are fairly bland and non-controversial and because funding issues and a long-term strategic direction are not addressed. The announcement, made in a written Answer to a parliamentary question from Nigel Waterson MP on 18 December 1995, stated that the most important functions of the public library service were: providing reading for pleasure; enlightening children and developing lifelong reading skills and habits in adults; encouraging lifelong learning and study; providing reference material including public information about local and national government and EU publications, current affairs, and business information, and providing materials for the study of local history and the local environment.

She also announced a wide-ranging policy paper on the public library service as part of the government's continuing review (Department of National Heritage, 1995b). The policy document covers: a framework for specification of service targets; performance publication and monitoring; cooperative arrangements and structures; critical importance of IT; potential for a cross-sectoral approach (Beauchamp, 1996).

GUIDELINES AND REPORTS: SCHOOL LIBRARIES AND SCHOOLS LIBRARY SERVICES

The range of reports and guidelines mentioned above are mirrored in the school library field. The most important are discussed below.

LISC: School libraries: the foundations of the curriculum

In July 1982, Max Broome, then County Librarian for Hertfordshire and former President of the Library Association presented a paper on school libraries (Broome, 1982) to the Library Advisory Council for England (subsequently the Library and Information Services Council for England, LISC(E)). This resulted in the establishment of a working party to look at the current state of school libraries. In due course, *School libraries: the foundations of the curriculum* (Office of Arts and Libraries, 1984) was published. This report which focused heavily on the school child and the learning process was influential in the development of school libraries and school library services. It was responsible for significant growth in school libraries in the mid 1980s and a clearer understanding of their role in learning. The report is still sound in many of its recommendations and basic philosophy, although time, in the guise of 'educational reform', has partly overtaken it.

Library Association guidelines: school libraries

Parallel to the guidelines on children's libraries discussed earlier are the Library Association's guidelines on school libraries, *Learning resources in schools*, published in 1992. The guidelines suggest that the emphasis on learning to learn, and learning to handle information bring information services into the centre of the delivery of the curriculum and into the centre of the learning process. The guidelines lay down recommended standards for staffing, accommodation, furniture, equipment, management and organization of resources, and a learning skills curriculum within individual schools. The introduction is quite clear about the implications for school libraries in delivering the National Curriculum:

> To achieve curricula of such scope and differentiation, children must be actively involved in their own learning and this requires a shift of emphasis from the learning of facts to the development of skills and an understanding of the processes of learning . . . This requires more detailed curriculum planning and more effective management

of resources, and thus creates an increasingly important role for library and information services both within the individual school and in every local education authority. (Kinnell, 1992, p.10)

The guidelines also recommend standards for schools library services, emphasizing their role as a support, consultancy, training and information network for all local education authority maintained schools and as being the most economic means of providing a wide range of support materials and professional advice, with books, audiovisual resources, computer software and CD-ROMs forming the core stock of an effective resources base for school libraries. They emphasize the professional support which could be given to schools and the local education authority, for example advisory support to heads, governors, teachers and parents on the management, organization and development of learning resources within schools, policy, strategic and financial planning and management and a particular key role as a training agent for the authority in fundamental areas of learning resource provision and use; learning skills and materials selection.

Better libraries

The LA guidelines are complemented by the HMI guidelines on good practice in school libraries, *Better libraries*, which state:

> Real learners need real libraries – libraries which bring to learning the active resources of people, of books, of the newest sources of information and knowing. Learners also need the skills that will help them to use their libraries well. (Department of Education and Science, 1989, p.5)

These were well received, as being accessible, sensible and easily transferable to any school.

Coopers & Lybrand report

The Department of National Heritage, concerned about the current state of schools library services following the general movement towards delegation of budgets to schools and the subsequent pressures on public library services, commissioned the consultancy Coopers & Lybrand to carry out a review of schools library services in England and Wales. The report, *Schools library services and financial delegation to schools*, recognized that almost all local authorities with educational responsibilities provide a schools library services, and highlights:

> The need for adequate learning materials in schools, to promote pupils' learning and personal development, has been stressed by Her Majesty's Inspectorate of Schools for many years, and the introduction of the National Curriculum has strengthened this need. The Schools Library Service offers a cost-effective way for schools to provide the necessary range and quality of learning materials for both teachers and pupils. (Department of National Heritage, 1994, p.v)

In the context of the effect of such issues on public libraries, the report, rather weakly, recommended that:

> There is some evidence of increased use of the public library service by schools following delegation; this needs to be monitored more closely at a local and national level so that a fuller picture is obtained. Local SLSs and public library services should draw up a code of conduct setting out their respective roles and responsibilities and circulate it to staff and schools. (Department of National Heritage, 1994, p.1)

The emphasis on the role of the public library in its own right, rather than as a support for the inadequacies of school libraries and the demise of the school library services, was spelt out in *Investing in children*:

> The public library is not intended to provide formal support for the teaching of the National Curriculum in schools. Formal support is primarily the responsibility of the schools themselves . . . The public library service in general is not adequately resourced to make up for the deficiencies of educational institutions that can not or will not provide sufficient textbooks and library books for their own pupils, nor does it have the professional staff in sufficient numbers to cope with the additional demands from pupils who are often inadequately briefed by teachers and unable to use books and other information sources for themselves. It has become clear that the short-term/high- volume demands arising from the National Curriculum have placed public library services under considerable strain at a time when their budgets are under pressure and demands on them from other client groups have increased. (Department of National Heritage, 1995, p.44)

CONCLUSION

There are signs that school libraries may be undergoing a positive reappraisal in the light of recent curricular development, for example the National Curriculum and General National Vocational Qualifications (GNVQs). However, there is a lack of reliable data to confirm this, other than anecdotal, and to inform the profession of national and regional trends. As suggested earlier, the role of the librarian in the school as an education professional is still not sufficiently widely recognized.

Secondary school libraries, along with other types of libraries, play a key role in supporting young people seeking accreditation for the National Targets for Education and Training (NETTs) launched in 1991. The existence of effective libraries are specifically required for schools seeking accreditation to GNVQ and BTEC. While the overall importance of NETTs as part of the government's overall educational policy is recognized by OFSTED, the role of the school library and librarian is again insufficiently recognized.

The historical perspective and current legislation and guidelines on children's and school libraries provide a framework for the discussion of the role of libraries in the development of the child and the role of the librarian in supporting children's and school library developments. The role of libraries is explored further in the following chapters.

REFERENCES

Aslib (1995), *Review of the public library services in England and Wales: for the Department of National Heritage*. London, Aslib (The Association for Information Management).

Barnes, M. (1995), Seeing the future: keynote speech at seminar 'Collaborating on the future for library and information services in the West Midlands region', Birmingham Rep, 17 January 1996.

Beauchamp, P. (1996), Public library review: paper given at seminar, 'Collaborating on the future for library and information services in the West Midlands region', Birmingham Rep, 17 January 1996.

Berkeley, V. (1980), 'Children among the hardest hit', *Library Association record*, 78 (4), 475.

Beswick, N. (1977), *Resource based learning*. London, Heinemann Educational.

Birmingham City Council (1991), *Report of the Director of Library Services to the Leisure Services Committee*, 24 October 1991.

Broome, M. (1982), 'The future of school library services': a discussion paper in Library and Information Services Council (1984) *School libraries: the foundations of the curriculum. Report of the Library and Information Services Council's working party on school library services*. Office of Arts and Libraries. Library Information Series no.13. London, HMSO.

Brown, R. (1979), 'Public library aims and objectives: children's services', *Library Association record*, 81 (8), August 1979, 382.

Children Act (1991), *The Children Act & local authorities: a guide for parents*. London, Department of Health, September 1991.

Colwell, E. H. (1947), 'Twenty eventful years in children's books', *Papers and summaries of discussions at the Brighton Conference of the Library Association*, 55–9.

Comedia (1993), *Borrowed time?: the future of public libraries in the UK*. London, Comedia.

Comedia Working Papers (1993), *Key themes and issues of the study*. The Future of Public Libraries Working Paper 1. London, Comedia.

Dearing, Sir R. (1993), *The National Curriculum and its assessment: final* report. London, Schools Curriculum and Assessment Authority.

Department For Education (1985), *Better schools*. London, HMSO.

Department For Education (1992a), *Choice and diversity: a new framework for schools*. London, HMSO.

Department for Education (1992b), *Education into the next century: the Government's proposals for education explained*. London, HMSO.

Department for Education (1995), *The National Curriculum*. London, HMSO.

Department of Education and Science (1967), *Children and their primary schools*. (Plowden Report). 2 vols. London, HMSO.

Department of Education and Science (1975), *A language for life: Report of the Committee of Inquiry . . . under the chairmanship of Sir Alan Bullock*. (Bullock Report). London, HMSO.

Department of Education and Science (1989), *Better libraries: good practice in schools*: a survey by HM Inspectorate. London, HMSO.

Department of Education and Science (1991), *The parent's charter: you and your child's education*. London, HMSO.

Department of National Heritage (1994), *Schools library services and financial delegation to schools: a report to the Department of National Heritage by Coopers & Lybrand*. Library and Information Series no. 21. London, HMSO.

Department of National Heritage (1995a), *Investing in children: the future of library services for children and young people*. Library and Information Services Council (England) Working Party on Library Services for Children and Young People. London, HMSO.

Department of National Heritage (1995b), *The public library service: Virginia Bottomley sets out libraries' key functions*. News release from the Department of National Heritage, 18 December 1995.

Dewe, M. (1995), *Planning and designing libraries for children and young people*. London, Library Association Publishing.

Edmonds, D. and Miller, J. (1990), *Public library services for children and young people: a statistical survey*. British Library and Information Report 72. London, British Library Research and Development Department.

Ellis, A. (1971), *Library services for young people in England and Wales 1830–1970*. Oxford, Pergamon Press.

Greenhalgh, E. and Worpole, K. (1995), *Libraries in a world of cultural change*. London, UCL Press.

Hopkins, L. (1995), 'Reviewing the public libraries review: editorial', in *Journal of librarianship and information science*, **27** (4), December 1995, 187–9.

Kelly, T. (1977), *A history of public libraries in Great Britain*. London, The Library Association.

Kinnell, M. (ed.) (1992), *Learning resources in schools: Library Association guidelines for school libraries*. London, Library Association Publishing.

Library and Information Statistics Unit (LISU), *A survey of library services to children in the UK, 1991–2*. Deborah Fossey, Richard Marriott, John Sumsion; 1992–3. Helen Pickering and John Sumsion; 1993–4. Claire Creaser. Library and Information Statistics Unit, Department of Information and Library Studies, Loughborough University of Technology.

The Library Association (1991), *Children and young people: Library Association guidelines for public library services*. London, Library Association Publishing.

Library Association (1992), Comments from papers presented at a one day seminar: 'Opening the national debate; library services to children and young people', 28/29 October 1992 (unpublished).

Library Association record (1979), 'Performance measurement: 1. children's services (excluding school services)', *Library Association record*, **81** (9), September, 455.

Line, M. (1993), 'What's wrong with libraries?', *Bookseller*, 20 August, 35–6.

McColvin, L. R. (1942), *The public library system of Great Britain: a report on its present condition with proposals for post-war reorganisation*. London, The Library Association.

Marshall, P. (1991), 'Children and young people: guidelines for public library services' in *International review of children's literature and librarianship*, **6** (3), 201–9.

Ministry of Education (1962), *Standards of public library service in England and Wales, Report of the Working Party*. (Bourdillon Report). London, HMSO.

Ministry of Education, Central Advisory Council for Education (England) (1963), *Half our future*. (Newsom Report). London, HMSO.

Myers, J. (1994), 'Stable, quiet retreats, or bustling with innovation?', *Library Association record*, **96** (8), August, 1994, 426.

Norris, K. (1933), *Hands full of living*. Amereon Ltd.

Northern Ireland Ministry of Education Advisory Committee on the Public Library Service in Northern Ireland (1966), *The public library service in Northern Ireland: report*. (Hawnt Report). Belfast, HMSO.

Office of Arts and Libraries (1984), *School libraries: the foundations of the curriculum*. Report of the Library and Information Services Council's Working Party on School Library Services. Library Information Series no. 13. London, HMSO.

Scottish Education Department (1969), *Standards for the public library service in Scotland: report of a working party appointed by the Secretary of State for Scotland*. (Robertson Report). Edinburgh, HMSO.

Shepherd, J. (1982), 'Children's librarianship and school library services' in Taylor, L. J. (ed.), *British librarianship and information work 1976–1980*. London, The Library Association, 131–51.

SOCCEL and AMDECL (1987), Library services to children and young people: paper presented to LISC(E). Unpublished.

Whiteman, P. (1986), *Public libraries since 1945: the impact of the McColvin Report*. London, Clive Bingley.

4

The role of the children's library

Judith Elkin

I had this very boring childhood. We lived in a boring house on a boring street in a boring town. School was boring. Every day was the same. I used to think, why does nothing exciting ever happen to me? Then I discovered my local library . . . (Swindells, 1993, p.23)

. . . libraries are still the most wonderful places. I use the word advisedly: they are full of wonders and delightful surprises. The very best present you can give any child is a library card. It is a key to everything there is . . . make your local library a second home. (Geras, 1993, p.23)

INTRODUCTION

Two renowned children's writers, Robert Swindells and Adele Geras write above about the influence of the children's library and knowledgeable childrens librarians in their own personal development. They recognize the pleasure to be gained by the wide access to reading which a freely available public library collection can bring. It is, perhaps, astonishing that such sentiments are so rarely expressed by others, particularly children's librarians themselves who are actually in such a powerful position to influence and advise the young.

It is now over 20 years since Janet Hill's inspirational *Children are people* (Hill, 1973) was published in the UK. Since then, other books have been written about British public library services to children (Fleet, 1973; Marshall, 1975; Ray, 1979) but none of these has taken a visionary approach. There has been little attention paid to the ways libraries have responded to the multifarious influences presented by society or any real attempt made to anticipate a future role or philosophy for public library services to children. Research in the area has been thin and has not kept pace with research in the school library field.

Books and literacy were highlighted in earlier chapters as being crucial for early development and lifelong learning, even in today's technological age. It was suggested that the role of libraries is paramount in ensuring that all children have free access to books and other materials, regardless of their age, wealth, health, gender or ethnic origin, and in promoting reading and connecting the right book to the right child.

Concern about the low profile of children's libraries and lack of understanding at national or government level of their role in the intellectual, social or cultural development of the child has been a source of concern for a number of years. The report, *Investing in children* (Department of National Heritage, 1995a), introduced in the previous chapter, attempted to redress this balance. This chapter assesses how effectively this has been achieved and analyses how practitioners have responded. First, it builds on previous chapters by looking at the role of libraries in both the public library and school library environment, within the political, economic, educational and cultural context already considered.

CHILDREN'S LIBRARIES

Viewed historically, there has been a significant shift in the philosophy underpinning the UK children's library service. While maintaining the fundamental right of young people to have access to a service (as enshrined in the United Nations Convention on the Right of the Child, 1980), contemporary children's librarianship suggests that children are deemed to be an 'investment' and 'at the heart of the core services'.

Traditionally, the library has been seen as a major contributor to the development of literacy, and that remains a primary aim of the service. At the heart of this philosophy is the belief that through its collections, which are uniquely objective sources of information, and ultimately through reading, the public library contributes to children's leisure needs and their intellectual, emotional, social and educational and language development. Again, there is a sense in which this notion has been extended in recent times. There is a prevalent belief that by developing literacy in the young the library can create the habitual adult reader and user of the library, instilling a positive view of libraries throughout adulthood.

Today, the public library fulfils a complementary social function through its programmes of activities, promoting social interaction among young people, between children and other groups in the community, while fostering an awareness of the culture of others. Children's libraries are concerned with the 'whole child', not just with school and learning. In considering the role of the children's library, UNESCO's *Public library manifesto* is a useful starting point, taking as it does a global perspective and responsibility:

> Freedom, prosperity and the development of society and of individuals are fundamental human values. They will only be attained through the ability of well-informed citizens to exercise their democratic rights and to play an active role in society. Constructive participation and the development of democracy depend on satisfactory education as well as on free and unlimited access to knowledge, thought, culture and information.
>
> The public library, the local gateway to knowledge, provides a basic condition for lifelong learning, independent decision-making and cultural development of the indi-

vidual and social groups. The Manifesto proclaims UNESCO's belief in the public library as a living force for education, culture and information, and as an essential agent for the fostering of peace and spiritual welfare through the minds of men and women. (IFLA, 1995)

Among the key missions which the Manifesto relates to information, literacy, education and culture are:

- creating and strengthening reading habits in children from an early age;
- supporting both individual and self conducted education at all levels;
- providing opportunities for personal creative development;
- stimulating the imagination and creativity of children and young people;
- promoting awareness of cultural heritage;
- fostering inter-cultural dialogue and favouring cultural diversity;
- facilitating the development of information and computer literacy skills;
- supporting and participating in literacy activities and programmes for all age groups, and initiating such activities if necessary.

This was echoed in the drafting of the International Federation of Library Association's (IFLA) guidelines for children's libraries:

> The children's library always reflects its own society – its educational and cultural goals . . . The international declaration of the child's rights in 1979 included ten claims, which are connected to their security and the universal balanced growth of the child. However, the declaration overlooks the right to culture, even though there are mentioned general educative training and free time activities. One of the basic goals for the children's library is to offer culture which might be presented in the form of text, picture or sound. (Teinila and Pissard, 1990)

Role of the children's library

The earliest clear statement of the aims and objectives of children's libraries in the UK was published by the Public Library Research Group (PLRG). It stated that the primary objectives of children's libraries were:

- to promote and encourage reading as a means for self development and to encourage an awareness of the pleasure of reading;
- to assist language development and improve reading standards;
- to promote and encourage the acceptance of books and related material as fundamental means in meeting information needs;
- to prepare children to make full use of the various agencies of books and information in later years;
- to provide the means of extending and deepening cultural awareness;
- to encourage children of all ages and backgrounds to use libraries;

with sub-objectives:

- to provide a wide range of books and other materials and present them in a manner and in surroundings attractive to children;
- to hold book-related activities thus helping children to make the connection between daily needs and information sources;
- to guide children in their choice of reading;
- to help children develop a critical facility;
- to establish and maintain contact with parents, teachers, under 5 groups, supervisors and all who care for children;
- to promote cultural events for children (Brown, 1979, p.382).

Contemporary with this, Adele Fasick in Canada was recognizing that public libraries for children were increasingly expected to:

- prepare pre-school children;
- provide cultural experiences (drama, film);
- help children to adjust to the community in which they lived;
- prepare children for living in a multicultural society;
- help children to adjust socially and psychologically to the demands of growing up;
- compensate for the deficiencies of home and school;
- provide programmes and materials to compete with television;
- provide entertainment and a meeting place for children with few other social outlets, especially during the school holidays;
- provide supplementary materials for school projects;
- provide books and services to enrich children's lives and support hobbies, sport, crafts;
- develop life-long interest in reading (Fasick, 1980, pp.97–8).

The LA guidelines, *Children and young people* (Library Association, 1991), published some ten years later, spell out the role of the children's library in considerable detail and establish a sound framework for considering services to children and young people. They begin by identifying four areas of child development where books and stories and, implicitly, libraries are vitally important:

1 **intellectual and emotional development;**
2 **language development** – particularly crucial in the pre-school years, and an area where the library can enhance the partnership between parent, child and teacher;
3 **social development** – children's attitudes to one another and to society are significantly shaped by reading;
4 **educational development** – the need for children to acquire reading and information skills is now being reinforced throughout the curriculum.

The LA guidelines identify the benefits children can gain from library materials, as:

- enjoyment: of story experience, of language, of associated art;
- knowledge of the wider world (through both fiction and non-fiction);
- understanding of other people: behaviour, cultures, situations;
- self-knowledge: identity (both individual and cultural), security;
- information: both problem-solving and 'unguided' discovery; confidence, in the acquisition of vocabulary, speech and language skills;
- shared experiences between adult and child;
- support for both formal and informal education.

They also specify that the way these are provided through public libraries is significant in terms of the added professional value, of:

- assistance, guidance, interpretation, enthusiasm and encouragement from trained staff;
- a far wider range of materials than home or school can generally provide;
- access to materials for every child, regardless of background;
- access to services at a choice of times and places;
- use of materials, the majority of which are available for loan at no charge;
- access, through one service point, to the greater library network;
- a neutral ground between home and school for independent and unhindered discovery;
- a place to learn and practice information skills;
- knowledge of a community facility that has potential lifelong relevance;
- experience of the library as an inviting place, with activities and events (Library Association, 1991, pp.8, 9).

The role of the children's librarian

Twenty years ago, Janet Hill was seeing children's librarians as rather precious, isolated from the reality of the world and children, on the one hand, and marginalized within the profession on the other. She was a pioneer in promoting the concept of community librarianship: children's librarians and storytellers going into the community, to where the children were, the parks, the swimming pools, the community centres and away from the four walls of irrelevant and outmoded public library buildings. She criticized children's librarians for demanding specialist staff and thus assuming that non-professional staff were incapable of dealing with children. She was scathing about the Library Association's Youth Libraries Group and the seeming lack of promotion of the true role of libraries and books:

I have been harsh about librarians. It is because so much *should* be asked of us all. Librarianship is potentially a most absorbing and exciting profession which demands real commitment from those of us who try to practise it. It is difficult not to be impatient with those who are content to continue working within well-worn grooves, conscientious, but anxious to avoid conflict, change, and anything which would disturb the even tenor of their professional lives. (Hill, 1973, p.151)

The LA guidelines (Library Association, 1991) are very up-front in their approach to the professional skills and dynamism required of the professional children's librarian. They spell out the knowledge, skills and expertise required of staff, to ensure the development and provision of an effective library service to children:

- an understanding of child development, including intellectual, emotional, physical, behavioural, language and social development;
- a detailed knowledge of children's books and related materials;
- a knowledge of educational trends, developments, terminology and local structures/patterns of organization;
- familiarity with contemporary child culture and storytelling, performance, public speaking, teaching and promotional skills.

The personal qualities of empathy with children and confidence in relating with and to them are also identified. The guidelines are significant in laying out an agreed framework for children's library services and it is noticeable that many authorities' policies, statement of service, etc., rely quite heavily on the wording of these guidelines. But they are only guidelines, *not* a full investigation or statement about the current state of children's library services and how some of the change elements referred to earlier have affected the quality and delivery of services. Neither do they attempt any strategic vision for the future. This has had to wait until LISC(E) set up its working party in 1993, to take a strategic view of the library needs of children and young people.

We shall discuss this later, but first we shall consider multimedia materials as part of a coordinated strategy of provision in children's libraries and take a quick look at the local authority management structures within which libraries operate. This will offer a context for discussion of the role of school libraries and schools library services.

The provision of audiovisual and computer and multimedia materials

There appears to be national agreement that children's libraries should be equipped to respond to the challenges of the information age, but to what degree have collections and services been established to satisfy those needs? Despite the attention which the media have received in the disciplines of education, sociology, psychology and technology, and the enormous output of documentation that has ensued, there is a dearth of material about the interaction of the media and children's librarianship in the UK. Surprisingly, there is not a huge opus from the USA, Australasia or Europe either.

Until 1990, virtually nothing had been written about the provision of audiovisual and computer materials to young people in the UK. What did exist suggested that services were piecemeal and woeful. The absence of data led the Department of Information and Library Studies at the University of Wales, Aberystwyth to undertake what was the first comprehensive national survey of public library provision through the children's service and the schools library service. An exceptionally detailed report of the research was published by the British Library who funded the project (Lonsdale and Wheatley, 1990a), and three articles were subsequently published (Lonsdale and Wheatley, 1990b, 1991, 1992). The following overview of provision is based on data from that study (which projected to 1995), together with a subsequent study undertaken in 1994 by the Department into the use of multimedia to support children's reading.

Perhaps the most fundamental issue concerns the availability and accessibility of audiovisual, computer and multimedia materials in children's libraries. At first sight the figures suggest a healthy degree of provision for the more traditional audiovisual materials (video, audio cassettes and CDs) with 72% of authorities holding collections, although distribution across the UK is notoriously uneven. Viewed another way, that nearly a third of library authorities do not offer even the most established formats is surely a matter of concern. Most alarming, however, is the figure for computer software: less than a third of authorities hold collections.

These figures hide as much as they reveal and give scant indication of the accessibility to materials. It is evident that there is a long way to go before the multimedia collections are made available to all children within an authority, with only half of the service points offering AV materials and a paltry 7% offering computer software. A few authorities have facilitated greater access by developing networking systems for computer software but these are not greatly in evidence.

Over half of authorities impose minimum age limits which appear to apply to a range of formats. Most noticeably video loans are restricted to 18 plus age groups and audio to young people over 15 years. This is in contrast to the more liberal attitude of North America, Europe and the Far East. In Singapore, for example, children as young as six years may borrow audio CDs and videos. With respect to computer software, over a third of providing authorities restricted material to in-house use only.

Open or closed access constitutes another factor determining availability. More than a third of authorities impose closed access, largely as a result of the perceived vulnerability of formats to theft (although there is little evidence to support this contention). Given the modest distinction between the current cost of software and hardback children's books, this is not an entirely convincing justification.

Expenditure is another indicator of depth of provision. There is a striking imbalance between books and non-book material. For every £100 spent on materials, approximately £6.00 is allocated for audiovisual materials and £3.00 for computer software.

Thus the general statistics of provision, although not entirely healthy, look considerably less optimistic when the issue of accessibility is explored. We must conclude that it is probable that a sizable proportion of children are being deprived of the facility of borrowing these very familiar and popular formats.

Availability and accessibility constitute but one dimension of the question relating to the provision of representative collections. Another issue concerns the nature and range of formats. A look at the incidence of formats currently held shows that a typical collection comprises audio cassettes, vinyl discs, video cassettes, and CDs together with one or two other formats. This represents the established traditional media. Predominant are audio cassettes (largely spoken word), reflecting a thriving publishing industry, and it is gratifying that the comparatively new audio CD is becoming so evident. Although video collections are widely available, this must be tempered by the fact that only marginally more than a quarter of authorities offer loans to young people. Video provision is a contentious area with respect to content, with libraries holding opposing views about competing with the commercial outlets, and about the levying of charges.

However, the major concern centres on the nature of computer software collections. There is a highly disturbing dominance of obsolescent formats such as BBC and the older domestic games such as Atari and Amstrad, presumably the result of a decade and a half of restrained funding. It is estimated that only about 10% of authorities have introduced IBM compatible software, and that approximately 5% offer CD-ROM software. The exceptionally low level of multimedia provision is especially worrying in the light of the rapid multimedia publishing developments reported elsewhere. Given the predicted cutbacks in local government funding there is little optimism that provision will significantly increase on a national front.

Management and training implications of developing the media have been paid scant attention in children's libraries. Issues such as budgeting, physical access to materials, loan procedures, security, ergonomics, networking and information skills training about the media for staff and children have been largely ignored in the professional literature. Guidance has largely emanated from within the fields of special and academic librarianship, and greater cognisance should be made of the management of the media in children's libraries. Recently, professional bodies such as the Youth Libraries Group of the Library Association has been organizing training programmes nationally to address these concerns and to recognize the importance of promoting a wider range of literacy skills.

MANAGEMENT STRUCTURES

Local authorities differ in the ways in which they organize the management and delivery of library services. They also vary in terms of whether they are part of free-standing departments, responsible purely for libraries, or are part of larger directorates. Judy White, in her study *Frogs or chameleons*, identified four main patterns currently operating within England and Wales: library services within education directorates; library services within leisure directorates; the extended library service including arts and culture; and the independent library service.

Her analysis, through case studies, of the strengths and weaknesses of each of these, may be summarized as follows:

- **Education directorates**: The influence of libraries is considerable as they are perceived to be part of the larger whole of the powerful Education department, with librarians having considerable autonomy, sharing values, purposes and attitudes and able to thrive and develop their skills as competent librarians to fit the local cultures and local ways of working. However, the declining influence of Education departments is leaving library services potentially more vulnerable and exposed to debilitating change and librarians within an education value system which may have closed off the possibilities of partnerships with other departments, e.g. leisure/ arts/ culture.
- **Leisure directorates**: Librarians are part of large departments which have strategic concerns for community and quality of life developments and can contribute to and benefit from cross fertilisation of ideas from other value systems and approaches. This means they can develop more creative and risky programmes and services within an environment which is flexible and open-minded.
- **Extended library services including arts and culture**: The library service with arts and culture is of sufficient size to be influential in terms of political position, status, budgets and outlook to enable it to build a key service not reliant on others for credibility; librarians share similar outlooks and approaches with those from cultural backgrounds.
- **Independent library services**: The independence of the service has been coupled with relatively large size and high credibility within the local authority structure, making it valued and with a relatively high status, with librarians encouraged to be innovative, exploratory and to take risks within the service, which has been viewed as different from other 'quality of life' services (White, 1993, p.33).

Children's library service structures

The LA guidelines on children's library services (Library Association, 1991) state categorically that whichever staffing structure is chosen within any library authority, it should evolve from wide professional discussion rather than from short term or financial expediency and that two general principles should underlie this discussion, given the importance of the client group. These are:

1 children's needs are important enough to *require* specialist posts;
2 children's needs are too important to be *left* to specialist posts.

The guidelines make the following recommendations:

- the management of children's services requires a senior specialist post;
- this post should be on the department's senior management team;
- this post must be supported by sufficient other specialist posts to enable full and consistent delivery of services to children;
- all specialist posts should include a wider professional involvement;
- the responsibility of other public service staff to children must be identified and monitored, especially beyond the point at which specialist delivery of the service ends.

The guidelines emphasize that any local authority reviewing its structures will have a number of crucial decisions to make:

- the structure must reflect a policy which supports and defines its library provision to children;
- there must be a clear line-management structure to deliver the service, and the functional role of specialist posts must be clearly delineated;
- the advantages and disadvantages of integration and separation of services to education and services to the public must be carefully thought through;
- the provision of specialist and generalist posts at all levels must be considered (Library Association, 1991, p.19).

SCHOOL LIBRARIES

Increasingly the nature of school libraries, catering as they do for a specific clientel within the school and meeting the teaching and learning needs of that clientel, have led to separate development for school libraries. It is useful therefore to take a separate look at the role of the school library and schools library services.

The Library and Information Services Council (LISC) Report, *School libraries: the foundations of the curriculum* was a most important document for specifying clearly the role of the school library within the school. Although published in 1984, the philosophy which it expresses is still pertinent today:

We are convinced that school libraries and school library services have a vital role to play in the process of teaching children to learn. We are disturbed by evidence that this role is not recognized everywhere and by evidence of underuse and lack of library resources in schools. We believe that the nation will pay a heavy penalty for many years to come if it continues to neglect the self-evident contribution which school libraries could make in producing citizens who are self-reliant, well adjusted and, above all, able to make use of information. (Office of Arts and Libraries, 1984, p.1)

Today's schoolchildren will one day be responsible for creating the nation's wealth and organizing its society. An ability to learn throughout life will be crucial in equipping them not only to contribute to the industrial life of the nation but to find happiness themselves and contribute to that of others. It is widely recognized that they must learn how to learn. A central feature of the learning process is learning to deal with information. Information exists in increasing quantity and comes from a variety of sources through an ever-increasing range of media. An ability to cope with these changed circumstances is not innate: it must be acquired. (Office of Arts and Libraries, 1984, p.1)

The library is not aside from, or a buttress to, the curriculum, but its skills are the very foundations of the curriculum. (Office of Arts and Libraries, 1984, p.8)

The more recent report by the Book Trust, *Books in schools*, published in 1992, largely endorses this philosophy:

We are, increasingly, an information-dependent society, and the ability to acquire and make use of information lies at the heart of personal and professional decision making . . . Reading and enquiry can become habits for life if children learn from an early age to use books and other resources both for information and for pleasure. It is in the primary school, therefore, that the foundations of independent learning must be laid and positive attitudes towards reading for pleasure developed. This can set the pattern for later learning. (Book Trust, 1992, p.41)

This was the approach emphasized in the introduction by Ross Shimmon and the foreword by Stewart Robertson to the Library Association's guidelines for school libraries, *Learning resources in schools* (ed. Kinnell), also published in 1992:

School libraries are, or should be, an integral part of the educational process. (Kinnell, 1992, p.4)

Good libraries empower. Using their resources can unfetter our imaginations; disclose hitherto unrealized worlds; promote knowledge; induce pleasure; make us laugh; impart insights; challenge our preconceptions; assuage fears; prick our conscience; inflame our sensibilities; and provide professional refreshment. What we learn from good books and other resources becomes part of us. Children and young people are entitled to the best – a range and depth of learning resources appropriate to their personal, social, emotional and intellectual needs. (Kinnell, 1992, p.5)

and reinforced in *Better libraries*:

Better school library resource centres are rooted in the active belief of all staff, clearly stated, that the library is essential to the healthy growth of learning and that the library and its use are the responsibility of all teachers and of all others concerned with promoting learning. (Department of Education and Science, 1989, p.6)

But, as long ago as 1989, the Scottish Arts Council's *Readership report* had warned:

Libraries, and schools also for that matter, are able, in spite of limited funds, to purchase banks of expensive electronic equipment. This would seem to be part of the current obsession with acquiring information, sometimes, one feels, for the sake of acquiring information and without necessarily a sure sense of what it is going to be used for. By contrast, books have had a raw deal – book purchase generally, in libraries and schools, is dropping. Perhaps it is time to re-invent the book – certainly as a multi-access, portable data bank and with search and index facilities, it is unbeatable for sheer convenience. But it is important to remember that books are sources of pleasure as well as information. (Scottish Arts Council, 1989)

The role of the school library

The Library Association guidelines on school libraries, *Learning resources in schools* (Kinnell, 1992) specify that school library resource centres:

- have a central place in providing a range of information resources in support of the curriculum and of pupils' personal and social development;
- are part of the national information network, contributing to the provision of access to information needed by individuals. They therefore provide a link between the school and the national information infrastructure;
- facilitate learning and teaching.

The guidelines suggest that the emphasis on learning to learn, and learning to handle information bring information services into the centre of the delivery of the curriculum and into the centre of the learning process. The functions of the school library resource centre may be summarized as:

- to assist in providing a comprehensive source of learning materials in different formats for use by pupils individually and in small groups and provide opportunity for loan for home use; to satisfy curricular, cultural and supplementary requirements;
- to organize all relevant learning and teaching materials within the school, providing for a centralized information system concerning all the learning resources available to the school;
- to act as liaison with outside agencies and information sources and encourage their use by pupils and staff;

- to acquire and disseminate comprehensive information to all staff on materials to meet professional needs and, in cooperation with them, to be actively involved in curricular development within the school as well as maintaining liaison with appropriate bodies in this respect;
- to make its team available for teachers to consult on the selection and use of appropriate material to achieve their learning objectives;
- to make opportunities for staff and pupils to learn how to use relevant materials, and to provide training in the exploitation of the facilities of a school library resource centre. The school library resource centre should provide a focus for the development of the school's information skills curriculum (Kinnell, 1992, pp.14–15).

The guidelines lay down recommended standards for staffing, accommodation, furniture, equipment, management and organization of resources, and a learning skills curriculum within individual schools.

Better libraries, the guidelines put forward by Her Majesty's Inspectorate of Schools, highlight the following as evidence of good practice in school libraries. Better libraries:

- are easy to get to and pleasant to be in;
- provide what readers want to read;
- are well matched to what learners have to learn;
- are well equipped to help the learning process;
- have skilled, enthusiastic staff who know how libraries work and have the time to see that learners' needs are met;
- develop and use pupils' skills as librarians;
- are funded to take sensible heed of costs and replacement needs;
- attractively present well-chosen stock which relates to learners' ages, abilities and interests;
- make good use of the expertise and stock of Schools Library Services;
- look regularly at what they have and how it is being used (Department of Education and Science, 1989, p.6).

The guidelines published by the American Association of School Librarians and Association for Educational Communications and Technology, *Information power* (1988), encompasses a number of specific objectives:

- to provide intellectual access to information through systematic learning activities which develop cognitive strategies for selecting, retrieving, analyzing, evaluating, synthesizing, and creating information at all age levels and in curriculum content areas;
- to provide physical access to information through a) a carefully selected and systematically organized collection of diverse learning resources, represent-

ing a wide range of subjects, levels of difficulty, communication formats, and technological delivery systems; b) access to information and materials outside the library media center and the school building through such mechanisms as inter-library loans, networking and other cooperative agreements, and online searching of databases; and c) providing instruction in operation of equipment necessary to use the information in any format;

- to provide learning experiences that encourage users to become discriminating consumers and skilled creators of information through introduction to the full range of communications media and use of the new and emerging information technologies;
- to provide leadership, instruction, and consulting assistance in the use of instructional and information technology and the use of sound instructional design principles;
- to provide resources and activities that contribute to lifelong learning, while accommodating a wide range of differences in teaching and learning styles and in instructional methods, interests, and capacities;
- to provide a facility that functions as the information center of the school, as a locus for integrated, interdisciplinary, intergrade, and school-wide learning activities;
- to provide resources and learning activities that represent a diversity of experiences, opinions, social and cultural prespectives, supporting the concept that intellectual freedom amd access to information are prerequisite to effective and responsible citizenship in a democracy (American Association of School Librarians, 1988, pp.1–2).

Information skills

Implicit in the guidelines from both the UK and USA are the place of information skills at the heart of the child's learning. These were spelt out in *School libraries: the foundations of the curriculum* in 1984:

> . . . one major thread of a pupil's school life is that of gradually developing the ability to pose questions, to seek sources of information, and to select, arrange and present. The child who can manage these skills well is not only likely to be a successful pupil, but also is preparing her or himself for all aspects of adult life, in which personal, social and occupational power and satisfaction depend to a considerable extent on an individual's ability to handle information . . . Thus learning to learn and learning to handle information are the key parts of the curriculum content of schooling, both for school and other study success and as preparation for adult life. (Office of Arts and Libraries, 1984, p.8)

At the centre of all school 'assignments' and virtually all adult jobs is a remarkably similar sequence of tasks. In some assignments certain tasks are more important or more difficult, and others less important, but there are few information-handling tasks from a seven-year-old's 'topic' to, say, a marketing manager's investigations . . . which do not require the stages analysed below:

The Nine question steps:

1. What do I need to do? (formulate and analyse need)
2. Where could I go? (identify and appraise sources)
3. How do I get the information? (trace and locate individual resources)
4. Which resources shall I use? (examine, select and reject individual resources)
5. How shall I use the resources? (interrogate resources)
6. What should I make a record of? (recording and sorting information)
7. Have I got the information I need? (interpreting, analysing, synthesizing, evaluating)
8. How shall I present it? (presenting, communicating)
9. What have I achieved? (evaluation). (Office of Arts and Libraries, 1984, p.9)

As Rogers says in his review of research into the teaching of information skills and its impact on education:

> The Marland definition of information skills is wide ranging involving library-user education, reading development, experimental and research training, study skills and media literacy. It remains the key point of reference in current thinking and research – either in terms of confirming its continuing validity or as a source of disagreement and a jumping-off point for redefinition. (Rogers, 1994, p.3)

The importance of learning and information skills was endorsed by *Books in schools*:

> A well-organized school library, with its own learning skills curriculum, can play a central role by creating an effective learning environment for all pupils and underpinning learning across the school. Through such a curriculum, pupils can achieve the necessary tasks of locating, selecting, interrogating, interpreting, and communicating knowledge and understanding . . . The library – or library resource centre – should be at the core of primary and secondary schools' work, responding to the school's changing needs, awakening and extending pupils' awareness of imaginative literature, meeting their reference needs across the curriculum, and helping to develop their information-handling skills. (Book Trust, 1992, p.41)

Libraries also play an important part in ensuring pupils progression through primary, secondary and into further and higher education. The development of individuals learning and information skills are essential elements of this progression but, despite the fact that the National Curriculum is founded on the principles of progression, no system is in place to ensure that pupils progressing through schools will encounter effective library services that can coordinate and support their learning needs. Because library provision in schools is largely hit and miss, it is rarely coordinated to ensure effective progression.

The revised *Handbook for the inspection of schools*, which now consists of three separate volumes for secondary, primary and special schools, will take effect in the summer term of 1996. Each of these handbooks contains a separate page on the school library and also contains separate statements to the effect that inspection teams will assess school libraries for the adequacy of their resources and their 'impact on the breadth of the curriculum and its ability to address the needs of all pupils' (OFSTED, 1995).

The role of the professional school librarian

All of the above emphasize the need for professional librarianship skills within the school situation, working alongside the teacher. Aidan Chambers has long been a promoter of the importance of libraries and professional librarians in promoting wider reading in schools. As long ago as 1983, he was saying clearly:

> a school's own library ought to be active, inspirational, and central in the formal and informal life of pupils and staff. Librarians in charge ought to be at least the equivalent in every way – money, status, prestige, and administrative power – with heads of departments and subject faculties. Librarians should never be appointed as part of the administrative staff. (Chambers, 1983, p.63)

The *Books in schools* report supports this:

> The best way to meet the information needs of a school is to have an information specialist on the staff . . . Professional librarians are able to identify clients' information needs; manage information; locate, acquire, and exploit all relevant learning resources; and make good use of local and national information networks. They are, therefore, well placed to manage a school's learning resources and support the teaching of information-handling skills across the school. (Book Trust, 1992, p.43)

The LA guidelines, *Learning resources in schools* (Kinnell, 1992) emphasize the educational reasons for the appointment of chartered librarians in schools and spell out their role as to:

- collaborate with teachers and other educationalists in the development and evaluation of pupils' learning skills across the curriculum;
- maximize the effective use of the school's learning resources by the whole school community;
- provide access to a comprehensive range of learning materials in different formats for use by pupils individually and in small groups, selected to satisfy curricular, cultural and individual requirements, and to offer the opportunity for borrowing;
- enhance cross-curricular initiatives supporting multi-cultural education and equality for all;

- organize all relevant learning and teaching materials within the school to facilitate their location, accessibility and use;
- maintain up-to-date professional awareness of learning resources availability and use through regular visits to the Schools Library Service, attendance at exhibitions, training sessions and contact with publishers and other resource providers;
- liaise with outside agencies and information networks and encourage their use by pupils and staff in order to extend the range of resources available to the school;
- acquire and disseminate comprehensive information to all staff to meet professional needs, and to advise staff on the selection of appropriate materials to achieve their learning objectives;
- provide facilities for the production of learning materials within the school by staff and pupils;
- promote and foster the enjoyment of reading from the earliest age and encourage the reading habit and enrichment of pupils' imaginative and creative life at all ages through a variety of resources, taking into account their interests and abilities (Kinnell, 1992, pp.21–22).

There is clearly a need to highlight the librarian's distinct curricular role as a coordinator of resource requirements and of the development of information skills. In addition, there is an important and frequently overlooked element of the work of schools librarians in their role in supporting 'differentiation' within the curriculum, i.e. supporting pupils with varied abilities and needs. The librarian in a school is usually the only person who helps individual pupils with *all* aspects of their work.

The role of schools library services

The LA guidelines, *Learning resources in schools: guidelines for school libraries* (Kinnell, 1992) recommends standards for schools library services, emphasizing their role as a support, consultancy, training, and information network for all local education authority maintained schools. They are the most economic means of providing a wide range of support materials and professional advice, with books, audiovisual resources, computer software and CD-ROMs forming the core stock of an effective resources base for school libraries, providing the following services:

- access to loan materials which supplement the core collection for school library resource centres;
- the opportunity to exchange these materials on a regular basis;

- materials which are borrowed by schools for a specific period of time to support project or topic work taking place within the curriculum, but which cannot be sustained by a school's existing resources;
- access to bibliographical information which would be unavailable or financially unsupportable in an individual school library resource centre;
- access to databases and IT support;
- display materials, exhibitions and support for special events, such as book weeks, author visits and other promotional events;
- a major contribution to materials selection in schools. This may be through a permanent exhibition collection of recommended materials aimed at the needs of an individual school (Kinnell, 1992, pp.62–63).

The guidelines again reinforce the need for professional skills within school libraries, by emphasizing the professional support which could be given to schools and the local education authority, for example: advisory support to heads, governors, teachers and parents on the management, organization and development of learning resources within schools; policy, strategic and financial planning and management and a particular key role as a training agent for the authority in fundamental areas of learning resource provision and use; learning skills and materials selection.

The two-year *Supports to learning project* (Heeks, 1990) studied the effect of the Education Reform Act 1988 on schools library services (SLS) and found the following points emerging:

- The National Curriculum had brought increased demands from schools, and confirmed the value of SLS in giving access to a wide range of learning resources and specialist expertise. The National Curriculum had provided a stimulus to the introduction of new services, and brought opportunities for more intensive curriculum support via SLS.
- Local Management of Schools had caused SLS to cost each aspect of service, carry out market research and, in some cases redesign services. On the debit side, it had reduced the catalytic role SLS had played in school library development.

It found the following four factors as key indicators of SLS effectiveness:

- committed and politically skilled leadership: commitment to carry the service forward, to envision the future, and to take staff through the times of anxiety and the political judgement to enable opportunities to be recognized and seized;
- positive relationships with the funding departments: the most positive relationships were found where the SLS was part of the Education

Department, giving opportunities for SLS to integrate their work with other departmental concerns;

- customer focus: client orientation throughout the services; sound information base, with efficient system for gathering, manipulating and updating management information; understanding of customer needs; methods for monitoring customer satisfaction; readiness to redesign services to meet the needs of different clients;
- dependable service of high quality: quality of service becomes a key factor as SLS have both to attract and hold customers (Heeks, 1990, Checkpoint 4).

CURRENT REPORTS

Public Library Review

The final report (Aslib, 1995) outlines 4 purposes for the public library and 13 core functions. Among these core functions are: 'Ways to enlighten children, by enabling and encouraging them to discover information and the advantages of reading'. The responses from the research noted: 'strong feelings were expressed about the importance of the public library for children and young people' . . . 'Enlightening children on the benefits of reading and information discovery' was regarded by three-quarters of sampled users and non-users as one of the top-ranking functions of the public library, and firmly in the 'core' of its service: 'It is a role which fits in well with the purpose many people see for the public library . . . to serve the interests of future generations.' SOCCEL, in its response to the Review, noted that all 13 of the core functions are fundamental to the provision of a good quality service for children and young people, in particular:

- **Charging for services**: services to children and young people need to be free of charge, including provision of new technology, due to this client groups inability to fund their own needs and their dependence on adults to enable them to use libraries;
- **Monitoring of service**: there is a need to ensure that libraries are providing services within guidelines and standards – especially services to children and young people since they are less likely to demonstrate their dissatisfaction;
- **Nature of regional co-ordination and co-operation**: Children's and Young People's services have, in some areas, a very strong regional structure and support quality service development through mutual collaboration;
- **Progress towards achievement of a coherent IT structure**: If libraries have a future for children and young people it is by the development of the substantial infrastructure to create a genuine information superhighway;

- **Diversification of funding**: Many of the ideas for 'new' funding are built on libraries current image from the public and building on the inward look-ing tendencies of the profession. Children's and Young People's Services continually break this image with their innovations, collaboration and energy which motivates their commitment. This in turn generates a wide range of sponsorship to children's services caused by CYP librarians ability to look outside of themselves.
- **Specifying the service**: The LA Guidelines for children's services provide an excellent outline for specification and only require a brief supplement to include model performance indicators and standards to be fully useful. Standards must be clear, explicit and enforceable, minima not maxima (SOCCEL, nd).

The Aslib Review recommended that the DNH and library authorities should implement the proposals and recommendations in the LISC(E) working party report on library services for children and young people, *Investing in children* and drew attention to the continuing demand for expertise in specialist areas, for example children's library services. It is a pity that the extensive survey conducted among the over-16s by the Aslib consultancy team, was not replicated for chil-dren: this remains a gap as no equivalent survey work was carried out by the *Investing in children* working party.

Investing in children

We said earlier that *Investing in children* was a highly significant report, with rec-ommendations which will affect the future direction of children's library services. It emphasizes very effectively the importance of the public library in catering for the needs of children and the future economic and cultural health of the coun-try:

> The role of the public library in meeting the needs of children and young people is of paramount importance to the future economic and cultural health of this country. Continuation of its service to them, untrammelled by barriers to access such as charg-ing, is a critical factor in the future development of the public library service as a whole.

> . . . it is our clear view that, at a time when unfulfilled reading potential affects the eco-nomic, cultural and social life of the country, the potential of a library, and in partic-ular the public library which is freely available to all, as a force in support of reading and information literacy cannot be too strongly emphasized. By making books avail-able to all who want them, together with specialist staff to make them accessible through advice and assistance in the choice and use of them, libraries are uniquely placed to make a significant contribution to the encouragement of reading amongst children and young people.

Public libraries are the only means whereby the widest choice of titles can be made available free of charge to the user . . . They are the one potentially constant source of supply of books which can also provide an environment in which to enjoy reading and gain value from it.

The public library is the only statutory library service that is available to pre-school children, the 'under-five' age group, where introduction to books and the pleasure of reading is vital. (Department of National Heritage, 1995, pp.15, 16, 19, 47)

But the report warns of its concerns about the current political climate within which libraries operate:

The Working Party is in no doubt about the importance and the value of books and reading for children and young people. But we are concerned that they are in danger because of: Government policies with regard to the teaching of reading, plus the demands of the National Curriculum; competition from alternative recreational opportunities; competition from information technology in schools. (Department of National Heritage, 1995, p.13)

The report has no reservations about the remit of British public libraries to facilitate the technological needs of the young, making the important connection between the multimedia world of the child and the responsibility to support that environment:

Children nowadays are accustomed to using computers and multimedia formats for both recreation and information; their high use of OPACs in public libraries has also been noted and their perception of the public library as a place that is 'switched on' to technology should be capitalised. (Department of National Heritage, 1995, p.62)

The Public Library Review similarly supported the notion that children's libraries should be responsive to Information Technology developments. However, it added a critical rider that public libraries were not fulfilling their responsibilities in this respect:

. . . young people increasingly operate in an IT environment with which they are familiar and adept. The Public Library Service is doing little in this area to meet either their needs or their expectations. (Aslib, 1995)

Investing in children takes a structured and managerial approach, as is fitting a serious report in the 1990s. It specifically builds on the Library Association guidelines and reminds us of the standards set in these. It is suggested that the major recommendations break down into the core role of the children's library:

- The satisfaction of children's and young people's needs as individuals should be recognized and promoted as a core element of the public library service, central to its role in the promotion of literacy and its role in relation to educational institutions.

and strategic management issues, locally:

- Each local authority should publish an integrated strategy for delivering library and information services to meet the identified needs of children and young people throughout its area;
- There must be clear objectives for services to children and young people, and clear priorities should be established for children's needs across ages and stages of development;
- A multi-service Charter for the Child, drawn up jointly by all departments of the local authority that provide services for children, and published by the local authority, should set out the child's entitlement to service . . . There should be model standards for services for children and young people, specifying minimum levels of provision and entitlement;
- The percentage of the total materials budget applied to services for children and young people should be determined locally and should be at least the same as the percentage of children and young people in the population served;
- Every library authority should have a strategy . . . to ensure and promote equal access to its resources for children and young people . . . for specialist training of staff engaged in work with children and young people;
- The public library's senior management team (or equivalent) should include a person with designated overall responsibility for services to children and young people;

and nationally:

- The Department of National Heritage should . . . initiate work on a model charter which can be adapted for local use and published by public libraries as a Charter for the Reader relating to children and their needs . . . take the lead in the development of national performance indicators which reflect the rights and entitlements of children, and include at least a basic indicator for a child's rights to reading materials and library services;
- Priority should be given to research which explores the benefits, impacts and effectiveness of library provision for children and young people.

Reactions to *Investing in children*

The above recommendations are clearly sensible, timely and pertinent, though tending to concentrate on good management practice now and extending current good practice, rather than a vision of *how* libraries for children might prepare for the future. While model standards and performance indicators are worthy and necessary in today's climate, there is little indication in the report of what might be acceptable as minimum provision. There is much meat here and, while some of the recommendations and statements are fairly predictable, they did need to be stated in a report emanating from a government department. The major concerns are: the lack of a long-term vision of how children's libraries might develop in the future; a rather cosy assumption that everything is rosy but just needs tightening up a bit; the lack of evidence in the report in terms of actual statistics demonstrating decline or increase in usage, expenditure etc.; or any argument for the need to increase investment in bookstock, staff or new services, such as developing technologies (Elkin and Denham, 1995).

Generally, the tenor of the report has been warmly welcomed by people closely concerned with children and their access to books and information through public libraries. The report stimulated a nationwide programme of discussion and focus of attention, internally, externally and politically. One authority was positively euphoric about the report: 'The working party are to be congratulated on the comprehensive coverage and its recommendations are wholeheartedly supported in their entirety . . . addresses the concerns of the profession for the future of library services to young people and the adoption of the recommendations would have far-reaching effects on the provision of a committed, quality service to young people'.[1]

Many authorities have used the report as a catalyst for local thinking, strategic planning and development. A number of authorities suggest that adoption of its recommendations would have far-reaching effects on the provision of a committed quality service to young people; others hope that the timeliness of presenting such a report from a national perspective may help to stave off any further cuts in expenditure at a local level. There is general recognition, though, that only if there is some commitment at national level from the Department of National Heritage and the Department for Education and Employment will the report have any real power.

Local authority responses to *Investing in children*

A survey of local authorities in England and Wales carried out by the author during 1995 showed that the majority of authorities had responded to *Investing in children* in a positive way, at the very least seeing this as a timely stimulus to discussion.[1] Some specific responses are discussed below.

Many library authorities have presented *Investing in children* or a summarized version to the appropriate committee of the local council, often flagging issues of particular concern to the individual authority and using the report to further policies or strategies already in hand. Because of the varied structures within local government, the appropriate committee, as previously outlined, may be a Libraries; Libraries and Arts; Leisure Services or Education Committee, or a combination of these.

In some cases, this approach proved particularly successful in moving services forward:

- **Hertfordshire's** committee report resulted in full support for work already undertaken, for an increase to the children's budget, increased access to IT and a requirement for the Education Committee to reinvestigate delegation of the schools library service;
- **Leicestershire** presented both the LISC(E) report (Office of Arts and Libraries, 1984)and the Library Association's guidelines (1991) to the Committee and both were endorsed. They are currently reviewing their services in the light of the recommendations; future expression of this will be seen in a service specification;
- **Nottinghamshire's** report to their senior management team was approved as a basis for a fundamental review of the public library service to children, with a service specification; a training needs analysis and development of a training and staff development programme in relation to children's library work at all levels. The paper presented to the Leisure Services Committee was approved and official responses sent to the Department for National Heritage, Department for Education and Employment and OFSTED;
- **Newcastle** presented a report to their Libraries and Arts Committee, where it was 'enthusiastically received' and viewed as timely in 'supporting development of future strategies and objectives' as part of the review of libraries and arts which was in progress.

In some authorities this was used for a very specific purpose:

- **Buckinghamshire** saw the report as offering a valuable source of guidance to the various project groups involved in discussions about local government reorganization.

Some authorities, though, received a fairly lukewarm response, while acknowledging the value of *Investing in children* as a catalyst:

- **Liverpool** presented a report to the Libraries and Arts sub-committee but otherwise report a 'low key response', while acknowledging that *Investing in children* supports their need for a strategy and charter for children's services;
- **Cornwall** set up a working party to look at providing a strategic plan for Cornwall but results at present are constrained by the current economic limits and political realities: 'despite a great deal of commitment from all our staff with the constant limits set by under-staffing, under-resourcing and lack of national and local political will to overcome this, libraries will continue to be the Cinderella of public services.'

- **Somerset** similarly is concerned that the recommendations of the report cannot be effectively achieved with inadequate and shrinking budgets.

Some authorities reported no internal reaction to LISC and others expressed disappointment that the report failed to come up with any hard arguments for increased expenditure on library services for children or with evidence that higher spending might equal a better service or have a greater impact on literacy and child development. There were concerns that the report judged services by inputs (the money, imagination and effort spent) rather than the outputs (what is achieved).

A number of authorities are now seriously considering an integrated strategy, as recommended in the report (Dorset; Calderdale; Croydon; Devon; Essex; Nottinghamshire; Warwickshire; Westminster).

- **Norfolk** are in the process of looking at the main recommendations with staff throughout the service, with a view to a joint strategy for children's services planned as a future project;
- A whole council initiative is a result of a committee report in **Hereford and Worcester**, with the Libraries as the lead department in a 'Commitment to Children' initiative;
- **Wolverhampton** reported to the Council's Chief Officers, seeking support for an integrated strategy and charter for the child;
- **Stockport** prepared a report for their Committee, drawing attention in addition to the Coopers & Lybrand Report on School Library Services, noting in particular the need for school library services to be 'constantly innovative': lukewarm response only is reported! (Department of National Heritage, 1994)

The *Public library review* and *Investing in children* have had little obvious effect on government policies, although some of the findings were utilized in the Library Association rally, mentioned below. The potential of the public library as a force to reach children *and* their parents/carers is still not fully recognized and the damage inherent in many of the cutbacks being experienced by public and school libraries is little understood.

The findings reported earlier about lack of strategic vision with regards to multimedia and computer provision in children's libraries is similarly an issue at this time. We are on the threshold of a new millennium, and while good work is being undertaken by library authorities, it is evident there is considerable truth behind the *Public library review's* assertion that: 'the Public Library service is doing little in this area to meet [children's] needs or expectations' (Aslib, 1995). In part this is a consequence of the underfunding of public services over many years. However, research shows that ideological reasons play a significant role, too.

Some authorities believe that it is not the responsibility of the children's service to offer media, that other departments should make that provision. There is a strong suggestion that staff feel uneasy about the new computer and multimedia technologies and are reluctant to venture into developing collections and services. A large range of issues need to be urgently addressed if children's libraries are to respond adequately to the challenges of the information age. There is genuine concern that, with the impending local government reorganization and predicted cuts in funding, the development of collections and services to support and promote the use of media by children will continue to receive inadequate attention. If this happens, then UK library services to children and young people are in great danger of letting the new information revolution pass them by.

CAMPAIGNS

An appreciation of the vital role of libraries in the development of the individual child and concern about lack of awareness in government and decision-makers circles about such issues, allied to increasing pressures on libraries from the National Curriculum, Local Management of Schools, local government reorganization and severe economic cuts in public services has prompted considerable outspoken commentary and personal and orchestrated campaigns.

Michael Rosen, writing in *Books for keeps* in 1993, contrasted the present decline in services to the huge changes which had taken place in attitudes to literacy, children's books and children in the period prior to 1988 or what Professor Ted Wragg calls 'Mad Curriculum Disease'. He traced the innovations in the early 1980s to the new and expanded institutions which grew up at that time: school libraries in many schools, class libraries, school bookshops, professional school librarians, school library support services, teacher-parent reading programmes, Children's Book Week, the Federation of Children's Book Groups. He also drew attention to the magazines and book clubs which supported these changes and were totally out of reach of government directives: *Books for keeps*; *Books for your children*; *Dragon's teeth*; *Letterbox library* and the autonomous networks of information and self-education that sprang up around teachers' centres, libraries and teachers' associations such as the National Association of Teachers of English:

> It'll be seen in years to come . . . that all this had a profound effect on what was written, who was writing, what was published and who was reading. We were on the verge, or perhaps in the middle, of a truly popular culture . . . The current government has declared war on the reading of books . . . their weapons: the closing of public libraries; the elimination of library support services; the forced amateuring of school librarians – professionals can't be afforded; budget restrictions on school book buying; the domination of fixed courses of study, set texts and testing that limits casual and pupil-led reading and browsing. (Rosen, 1993, p.5)

He defended the good things about reading: 'the recreative, imaginative, possibility-opening, autonomy-encouraging' features which reading based on current government initiatives stifles:

> We have to make as wide a range of experiences as possible available to children - ones that include all of the cultures and classes of the children themselves . . . .it means fighting to save every part of the elaborate support structure described earlier, because it's mainly through that structure that children receive the multi-cultural, the offbeat, and the dissident. (Rosen, 1993, p.7)

A concern about what cutbacks, particularly the closure of libraries might mean for the individual was highlighted by author Nicholas Fisk:

> There they are, millions of people who all belong to local libraries. What are they looking for, for heavens sake? They are head-hunting. They want access to other people's heads, brains, minds, emotions. They want to know what it was really like in the trenches in WW1 – how to do Malaysian cooking – how to mend a moped. They want to learn about lush love affairs, astronomy, Sherlock Holmes, the new Ford or Fiat. It's all there in the local library, and along with the cassettes, records, magazines and help with Regulation C225/348/para vi (garden sheds, erection of). And if it isn't there, they will get it for you. Fill in the card . . . I need the public libraries. You don't? Very well, close them. And while you're at it, close your mind. But over my dead body. (Fisk, 1993, p.23)

This has been mirrored in concerns about the inadequacy of bookstocks, particularly in school libraries, for example in *Books in schools*:

> Rarely have so many pupils had so few books. Today, no school can afford to give a pupil a book on science, maths, history and English to take home to study. That is one of the conclusions from this new report on the state of books and reading in schools . . . at the core of this report is the belief that reading is the key to learning and books are the key to reading . . . We are in danger of creating a book-starved generation. (Book Trust, 1992, pp.3, 70)

The editorial in *Books for keeps* at the end of 1995, summed up clearly the pressures on books:

> Recent times have been more than a little hard on the friends of text. Books budgets in schools are increasingly under pressure as resources are diverted into media which should be complementing literacy not competing with it; library provision and specialist expertise steadily diminishes or must be eked out across ever-widening remits; the government persists in inflating wholly fictitious arguments about differing approaches to reading in order to divert attention from the over-size classes which undermine any approach; even the book-trade itself sometimes seems to be doing us no favours. (Powling, 1995, p.3)

Library Association campaigns

The above quotations were emotive words from a number of leading writers and educationalists, but they summed up the often unexpressed feelings of the general public about the value of public libraries. It was just such concern about the political framework which was threatening libraries of all kinds which led the Library Association to organize Save Our Libraries Day in February 1992, National Library Week in November 1993, and the Library Power campaign in 1995, all with an impressive range of national events and press coverage.

Save Our Libraries Day in 1992 focused on the cuts in public library services, with the results of a survey of public libraries showing that 50% of respondents reported that cuts were being planned, usually on an already depleted service: many library authorities were heading towards a situation where they would be unable to offer the 'comprehensive and efficient' public library service they are obliged to offer under the 1964 Act. Yet the staff in public libraries are still issuing an average of ten books per year to every man, woman and child in the country at half the cost of a newspaper! Particular attention was drawn to the cuts in opening hours, comparing the number of libraries open 60 hours or more in England and Wales in 1974/75 (229) with those open 60 hours or more in 1991/92 (18) (Save Our Libraries Day, 1992).

In 1993, The Library Association mobilized the resources of libraries of all kinds to help put libraries higher up the political agenda, to encourage non-users to see what libraries could offer: 'Libraries are all about producing a literate society with liberated minds . . . Libraries empower people, by letting them make up their own minds. Without them we would be continually reinventing the wheel' (National Library Week, 1993).

The Library Association's approach was more specific in 1995, with the Library Power campaign launched in January and culminating in a focus week in May. It aimed to put the spotlight on the role of libraries in the education and overall development of children and young people. With the theme of 'switching on young minds', Library Power focused on libraries empowering young people with information, nurturing independent thought and imagination as well as providing vital support to education in delivering the curriculum. Through a national framework of competitions, activities and events in libraries and in schools around the UK, Library Power attempted to reach parents, decision makers in education, young people, their carers, local and national government and the national and regional media. The media coverage was good but too recent to assess long-term benefits in terms of a higher profile and understanding of the role of libraries.

Mary Hoffman, writing about the Library Power campaign, stated categorically:

If 'Library Power' seems a bit of an oxymoron to you, it's because libraries and librarians have such a poor public image. How did the stereotype of a dull person in a dull place ever take hold? Libraries are the most subversive places in the world, much more so than the smoke-filled backrooms, because they hold everything you need to teach you your civil rights and empower you to use them.

And this is just one tiny aspect of what they do. They are also time-machines to take you back into history or forward into unimaginable futures. And supersonic jets to take you anywhere in the world at the turn of a page. And they are so full of mind-expanding substances, it's a wonder to me that they aren't regularly raided and closed down.

Well, actually they 'are' sometimes closed down. Or at least they have their hours and staff reduced and their book funds frozen. This happens or is threatened to happen about once a year. As the days shorten and local councils start to think about setting their budgets, local library campaigners dust down their old banners, get out their writing paper and heave a great sigh. (Hoffman, 1995, pp.18–19)

Concerns about further government cuts stimulated the Library Association to campaign about the future of public libraries, with a rally at the House of Commons on 18 October 1995:

In the short term we want to focus attention on the damage being done to libraries by local authority spending cuts . . . In the longer term there are some fundamental issues to be addressed about the position that we want libraries to occupy in the next century. Without a vision for the future and a major injection of cash they cannot be fully wired up to deliver information to everyone through the new technology. If we wire up homes and businesses but no libraries the gap between the information rich and the information poor will grow alarmingly. (Library Association, 1995)

Once again, this campaign received good media coverage but little response from government circles, other than the statement by Virginia Bottomley, Secretary of State for National Heritage, in which she defined what the government expected public libraries to deliver to their users and announced a wide-ranging policy paper on the public library service as part of the government's continuing review (Department of National Heritage, 1995b).

CONCLUSION

The role of children's and school libraries in the educational, cultural and personal development of the child has been highlighted in a number of reports and sets of guidelines. The professional dynamic of providing a high quality service to children through public and school libraries has also been emphasized. The present political and economic climate provides a gloomy and depressing framework for the development of the quality of library service required to meet the needs of recent educational change, particularly the National Curriculum and Local Management of Schools. The reality of cuts in numbers of libraries, opening hours and book stock have been highlighted in recent campaigns in various sectors of the children's book world. Later chapters will look at collection development, marketing and promotion and will give examples of current practice within children's library provision.

We are on the threshold of a new millennium, and while much good work is being undertaken by some library authorities with respect to multimedia materials, it is evident there is considerable truth behind the Department for National Heritage's assertion in its *Public library review* that 'the Public Library service is doing little in this area to meet [children's] needs or expectations' (Aslib, 1995).

In part this is a consequence of the underfunding of public service over many years. However, research suggests that ideological reasons play a significant role too. Some authorities believe that it is not the responsibility of the children's service to offer media, that other departments should make provision. There is also a strong suggestion that staff feel uneasy about the new computer and multimedia technologies and are reluctant to venture into developing collections and services. That there is a strong undercurrent of unease about the new technologies is a consequence of the deficiencies in the education and training of children's librarians.

A large range of issues need to be urgently addressed if children's libraries are to respond adequately to the challenges of the information age. There is genuine concern that, with the impending local government reorganization and predicted cuts in funding, the development of collections and services to support and promote the use of media by children will continue to receive inadequate attention. If this happens, then British public library services to children and young people are in great danger of letting the new information revolution pass them by.

Notes

1   I would like to thank colleagues in the 65 local authorities who responded to my letter requesting information about their current library service to children and young people, and in particular requesting information about local responses to the LISC Report *Investing in children*. Where confidentiality was requested, I have respected this. Other information is taken from the first issue of ASCEL Newsletter (ASCEL, 1995).

2   A full list of library authorities and the names and addresses of the principal children's and education librarians can be found in the *ASCEL Directory 1995/6* (Westminster Libraries, Schools Library Service, 62 Shirland Road, London W9 2EH).

REFERENCES

American Association of School Librarians and Association for Educational Communications and Technology (1988), *Information power: guidelines for school library media programmes*. Chicago and London, American Library Association.

ASCEL (1995), *ASCEL Newsletter*. vol. 1. 1995, ed. Christine Hall (Westminster Libraries, Schools Library Service, 62 Shirland Road, London W9 2EH).

Aslib (1995), *Review of the public library services in England and Wales: for the Department of National Heritage*. London, Aslib (The Association for Information Management).

Book Trust (1992), *Books in schools*. Book Trust Report Number 1; British National Bibliography Research Fund Report 60. London, Book Trust.

Brown, R. (1979), 'Public library aims and objectives: children's services', *Library Association record*, **81** (8), 1979, 382.

Chambers, A. (1983), *Introducing books to children*. 2nd edn. revised and expanded. London, Heinemann.

Department of Education and Science (1989), *Better libraries: good practice in schools*: a survey by HM Inspectorate. London, HMSO.

Department of National Heritage (1994), *Schools library services and financial delegation to schools: a report to the Department of National Heritage by Coopers and Lybrand*. Library and Information Series no.21.

The Department of National Heritage (1995a), *Investing in children: the future of library services for children and young people*. Library and Information Services Council (England), Working Party on Library Services for Children and Young People. London, HMSO.

Department of National Heritage (1995b), *The public library services: Virginia Bottomley sets out libraries key functions* . . . News release from the Department of National Heritage, 18 December 1995.

Elkin, J. C. and Denham, D. (1995), 'Investing in children: a real strategy for future development?' *The new review of children's literature and librarianship*, **1**, 13–34.

Fasick, A. (1980), 'Research and measurement in library services to children', *International library review*, **12** (1), 1980, 95–104.

Fisk, N. (1993), 'Dear Mr Peach . . .', *Books for keeps*, no. 83, November 1993, 23.

Fleet, A. (1973), *Children's libraries*. London, Andre Deutsch.

Geras, A. (1993), 'Dear Mr Peach . . .', *Books for keeps*, no. 83, November 1993, 23.

Heeks, P. (1990), *School library services today: the first report of the Supports to Learning Project*. BLR&DD Report 6024. London, British Library Board.

Heeks, P. and Kinnell, M. (1993), *School libraries at work*. Delivering the National Curriculum Project, The British Library.

Hill, J. (1973), *Children are people: the librarian in the community*. London, Hamish Hamilton.

Hoffman, M. (1995), 'Power to the book people', *Books for keeps*, no. 94, September 1995, 18.

IFLA (International Federation of Library Associations) (1995) *UNESCO public library manifesto*.

Kinnell, M. (ed.) (1992), *Learning resources in schools: Library Association guidelines for school libraries*. London, Library Association Publishing.

Library Association (1991), *Children and young people: Library Association guidelines for public library services*. London, The Library Association.

Library Association (1992), Comments from papers presented at a one day seminar: Opening the national debate; library services to children and young people', 28/29 October 1992. (unpublished)

Library Association (1995), Press release.

Library Association. School library information pack, regularly updated.

Library Association record (1979), 'Performance measurement: 1. Children's services (excluding school services)', *Library Association record*, **81** (9), 1979, 455.

Library Power (1995), Press release and publicity packs from the Library Association.

Lonsdale, R. and Wheatley, A. (1990), *The provision of audiovisual and computer materials to young people by British public libraries*. (British National Bibliography Research Fund Report 49). London, The British Library.

Lonsdale, R. and Wheatley A. (1990b), 'The provision of audiovisual and computer services to young people by British public libraries: nature, range and availability of materials', *International review of children's literature and librarianship*, **5** (3). 159–79.

Lonsdale, R. and Wheatley A. (1991), 'The provision of audiovisual and computer services to young people by British public libraries: collection management and promotion of services', *International review of children's literature and librarianship*, **6** (1), 31–55.

Lonsdale, R. and Wheatley A. (1992), 'The provision of computer materials and services to young people by British public libraries', *Journal of librarianship and information science*, 24 (2), 25–37.

Marshall, M. (1975), *Libraries and literature for teenagers*. London, Deutsch, 1975.

National Library Week (1993), Press release for National Library Week, 1-7, The Library Association, who also published a calendar of events and a newsletter.

Office of Arts and Libraries (1984), *School libraries: the foundations of the curriculum*. Report of the Library and Information Services Council's Working Party on School Library Services. Library Information Series no. 13. London, HMSO.

OFSTED (1995), *OFSTED framework and handbook*. London, OFSTED.

Powling, C. (1995), 'Backing the book', *Books for keeps*, no. 95, November 1995, 3.

Ray, S. (1979), *Children's librarianship*. London, Clive Bingley.

Rogers, R. (1994), *Teaching information skills: a review of the research and its impact on education*. London, British Library Research, Bowker Saur.

Rosen, M. (1993), 'On the importance of books in schools', *Books for keeps*, no. 79, March 1993, 4–7.

Save Our Libraries Day (1992), Press release and publicity materials from the Library Association.

Scottish Arts Council (1989), *Readership report 1989*.

SOCCEL and AMDECL. *Library services to children and young people: paper presented to LISC(E)*, no date.

Swindells, R. (1993), 'Dear Mr Peach . . .', *Books for keeps*, no.83, November 1993, 23.

Teinila, L. and Pissard, A. (1990), *Goals for children's libraries: draft of IFLA guidelines for children's libraries*. International Federation of Library Associations.

White, J. (1993), *Frogs or chameleons: the public library service and the public librarian: a research report investigating the status of public libraries and the careers of public librarians in England*. London, The Library Association.

5

Trends in publishing and supply of children's books

Judith Elkin

Book manufacturing facilities and sound publishing industry are vital to national development; booksellers and libraries provide necessary services to publishers and the reading public; free flow of books between countries is of fundamental importance; books serve and promote international understanding and peaceful cooperation. (UNESCO, 1982)

Given the international reputation Britain has for its children's publishing it seems ironic that it is barely recognized and certainly little valued in this country by those who could make it a powerful and creative tool where it would be most effective – in schools. (Eccleshare, 1992, p.5)

INTRODUCTION

In terms of quality and originality of writing, illustration and production UK children's book publishing has long led the world and the industry is viewed with envy by other parts of the developed and developing world. Yet, as in other countries, the publishing industry has been vulnerable to economic and political pressures. When the target audience is the child, with little direct influence or power, these pressures are writ large.

Children's book publishing in the UK has traditionally relied heavily on the institutional market, on public and school libraries, rather than on the retail trade. A study of the current state of children's and education book publishing shows clearly that political pressures of educational change and economic recession have put an enormous strain on publishers, booksellers and library suppliers. Yet, at the same time, fortuitously or perhaps through a timely entrepreneurial approach, new markets have opened up. The scale of change has been unprecedented and is worrying many observers concerned with the future education and well-being of children.

This chapter looks at the current state of publishing, bookselling and library supply for children's and schools books in the UK, with particular reference to the forces of change which are affecting the changing environment of children's and schools' librarianship outlined in previous chapters. A brief study of children's book publishing in the past 25 years provides a backdrop to discussion of current issues and raises a number of instances of critical concern.

TWENTY-FIVE YEARS OF CHILDREN'S BOOK PUBLISHING

It is easy to assume that today's crises in public expenditure have not been faced before. A study of children's publishing over the last quarter of a century shows this to be only partly true. In 1990, Brough Girling was saying: 'I have been concerned with the British book trade for only about 20 years, but I can't remember a time when it did not think it had its back to the wall' (Girling, 1990, p.1526).

1971–9

Children's books of the year, which has been published almost annually since 1971, allows a study of the vagaries of publishing and book production, against the background of a changing institutional and public market. As each year sums up the major publishing triumphs, and disasters, in terms of children's books, the year-on-year snapshot provides a fascinating overview of the major titles being published. The provocative introductions each year from knowledgeable critics and observers chart the underlying trends in publishing, economics, sociology and politics as they were affecting children's books. Three names have dominated this: Elaine Moss, Barbara Sherrard-Smith and Julia Eccleshare. Each in their own way brought an individuality and a critical eye to the world of children's books, born from a deep understanding of children and a love and respect for reading.

Even in 1971 the National Book League (later The Book Trust) was campaigning for a rise in the amount of money spent on books in schools, to counteract the annual fall in the rate of local authority expenditure on class and library books (Educational Publishers Council, 1971). In June 1972, Mrs Thatcher made the suggestion that national standards might in due course be set up for book and equipment expenditure in schools, rather than leaving it to the individual whim of the local education authorities. The Secretary of State for Education responded to growing concerns about illiteracy, by setting up the Bullock Committee to enquire into aspects of teaching of reading and the use of English in schools.

Writing in the introduction to *Children's books of the year 1973*, Elaine Moss stated: '1973 may go down in the history of children's books in Britain as the year in which publishers made the most of book conditions that still prevailed, feeling in their bones that an enforced restructuring of the whole children's publishing scene was just around the corner . . . the present cuts in educational expenditure and the staggering rise in the price of books (children's novels, hardbound, must approach and will probably exceed the £2 mark in 1974) . . . spell disaster' (Moss, 1973, p.9). This was the era of the three-day working week in the UK, world economic problems and shortage of power. The steep rise in the cost of hardbound books accounted for a large number of paperback originals and the simultaneous publication of many titles in paperback and hardcovers.

Despite gloom and doom, the forecast catastrophe never arrived but heralded a period of sustained cutbacks in local authority expenditure, affecting both public and school libraries and schools library services and a regrouping and refining of publishing companies. This had inevitable effects, both immediate and longer term. One of the fears highlighted in 1975 was that the reductions in numbers of children's books published, combined with acute cash flow problems, would force children's publishers to choose between the quick safe sell and financial insecurity: 'The palmy days, when a backlist full of enduring sellers, reprinted year after year, financed experimental publishing of exciting new authors and artists, of books from overseas, and books from minority tastes, are fast disappearing' (Moss, 1974, p.7).

In reality, 1975 saw a rise in the number of children's titles being published (2688) and inflated prices (one novel topped the £4 mark), but this was paralleled by school and children's library book funds being slashed. This was the year of the Bullock Report *A language for life* (Department of Education and Science, 1975) in which whole chapters were devoted to the book as a gateway to a full life, and much stress was laid on availability of books at home, at school and from the public library. The report endorsed the existence of school bookshops and helped to stimulate the school bookshop movement. The following year, the School Bookshop Association was launched and with it, *School bookshop news* (later *Books for keeps*). Sales of paperbacks continued to flourish, including paperback originals and paperback non fiction, despite the recession: 'Could it be that paperbacks, spread nationwide, will hold the breach, generating and sustaining young readers' enthusiasm for books, whilst the home market for hardcover books goes into recession and out again?' (Moss, 1975, p.12).

There was a growing worry that sales departments and accountants were increasingly dictating to hard-pressed editors, at the expense of originality : 'No sales department prediction graph would have supported an editor with the flair to recognize the freak potential of *Watership Down*, a quality bestseller . . . The balance between visionary editorial hunch and hard sales department estimates must be preserved if standards are not to slide' (Moss, 1976, p.5).

By 1977, Elaine Moss was relishing (albeit prematurely) the news that: ' . . . the momentum of quality children's book publishing was so strong before the slump . . . that its best features (a constant flow of new authors and artists, good design, high standards of production) have been maintained' (Moss, 1977, p.5), while identifying that the axe had fallen, probably for ever, on the slow-selling backlist.

By 1978, despite the foregoing problems, perhaps even because of them, the number of children's books being published had risen by 50% compared to 1971 (3010 titles), but frequently at the expense of quality: 'little to do with the growth of the child' (Moss, 1978, p.5). This period heralded the rise in international co-production, a further factor which was to change the profile of British children's book publishing irretrievably.

The following year saw yet more stringent cuts in an already contracting library market: ' . . . in real terms the library service to children diminishes by the hour' (Moss, 1979, p.5). However, the trade in picture books remained undiminished and the year saw the beginning of the quality pop-up book which, in Moss's eyes: 'apart from the subliminal message to children that things shaped as books can be fun, have nothing whatever to do with the magic of the word . . . the feeling that presentation mattered more to publishers than content was inescapable' (Moss, 1979, p.6).

1980–88

Cuts in public expenditure in 1980 and 1981 continued, although the numbers of titles of children's books published rose again (3485 by 1980): 'The pattern throughout the country is one of diminishing resources, and savage cuts have been imposed on public libraries, the traditional and reliable markets for children's books, especially hardback fiction' (Sherrard-Smith, 1981, p.5).

This was accompanied by a worsening scene in many schools library services, with only 11 out of the 68 local authorities which were operating a schools library service managing to keep allowances for books in line with inflation. In 1982, Barbara Sherrard-Smith was concerned not only about the proliferation of 'novelty' books: 'A book that doesn't move, bang, squeak or pop up seemed not to be really desirable' but also about the closure of some children's lists from established publishers such as Chatto and Windus and the closure of High Street booksellers: 'at the present time, 90% of children never go into a bookshop and, in the inner city areas, many have never seen a new book, never experienced the look, the feel, the smell of its fresh paper' (Sherrard-Smith, 1982, p.7).

In 1984, 4479 children's book titles were published, but at a cost, warned Julia Eccleshare: ' . . . by allowing a much shorter life for each title on the assumption that you can sell enough for a small print run to make money. The result in this policy will be a profound change in our literature. Books, except for an exceptional few, will not pass from generation to generation. They will hardly pass from one school year to another, as they will simply not be available. The sharing of books across the years and the common core of a shared reading experience will be lost' (Eccleshare, 1985, p.1).

Cutbacks in school and library budgets were still on the increase: 'A chill economic wind is blowing, leaving minimum education and library budgets for buying children's books . . . another year of growth of titles set against a shrinking spending capacity by schools and libraries and reduced support for the arts by central government' (Eccleshare, 1986, p.1). The year 1986 was marked by an increasing emphasis and discussion on learning to read, with new reading schemes appearing from a number of leading publishers, such as Oxford University Press, Nelson and Ladybird. Eccleshare noted the marked dearth of new writers and illustrators: 'Instead, the pattern seems to be that a few writers are writing more and more books . . . ' (Eccleshare, 1986, p.2). Another worrying trend lay with few books for a multi-cultural society: 'too much emphasis on the external "signals" – steel bands and the like – and not enough concentration on daily life' (Eccleshare, 1986).

By 1987, Eccleshare was still bemused by the numbers of new children's books appearing with: 'almost hysterical zeal . . . an ever-increasing flood. Some of this increase reflects a healthy experimentalism which is being practised by publishers, some of it reflects hopping on a band wagon which seems to have rolled-by long since . . . too many books by the same authors and illustrators and too few by anyone new' (Eccleshare, 1987, p.1).

This concern about the unchecked flood of new titles was echoed in a number of articles in the Bookseller: between 1986 and 1987 the output of children's books rose from 4510 to 5014 titles; between 1983 and 1987, children's paperback fiction sales by UK publishers rose by 139.4%: more growth in turnover than any other publishing sector. This represented a total sales figure of £157m and 9.4% of total sales: in unit terms this represented 23% – nearly one in four books sold. For a number of general publishers, a flourishing children's list contributed significantly to their annual turnover in 1987: 40% at Deutsch; 50% at Bodley Head; 50% at Heinemann; about half the Penguins sold were Puffins. For specialist publishers, turnover was also good: £7million for Walker Books; with Usborne reporting 'an amazing year . . . not a sign of doom and gloom anywhere'. Taylor echoed concerns that sales to libraries had declined or were stagnant: a particularly worrying sign for hardback publishers who relied for 75% of their UK turnover on institutional sales (Taylor, 1988, p.995; Girling, 1990, pp.1526–8).

1988–95

Perhaps the most fundamental change to education for four decades came in 1988 with the Education Reform Act: 'Under the shadow of profound and much debated changes in the very basis of education . . . reading and therefore books, are finding a new centrality . . . now, more than ever, it is vital to show that the best books, the best stories, are both the soundest source for teaching reading and the surest way of maintaining literary skills and appreciation' (Eccleshare 1988, p.1). 'For better or worse, books for children are fairly and squarely in the public eye. With the coming of the 1988 Education Reform Act and the laying down of the core curriculum which includes English, what reading is for and various ways of how it might best be learned and developed has been ordained . . . stress lies firmly on reading for meaning and enjoyment . . . speaking and listening, writing, and reading, are the central planks of the English curriculum. Well written books, in all genres, are needed to provide the necessary source material' (Eccleshare 1989, p.1). In 1989 there was a welcome upsurge of books for teenagers, resulting from a new recognition of their spending power, with new lists from Virago, the Women's Press, Magnet, and Puffin Plus.

As will be seen later, the early optimism was not sustained. Eccleshare summarized the decade in 1990 by noting some of the enormous and profound changes that had affected the publication of children's books and their attendant commercial success. Children's books had become:

> . . . part of the mainstream operation with all the attendant advantages and disadvantages . . . These publishing changes . . . and the philosophical thinking of the 1970s have shaped the kinds of books which have been published . . . The 1970s wrenched books away from the elitist, literate image created by the 1960s' 'golden age'. The 1980s have, as many corrections do, overcompensated by taking the cause of social realism so seriously to heart that the message has far too often outweighed the medium. (Eccleshare, 1990, p.6)

Eccleshare recognized that the growth in paperbacks for children published at prices that parents and children could afford, had led to a growth in children's books and therefore child readers, at a time when decline in institutional sales might have predicted the opposite: 'It may be that this expansionist, non-elitist style of publishing has been the very thing that has prevented books from being replaced by the long threatened electronic media – audio, visual or both' (Eccleshare, 1990).

In 1992, children's literature was dominated by the rhetoric and invective about how children learned to read, with the introduction of assessment tasks at age seven, pushing teachers:

> towards 'teaching' which may in turn become 'bullying' children to learn to read with tricks and techniques which have little to do with the enjoyment of story or the understanding of the particular and special qualities of books. (Eccleshare, 1992, p.5)

Eccleshare celebrated the fact that in some areas authors, illustrators and publishers had kept faith with the true purpose of books for children, notably in poetry and in picture books, noting that the latter must be:

> the best possible way of holding the dyke against the tidal wave of home learning programmes and reading schemes with which parents are daily tempted . . . Reading is special and so are books. They are all too easily classified as luxuries, the prerogative of the educated elite. But reading is central to all understanding and good writing, though often dismissed as 'unavailable', is in reality no more difficult to read than bad

... The literary standards and expectations which have lain behind the children's books tradition in this country have preserved reading. The danger lies in making reading as close to other media as possible in the mistaken belief that it will then be more attractive to children who, it is known, consume television visually and music aurally far more easily than they read. (Eccleshare 1992, p.6)

but also warning that:

Children's reading is under siege. Not, as might be imagined, from the long-dreaded combined forces of Sega Megadrive, Nintendo Game Boy and the rest but from a far more insidious and therefore dangerous enemy – the Government ... the authorities who are currently controlling the education of the next generation have, at a stroke, obliterated the 'golden age' of children's literature ... by drawing up a 'list' of recommended books for children of different ages which are, almost without exception, not one but two generations old. In so doing they are making reading old-fashioned, illiberal and unappealing ... in ignoring the best writing for children, they are denying the existence of the multi-cultural and non-sexist fiction for children which has reflected the changes in society over the last twenty years ... It is hard to see how an area of such excellence, widely acknowledged throughout the world as the market leader, can be so deliberately rejected at home ... Children's books have always been published for didactic purposes as well as for entertainment. But it is equally important to recognize children's ability to imagine, interpret and discriminate in what they read ... Recently there has been a danger of children's books lapsing into seriously underestimating the intelligence of children. (Eccleshare, 1993, pp.5–6)

Chester Fisher, of Franklin Watts, reviewing the period 1980 to 1992 in the British children's book world charted the growth in publishing from 3000 new children's titles in 1980 to 6000 titles by 1989 – 100% increase. While acknowledging that such figures looked healthy, he noted that growth in titles sold was largely achieved through paperback sales and the increase of direct sales to homes and to schools, counteracting, to a certain extent, the decline in available funds to libraries:

Libraries throughout the 1980's saw a steady decline in available funds and were gradually limited to buying only the most necessary books. Fiction and picture books tended to suffer more than non-fiction. Titles of minority interest ... were excluded. Bookshops also experienced a decline in the purchasing of children's hardback books by the general public and publishers were generally forced to cut their initial hardback print-runs. (Fisher, 1994, p.31)

He analysed the subsequent decline in profits and publishers' responses: more titles per year to maintain turnover and profit levels; reprint titles forced rapidly out of print, when sales dropped below economic levels; a swing to new title publishing (a change from 60% backlist: 40% new title publishing in 1980 to 40% backlist: 60% new titles in 1992); demands of the international rights market; strict cost controls.

These trends have largely continued unabated. The state of school and public library book expenditure has also remained an issue to the present day.

1995–

Largely as a result of the foregoing, a survey was carried out during 1995 of the major publishers of children's and school books and the major library suppliers and booksellers in the UK to establish how changes in education, in funding and in the marketplace had affected children's and educational book publishing and supply over the last ten years. Respondents[1, 2] were particularly asked to address the following, with relation to their own environment: The Education Reform Act and the National Curriculum; Local Management of Schools; demise of schools library services; cuts in public library expenditure; paperback versus hardback publishing; new title publishing; direct purchasing of books in schools; impact of new technology, particularly CD-ROM; increased interest in reading and literacy standards; Net Book Agreement. The overall responses echoed an article by Paula Kahn of Longman: 'In a short period of time the market has changed from a relatively stable one into a high risk, high investment, competitive environment in which a publisher has to have a major market share simply to survive' (Kahn, 1992a, p.258).

The rest of this chapter will look at how the issues raised above have affected publishing, bookselling and library supply.

EDUCATION REFORM: THE NATIONAL CURRICULUM

The Education Reform Act of 1988, as outlined in Chapter 3, set out to transform the education system in the UK, with reforms dedicated to reshaping the nature and management of education throughout the primary and secondary sectors. The major changes which have particularly affected libraries and access to books and other resources have been the introduction of a National Curriculum and Local Management of Schools (LMS). The National Curriculum involved changing from a predominantly school-based syllabus, where teachers had freedom of choice (up to GCSE level) over content, methodology and source materials, to a centrally determined and centrally evaluated system similar to those already well established on the continent. The effects of the National Curriculum and subsequent revisions of the curriculum on publishing can be seen as different, but equally critical, for education and textbook publishers and mainstream children's book publishers in the UK.

Educational publishing

John Davies of the Educational Publishers Council says that the introduction of the National Curriculum had a profound effect on educational publishers. It focused publishing attention on the various curriculum areas of science, history and geography, with a corresponding reduction of interest in, and sales of, non-curriculum areas and encouraged the use of published schemes. To meet the needs of the National Curriculum, books and teaching materials had to be produced and revised at breakneck speed to very tight timetables and against problems in obtaining relevant and accurate information: 'The pace of curriculum change since 1985 has been such as to continually shorten the life expectancy of each successive wave of new publishing that has been created to meet the specific needs of the ever changing curriculum' (Davies, 1995a). One publisher regards the introduction of the National Curriculum as a 'publishing nightmare', with established backlists invalidated almost overnight, with no consultation from the National Curriculum Council in the early days and precious little more from SCAA (Schools Curriculum and Assessment Authority): 'In particular, the timescale for producing books to match the new curriculum has been heavily underestimated in the push for political progress. This has been further exacerbated by sea-changes in thinking right up to and including the Dearing report.'

Publishers uniformly respond that the National Curriculum had a huge effect in changing what was being taught in schools and the ensuing need for resources to support this. But it has often proved more effective in pinpointing a subject (e.g. Medieval Britain, the Egyptians) than in altering methodology, for example science teaching is still heavily content-driven. While certain areas, such as history and science have been boosted by the concentration of the National Curriculum, books on other more general areas, such as nature, animals, sport, no longer strictly necessary in National Curriculum terms, are disappearing. One publisher bemoans the fact that all publishers are now going for the same titles – 'severely dampening innovation and experiment, a fact that has gone largely unmentioned'. There is a growing concern that non-fiction books in schools and public libraries will be completely dominated by the requirements of the curriculum and by the emphasis placed by the National Curriculum on the use of text books.

Mainstream publishing

The breakneck task of preparing materials for courses was particularly pertinent for publishers of course text books but also applied to mainstream publishers. Jill Coleman of A & C Black, considering the impact of the National Curriculum on publishing information books for primary schools, says:

> It's hard to believe that it was only in 1989 when the first National Curriculum documents started arriving. Until then, the commissioning editor for non-fiction had two strategies to choose between when deciding which books to publish for primary schools. She could tackle one of the old favourites in a new and hopefully interesting way . . . she could commission books in new areas, a task not unlike fortune telling. (Coleman, 1993, p.24)

Like many publishers, A & C Black looked at proposals for the National Curriculum with mixed feelings: would it give them more information on which to base commissioning; would it confine them to the same topics year after year; would every publisher be producing identical and competing books? In reality, they found that the early documents for science had a tremendous impact on publishing, because, for the first time, there was to be a set curriculum for primary schools, with a range of specific subject areas to be covered. Early series developed to cover gaps in the market sold well. At the same time teachers and advisers were exploring new ways to teach the new science curriculum and this led to new publishing projects. Because there was such a wide variety of topics to be covered and it was possible to approach topics in a number of different ways, information book publishers did not find themselves producing identical products. There was some disappointment when the English curriculum guidelines appeared in 1990 that, although specific mention was made about children reading for information, no information books were included on the set reading lists. This was in marked contrast to the antagonism to the backlists from other publishers, writers and librarians, discussed further below.

A & C Black found frustratingly:

> Some of our backlist titles such as *Beans* and *Wideworld* fit very well into human geography at key stage one and two, but it has been hard to persuade teachers of this. They seem to think that the guidelines are new, so, as far as they can afford, they would like to have new books . . . on the whole, changes to the documents have been more of a headache to textbook publishers than they have for information book publishers. The library book is much more flexible than the text book which is expected to cover the complete curriculum and can be made redundant by a few changes to the attainment targets. (Coleman, 1993, p.24)

Timing has been a problem for each of the subjects introduced. It takes between six months and two years to produce a new information book, and there were rarely more than a few months between the publication of the final Orders and their implementation. Publishers have either had to base their new series on consultative documents, hoping there wouldn't be too many changes, or be late with the new books. Extra money for new books has generally been too little and made available over too short a time, encouraging panic buying of books which may have been hastily put together, or indeed reissues of old books with new National Curriculum covers:

> The National Curriculum has been more of a positive stimulus than we expected. But many worries still remain. As information book publishers, we have supported the cross-curricular approach in primary schools but now increasingly find ourselves talking in terms of subject areas . . . will there still be a place for the inspired author who isn't easily fitted into a National Curriculum category? (Coleman, 1993, p.24)

Encouragingly, the National Curriculum documents stress wide and varied reading. But will the attainment targets and the vast spectrum of topics which need to be taught in a short space of time push teachers towards using textbooks?

> Many of the large text book publishers are producing expensive new course books for primary schools, a market which used to be relatively unimportant to them. This is a worrying sign for information book publishers . . . I do feel that children who select the library books which they have decided are appropriate for a topic are learning skills they couldn't learn by using text books, and are in control of the process rather than following a set programme. (Coleman, 1993, p.24)

For many mainstream children's book publishers, it is the way that the books need to be marketed, as a result of the National Curriculum, which has changed most fundamentally. Booklists and catalogues have needed to be redesigned so that teachers can see how individual titles can fulfil the criteria laid down by the new Orders, especially for reading, but for other areas of the National Curriculum, too.

Prescribed reading lists

In 1993, the government published the list of prescribed books (generally referred to as the SATs lists) to accompany the English curriculum. There was an immediate outcry from a number of quarters uneasy about the 'routinisation' of these restricted reading lists and objecting to the 'totalitarian' approach. Michael Rosen in a perceptive article declared:

> This government, despite all the rhetoric concerning literacy levels, has declared war on the reading of books . . . The Government through its English studies junta in particular, is positing a model of reading based on authority. The set text, the cloze procedure and the removal of the expertise to help teachers and pupils into personable reading, is a way of suggesting that books are sites of authority that should not really be challenged. (Rosen, 1993, p.7)

This view was reinforced in a letter to the *Guardian*, from a number of leading children's writers, including Joan Aiken, Helen Cresswell, Michael Foreman, Leon Garfield, Brian Patten:

> We are writers whose names or works have been put on the new English National Curriculum lists. We would like to dissociate ourselves from these lists. In a democratic society, the distribution of literature is informed by open debate. This enables readers to engage with the arguments recommending or disapproving of any given work. However, this list comes without any critical commentary and yet it is armed with commands that our books should be read. We reject this authoritarian approach to reading . . . These lists will not contribute to teachers' understanding and enthusiasm for literature as their choice of books in schools would largely be a consequence of obeying orders from on high . . . No matter how flexible these lists may seem to be,

they dictate a view of what a national literary heritage ought to be. They are unrepresentative of many cultural traditions that have prevailed in the past or are important today. In any case, we reject the attempt to use literature to express notions of a national heritage when writing has always consisted of a mosaic of international traditions and forms . . . If authors are to be recommended to teachers – or for that matter rejected – then there are other ways of doing so, more in spirit with literature itself. (The *Guardian*, 19 May 1993).

For publishers, the extraordinary way these 'reading lists' were introduced played havoc with sales and stock control initially. For many, the first they knew about the lists was when they were contacted by the press for comment; there was no time to prepare for the huge demand from schools and libraries and from parents. Some books were best-sellers anyway, but others had gone out of print due to lack of sales. One book that had gone out of print for selling less than a thousand copies in the previous year shot up to 24,000 copies in the year the SATs list came out; an 'almost hysterical' approach, says one publisher. An enormous number of picture books from the list were sold, but it appears that these were largely substitute sales rather than additional sales, in other words this was at the expense of other titles.

Revisions to the National Curriculum

The announcement in 1992 that there would be revisions made to the National Curriculum, instigated a slump in overall purchases in schools, as schools were not prepared to buy teaching materials and books while the whole concept of the National Curriculum was under review. The Dearing Review sought to respond to many of the concerns from teachers and to give more scope to schools to respond to the needs and talents of their pupils by removing 'unwarranted complexity and addressing the problems caused by too many attainment targets and statements of attainment' (Dearing, 1993) The accent was on simplification and the promise of stability and consolidation. The crisis here for publishers was that, once again, the current stocks of books and learning materials closely tied to the National Curriculum were rendered useless to implement the new Orders. Even the fundamental terminology of the curricular process has been significantly altered. Statements of attainment are defunct. Level descriptions have been ushered in. Available books are thus speaking the wrong language and are crowded with references which are no longer relevant. Terms which recur throughout the Dearing documents are reduction, removal of overlap, mergers, improvements, restructuring, rationalizations, shifts of emphasis: 'Each time they are introduced, they put another nail in the coffin of existing texts and cause them to become obsolete' (Davies, 1995a).

For most textbook publishers the main effect has been felt in the rapidity and frequency of change during the 'consultation' period before the Dearing Review in 1993. Publishers have had to reinvest substantially in order to provide teachers and children with new or revised books which meet the requirements of each new version of the National Curriculum. Timescales for development have been very tight. Other publishers suggest that changes have shortened drastically the sales lifetime of newly published titles. The fact that many books were rendered redundant was similarly nightmarish for booksellers.

However, the announcement, albeit two years on, that the much-reviled lists of recommended books from Key stages One and Two had been abandoned, was received with considerable pleasure: 'At long, long last the Government appears to have accepted that the canonical approach it struggled so hard to impose on teachers is politically objectionable, misunderstands the nature of literary evaluation, breaks that crucial personal bond between a book and an apprentice reader and actually sidelines the proper working out of a reading pedagogy' (Powling, 1995, p.3).

The New Orders for English state: 'Pupils should be given extensive experience of children's literature. They should read on their own, with others and to the teachers, from a range of genres that includes, stories, poetry, plays and picture books . . . These materials should be used to stimulate pupils imagination and enthusiasm' (Department for Education, 1995, p.6).

It is hoped that with all of the changes to the National Curriculum now determined, schools will be in a position to turn their attention to the books they require to meet the new curriculum. The government has nominated books and teaching materials as items that might be purchased under the 1995–6 earmarked grant for School Effectiveness and the Basic Curriculum but what this means in monetary terms is as yet unclear: 'At current levels of expenditure, it will take a school in the region of 5 years to achieve book resourcing such as to provide every child with a core text for each of the National Curriculum subjects' (Davies, 1995b; *The Bookseller*, 1995c).

EDUCATION REFORM: LOCAL MANAGEMENT OF SCHOOLS

Local Management of Schools (LMS) which shifts many responsibilities from local education authorities to governors and headteachers, including the control of the school budget, has been described as the biggest revolution in education since the introduction of state education. This devolution of decisions to schools may have been helpful in book purchasing terms, where parents, teachers and governors value books. However, when cash is tight, the book budget is standardly squeezed in favour of retaining teaching staff. In publishing terms, local management of schools means that publishers now have to reach schools directly, by marketing their products intensively, including direct sale and supply. Direct sale increases publisher's margins but adds costs in terms of the increased number of accounts to monitor and service. In practice publishers are finding many individual schools poorly prepared for this, lacking selection expertise and book knowledge and without the advice of experienced librarians to rely on.

This has been exacerbated by the terms of local management of schools which allow schools to purchase from whatever source they see fit. Most schools previously were obliged to use a local authority nominated contractor or contractors. While this has opened up the market, it does not necessarily ensure quality of service or best advice. Before LMS, most publishers worked with a few suppliers and local authority direct purchasing organizations who supplied most of the schools in the UK. As LMS was introduced, publishers were faced with a much more fragmented market, as schools began to respond by selecting their own source of book supply, some quite unknown and perhaps supplying only a tiny number of schools. Promotion, as a result, has been nightmarish for the publisher and extremely difficult to organize and control, although some publishers report that they feel more in touch now that they are directly in contact with schools rather than dealing through suppliers.

Most of the major educational publishers appear to have made strenuous efforts to service individual schools rather than third party suppliers. One such publisher states that: 'Not only are we able to offer faster and better service but our margins are improved and we have the opportunity to develop customer loyalty.' Direct purchasing from publishers has risen from 15 to nearly 50 per cent. For some publishers, it is as high as 70% to primary schools. It is suggested that it is in the non-fiction area that this has been particularly noticeable. Direct sales of encyclopaedias to schools are at a level, for example, which would have been unprecedented through traditional schools library service sales.

One publisher describes LMS as a bit of a 'curate's egg' as schools are happier to be in control of their own budgets but find book expenditure difficult to balance against other pressures facing schools – not least maintaining minimum staffing levels. Schools are submitted to many more selling visits, for example from cheap book merchants and other industries: the Heads are more stressed and in secondary schools, the bursars more powerful.

The focus of the activity of the Education Publishers Council has changed too, because:

> Educational divisions have had to take a long hard look at their relationship with the customer, and have had to learn quickly from their business and professional colleagues how to use a marketing database, how to make effective use of direct mail and direct selling. They've had to retrain their sales force and rethink their promotion and information materials. The customer rules and the customer is now a teacher. (Kahn, 1992).

For booksellers, too, the issue of now having to cope with hundreds or thousands of accounts rather than only a few, often dealt with through a centralized service, has greatly increased administration. One major plus reported by booksellers, though, is that schools no longer stick rigidly to the financial year and this has helped to even out the buying pattern over the year.

Demise of schools library services

In library terms, one of the most serious implications of LMS has been the demise of schools library services (SLS). Without a centrally retained funding system within local education authorities, schools library services are having to reshape as businesses from which schools buy the services they require: loans, advice, consultancy, purchase. While there is some logic and potential efficiency to be gained from a clear and strategic focus, in practice the gains are far from obvious: some authorities have already established impressive reshaped schools library services; others are struggling against substantial odds. It is hard to convince schools that library services are no longer free; they have to be purchased.

Although hard evidence is difficult to find, it appears to be generally accepted in the book world, among publishers and library suppliers, that without a good SLS, some schools will make ill-advised purchasing decisions, which will leave them with less money to spend on good children's literature. This is clearly recognized by the Educational Publishers Council:

> At present there is real cause for concern about the future of library book provision in schools and particularly about that part of it that is provided by professionally expert and cost effective schools library services. These have been depleted by moves to local management and could vanish entirely under local government reorganization . . . School library publishers are very concerned about the cash stagnation in school library service book spending which, compounded with real decline in public library book funds, makes investment in new product difficult. (Davies, 1995c).

Publishers generally have supported schools library services, recognizing the value of a centralized service and particularly the advice and guidance which can be given to schools through SLS. In the early 1990s, publishers such as Watts, Wayland, and A & C Black combined to present their concerns about the situation by sponsoring leaflets to schools and governors alerting them to the strengths of the schools library service system. Without a SLS, the purchasing power of a local authority becomes fragmented and difficult to access for publishers, exacerbating promotional efforts. 'Disastrous', says one publisher who has recently entered the juvenile non-fiction ranks and believes that this is where the demise of SLS will be most severely felt: 'All library books will be seriously affected if the school library services are cut back . . . Their collapse would make information books more dependent on other markets, such as foreign sales, and therefore less relevant to British children and to the National Curriculum' (Coleman, 1993, p.24).

Worryingly, though, one library supplier notes, with considerable concern, that schools library services, on the whole, are now not able to run the quality of service possible pre-LMS: 'The old SLSs ran some wonderful services and now they are gone and what is in their place and what schools are paying for, is not nearly so good.' One of the major problems appears to be that school library services, in the past, played substantially different roles within individual local authorities. The result was that there was no clear and universally accepted view of what a good SLS should provide: some loaned fiction; some purely non-fiction; some ran book purchase schemes; some offered project boxes; some authorities had no SLS. In other words, there was no united front with which to fight the loss of centralized funding. Post-LMS, this fragmented approach continues, but almost universally with fewer staff and less money. Both professional and support staff have been reduced: 'Teachers see themselves paying for a poorer, or less flexible service . . . the loss of the friendly, helpful, well-known librarians with whom they had built up a relationship over the years, has gone . . . it is easy to let the subscription to SLS lapse.' Individual local authorities are aware of this as a major issue in the survival of school library services but at a time of economic restraint, the investment needed to underpin quality SLSs has been absent.

ECONOMIC PRESSURES

Public library cutbacks

Cutbacks in public libraries have had a particular effect on hardback publishing, an area where there was never a large retail market. Hardback print runs have been reduced, although there has often been a corresponding increase in demand for paperbacks from libraries. With tight book funds, there is a tendency for libraries to await the appearance of the paperback edition. This, of course, may not happen: if a book performs badly in hardback, a paperback edition can never be guaranteed.

The decline in hardback sales can be seen by a look at the comparative figures for print-runs for 1980 and 1992:

In 1980, junior fiction titles had a first printing of about 5000 copies, followed by a reprint of 2000 after eighteen months to two years, then a regular reprint of 1500–2000 copies every 2–3 years. Paperback editions would be done of the most popular titles. By 1992, the average first printing was 2000 copies, with no guarantee of a reprint. It is therefore essential that new fiction has a guaranteed paperback edition after two years to spread the origination costs. With non-fiction, the average first printing in 1980 was around 8000 copies with a reprint of 3000 copies after 18 months to two years and then regular reprints every two years. By 1990 the first printing was down to 5000 with reprints of 1000–2000 after 12 months and no certainty of further reprints. The average life of the non-fiction title has also been reduced from 10 years to between three and five years. Inevitably this has meant a reduction in profits for the publisher, forcing them to publish more titles per year to maintain turnover and profit levels or to publish in paperback. It has to be noted that a paperback must sell at least three times as much as a hardback to produce a similar profit. (Fisher, 1994, p.31)

There has been a steady shift over the last fifteen years from the majority of books coming out in hardback to the majority being produced in paperback. Shortage of funds and price sensitivity are said to be the main causes of this, and a number of publishers suggest that this is being driven by the buyers rather than by the economics of publishing. There is growing concern that this trend obstructs new authors, by offering considerably fewer opportunities to break through the barrier of first publication. One publisher states that 'the writing was on the wall' when they started selling less than 1000 copies of a new novel in hardback.

Some publishers still suggest that the economics of publishing continue to favour a traditional approach of a hardback edition, followed later by a paperback edition, but a number admit that they are following hardback editions with a paperback more quickly than in the past; others are increasingly moving to simultaneous hardback and paperback or straight into trade paperback novels to try to keep the print quantities above 2000:

> Perhaps the biggest change in children's publishing in the last 15 years is what has happened to the serious or literary hardback work of fiction, particularly the first novel. The paperback original has arrived . . . it's seen as user-friendly . . . Flexibility is the keyword on the lips of many publishers. They think hard about what kind of format fits the book and the author. (Hoffman, 1995, p.26)

Even such publishers as Oxford University Press, traditionally recognized as hardback publishers, launched a new trade paperback list in 1995 (Bookseller, 1995a) with the announcement that all new original fiction would be published in paperback and no more hardbacks for a while. Other publishers state that non-fiction books and dictionaries, anthologies of stories and poetry and picture books, still seem to move in hardback.

The general increase in the number of paperback imprints and books published has meant that all paperback publishers are fighting harder for shelf space, both in the library and in trade markets. For many years, there were only two main paperback publishers, Puffin and Collins, with their lists selected from everything that was published by almost any publisher. Now there is a tendency to move into a paperback edition in-house, particularly with picture books, to justify the enormous origination costs, whereas a few years ago these would have stayed as hardback editions. Stephanie Nettell, writing in the Bookseller says: 'Although libraries *prefer* hardback picture books, funding dictates paperbacks; yet librarians believe there's a readership for both' (Nettell, 1995, p.25). This is an interesting comparison with Germany and Holland, where publishers do not put picture books into paperback: the general public expect to pay for hardbacks, because they last!

New title publishing

The accent in recent years has been towards more new title publishing and less maintenance of backlists. In the early 1980s the turnover of many publishing companies was derived 60% from the backlist and 40% from new title publishing. By the early 1990s this had been reversed. Publishers strive to reverse this proportion and re-establish the importance of the backlist but if backlist sales drop, then the tendency is to continue to push new titles at the expense of the reprint. Chester Fisher admits that: 'a new title orientation can force publishers to offer quantity rather than quality in their publishing. This is especially true in the picture book and non-fiction fields. Book purchasers, especially librarians, have a duty to reject this trend' (Fisher, 1994).

Certain publishers of course have always had a big output of new titles and for publishers like Oxford University Press this has remained the case, but with a strong backlist, too. Oxford note the growth in repackaging of the classics as a positive recent trend, with, for example, Book Fairs Ltd having the buying power to stimulate the publishing of a number of titles, such as *The ship that flew* and *The gauntlet*. A trend of the last two years has been new series from several publishers responding to the perceived demand for fast, immediate reads, perhaps in an attempt to compete with the rise in multimedia technology. Series, such as Puffin's *Boyfriend series*, and others from Collins, Hodder and Random House provide one approach to reading but are a worrying trend if this is all that is to be on offer in the future. Allied to a certain nervousness in children's book publishing which means that few risks are being taken with new authors or new ideas, inevitably the range and quality of titles diminishes.

Perhaps the major problem, though, is that for all the reasons mentioned earlier, particularly cutbacks in spending, alongside increased numbers of individual titles being published, print runs inevitably become shorter and titles stay in print for a very short time. It is now not unusual for a title to be out of print within 12 weeks of publication and then out of print until a paperback edition appears. Libraries with lengthy reviewing procedures may never have their order fulfilled.

Multicultural/special needs

The importance of children's books reflecting the different cultural mix of our society was mentioned above, but the pressures of educational change and their influences on the publishing and bookselling world, have hit multicultural books particularly hard. The very focused subject nature of the National Curriculum does not support the cross-curricular, underpinning nature of multicultural awareness; LMS does not encourage a liberal, multicultural approach; the social and political drift to the right similarly acts against the best thinking of multiculturalism and anti-racism. This is best expressed in an article in *Books for keeps*, in which Rosemary Stones (1994) writes about and applauds the evolution of the updated *Multicultural guide to children's books* (Elkin, 1994):

For everyone concerned with children's books – writers, illustrators, teachers, librarians, parents – the '70s and early '80s had been a period of intense and sometimes acrimonious discussion as the need became accepted (mostly) for all children to have access to a literature free from racial stereotyping on the one hand, and reflecting the diversity of the multicultural society that we are, on the other.

There can be no doubt that the most significant development of the last decade has been the emergence of a new generation of British born Black poets and writers . . . the number of talented contributors to the field (black and white) continues to grow . . . while the last decade has seen the publication of a wealth of multicultural books, it has at the same time seen a massive attack on the educational and public library structures which underpin their availability . . . the deprofessionalization of the school library service, LMS, the opting out of schools, the exigent demands on the time and morale of teachers of the National Curriculum and, in the public library arena, substantial cuts in resources . . . We must also add to this a new social climate of ridicule and alienation around equalities issues which it has become socially acceptable to dismiss as 'political correctness'. (Stones, 1994, pp.4–5)

Publishers have drawn back from non-sexist and non-racist books, because of the recession . . . Publishers are going for safe commercial ventures . . . There are fewer titles by new authors and fewer with black children taking the main roles. (*The Bookseller*, 1995c)

This is reinforced by Beverley Naidoo: 'Discrimination on the basis of "race" is still deeply prevalent throughout Britain. But unlike my own childhood (living in South Africa), there are more possibilities today of young people hearing other voices which challenge racism and which value diversity and equality' (Naidoo, 1994, p.11).

In parallel to this, Viv Edwards criticizes the missed opportunities of the late 1980s and the Education Reform Act of 1988 for 'stifling' the enthusiasm for diversity, which is now so desperately in need of being rekindled: 'Not least of the omissions has been the failure to prepare teachers adequately for the needs of multi-lingual classrooms' (Edwards, 1995, p.24).

Pat Thomson makes a similar case for children with disabilities:

Disabled readers have every right to see themselves represented in books. It is sobering to think that 20 years ago there were twice as many male characters as female in children's books and working mothers were all but unknown. That battle is being won and the efforts to give black characters their rightful place in literature is being vigorously pursued. What progress has there been for disabled people? . . . There is still a tendency for a book with a disabled character in it to be a 'problem' book and there is an infuriating genre which might be termed a 'second fiddle' book. In these, there is indeed a disabled character but they exist only to promote the personal development of the main, able-bodied character. (Thomson, 1992, p.24)

NEW TECHNOLOGY

New technologies have already altered the production and distribution of books dramatically over recent years. Publishers have had to be aware of adaptation of product to other media. This can be expensive in terms of parallel publishing and investment lost in the early stages, although clearly there are significant opportunities here and for some publishers, new markets have opened up. One publisher states that the new technologies have had a: 'major impact! . . . This is a whole new market looking for the right kind of publishing . . . Undoubtedly, the reputable publishers will be the front runners in the school market given their expertise in developing curriculum materials rather than games and entertainment.'

Another publisher highlights 'edutainment', the blurring of boundaries between school and home as a huge growth area. The impact of new technology is most felt by the non-fiction publishers, for example Dorling Kindersley's launch in autumn 1994 of their CD-ROM titles, which bring together an exciting combination of words, pictures, sound effects, animation and video (*The eyewitness encyclopaedia of nature*; *The eyewitness history of the world*). Wayland have also launched their first CD-ROM, *Violent earth*, which focuses on natural disasters and features interactive diagrams, maps and photographs, documentary film, on and off-screen activities, timelines and hyperlinked glossary. Audio books already have a significant place in the fiction field. Virtual reality is with us, too, for example a recently released version of *Wuthering Heights*.

The commercial market for CD-ROMs is increasing rapidly, particularly to fill gaps in library resources and for remedial support. There is a danger, though, that where schools devote their 'book' budget to CD-ROMs there may be less money for fiction and picture books for the school library. Print-based reference books, particularly dictionaries and encyclopaedias, may be particularly vulnerable, although publishers suggest that CD-ROM sales have not yet dented print sales.

It is interesting to note that a number of publishers and suppliers draw attention to the fact that schools, despite huge investments in the technology, are still far away from having the hardware to teach children continuously via new media and that the majority of teachers are not computer-literate to the extent required to maximize use of a range of technologies. Most direct teaching and learning remains based on print. In many schools, the machines are unused or sited inaccessibly in departments where they are little used. Most suppliers have the facilities to show CD-ROMs in their showrooms but remain cautious about the possible need to provide helpdesks to schools.

BOOKSELLING AND LIBRARY SUPPLY

Bookshops

UK retail bookshops, except for a few notable exceptions such as Heffers in Cambridge and the Waterstones chain, have generally reduced their stockholding of hardback children's books in recent years. There are few specialist children's bookshops and only a very few specialist staff. In 1993, retail sales of children's books at about £260 million accounted for some 10% of UK retail sales (Eccleshare, 1995).

Mary Tapissier, from Hodder Headline, says:

> Upheavals in education with the advent of parent governors, endless debate on the curriculum and waves of testing should have been good things for the children's book trade. Never before have parents been made so aware of what their children need in order to read and learn. Yet only a few shining examples in the stockholding book trade have turned this increased market awareness to their advantage. The school book fairs have proved that children and adults will buy books if presented with the opportunity. They will even buy first novels by unknown authors! . . . Dedicated independent children's booksellers and book fair selectors both know that attractive display, specialist advice to customers and wide choice – that 'good mixed diet' from which all children benefit – pay off. There is a passionate vocational element in children's publishing and, here and there, in children's bookselling. (Tapissier, 1994, p.26)

For some time, Elizabeth Attenborough has talked about 'bookseller malaise', an almost palpable inability to seem to want to sell or promote children's books and a significant lack of real book knowledge, to help the customer, whether child, teacher or parent:

> The low status of children's books is part of a wider problem: it reflects the way our society sees children themselves, and those who work with or for them . . . The book trade should play a leading role in changing that, and to do that it must unequivocally embrace children's books as an important part of its whole, a part that needs special care and attention to make it work. If children's books look second class to the book business, why should the public think them any more important? (Attenborough, 1989, p.262)

Brough Girling agrees but suggests that perhaps children's books should be given lower status:

> Because we confuse children's books with 'education' we mistakenly feel that knowing about them requires a special expertise, involving at the very least a degree in child development or a doctorate in education psychology. If we forget all this and regard children's books as just very good 'pretending game' toys – that is after all how they see them – we'd enter the fray with a lot more fun and enthusiasm . . . For children, all reading, if it is done for pleasure, is holiday reading . . . Product knowledge is all

that's needed. (Girling, 1989, p.401) . . . The birth of the children's paperback put books within children's own reach – and that has made a radical difference to children's reading. Children have now become book consumers. They have learnt to select and buy books for themselves; they can develop their own reading tastes and habits. (Girling, 1990, p.1528)

How many booksellers display their children's books downstairs, where pushchairs can't go? How many have trained members of staff who know the stock and know children? How many more leave the children's section to the junior, who will be moved to the 'main' part of the shop when he or she gets more experience? . . . It seems to me that we have an enormously flourishing children's publishing industry, and an enormously enthusiastic and ready audience, but with big gaps between those two points that must mean that we are missing enormous opportunities. (Attenborough, 1989, p.262)

A recent survey showed that the most likely place of purchase for children's books in the UK is W H Smith, with 47% of all purchases (Fisher, 1994). But a report in *The Bookseller* demonstrates the narrow range of titles available in WH Smith's stores. With regard to picture books, Helen Randles, the product manager for younger children's books states:

We decided to cut the picture book range from around 480 titles to 165, which was the number we felt that we could display properly. We created stronger, more eye-catching displays so that customers could see the books better. It was a huge gamble to take, but we were sure that customers were finding it difficult to choose when the books were so cramped. (Randles, 1995, p.90)

In the first three months W H Smith's sales of picture books increased by 60%: 'We are happy now that we are giving the picture books that we do stock a real chance for anything from three to six months' (Randles, 1995).

Attenborough is particularly concerned about who will guide children in their reading, if booksellers, teachers or parents have no real understanding or knowledge about children's books: 'The trained, interested and enthusiastic librarian will have the knowledge and the experience to help them find other books for their child to enjoy, but only in a minority of places will parents be able to find that sort of response in a bookshop' (Attenborough, 1989).

Forget the dumpbins, forget the mobiles, forget the pretty posters – or at least to start with. No amount of extras in a bookshop can make up for any lack of knowledge or enthusiasm for the books themselves. Knowledge, knowledge, knowledge; it seems to me that that is the magic ingredient needed to make a success of a children's book department. (Attenborough, 1994, p.24)

In similar vein, writing in the same series of articles, David Lloyd of Walker Books speculates:

If I'm ever lucky enough to become a bookseller . . . all the departments in my shop will have their notable and special qualities, but no-one will ever doubt the pre-eminent importance of children's books; everyone will properly and intelligently understand that this is where the great adventure begins. And if you get the beginning wrong, you might as well forget the rest. (Lloyd, 1994, p.24)

Specialist library supply

The picture in the specialist library supply market perhaps mirrors some of Lloyd's dreams. Suppliers like Peters Library Service and Books For Students give expert advice to librarians and teachers but, as they are library supply rather than retail booksellers, this level of advice is not available to the general public. For library suppliers, the cutbacks in library expenditure are cutting deeper and deeper, although specialist children's library suppliers are suggesting that, to date, cuts have been less severe in the children's area than in adult book expenditure, perhaps because children's book expenditure tends to account for only about 20% of total bookfund and most authorities tend to try to protect that. However, the effect of local government reorganization on bookfunds is, as yet, unclear. Potentially, it could prove disastrous, as smaller authorities are less able to effect the economies of scale and maintain current standards of service. It will certainly be the major element of change experienced in many public library authorities in the foreseeable future.

Library suppliers are particularly concerned with the effect of public library cutbacks on book purchase and approvals schemes. The traditional approvals schemes are becoming more and more expensive for both the supplier to service and the library to manage. A number of library suppliers are suggesting that it would be cheaper for them and would save the authorities staff time, if the supplier could select books:

> We can easily build up an authority file and do the selection for them. This would have positive implications for publishers – it would eradicate returns, so everything bought by a supplier would go to a library customer. The backing we give to certain titles would encourage publishers to keep these books in print. As suppliers we have a better overall view of what is available and what is planned for publication in any year, so we would potentially control a local authority's budget better than they would! This may all sound very radical but bibliographical services are discussing this possibility with us – of course the children's specialist is aghast at the thought and would fight any change from the approvals system. However, cuts and local government reorganization might be bigger than any of us.[2]

An interesting and imaginative response reflecting the professionalism evident in some areas of library supply but highlighting the radical rethinking which is being forced in all areas of the children's book world.

The National Curriculum has, inevitably, had a significant effect on suppliers, too, with a changing emphasis on which subjects are bought. Prior to the National Curriculum, says one major supplier, schools library services and public libraries bought books across the board (accounting for 95% of the business). Public library sales tended to concentrate on more recreational non-fiction and tended to purchase a greater proportion of fiction and picture books than the schools. The National Curriculum has forced public libraries to divert funds away from picture books towards non-fiction to support homework. Both schools library services and public libraries concentrate on buying the major topics of the National Curriculum.

As regards Local Management of Schools, the early years for many suppliers were 'wonderful', but perhaps falsely so. Extra funding was made available and schools library services took advantage of this. In addition, schools were beginning to spend their own delegated funds and the market 'seemed buoyant': 'Library suppliers and publishers were fooled into thinking how wonderful LMS was.'

However, most schools library service budgets in the current year have dropped dramatically and schools themselves are having to cut back. As one supplier says:

> We do not have the resources to go after every school account in the country, but will target various counties and schools where we feel there is potentially a good return. We are able to offer schools a wide range of books and a wide range of servicing, including acquisitions disks to load onto whichever computer system they have. We feel, therefore, that we will always be able to keep a good level of business and not lose out to direct purchasing completely . . . As library suppliers we only see the schools who are committed to spending money on library books, so the teachers we see tend to be keen and interested in children's books. However, we are aware that we only see a small percentage of schools. *What are the rest doing?*

Suppliers can find themselves in a cleft stick with respect to schools, clearly wanting to expand business into schools, while maintaining a reasonable profit margin *and* loyal customers for an uncertain future. On the whole, teachers are not business minded and suppliers can find themselves faced with requests for schools to spend whole days in a showroom, selecting stock. Not only are showrooms limited in the space available but schools may expect to bring 20 people to spend relatively small sums of money and expect to be looked after with free lunches:

> Any profit we might make will go on lunches, but if we refuse the visit how much damage might it do? LMS has meant many more visits by customers for small amounts of money . . . our customer base is expanding rapidly . . . with librarians, once you have met them and they have used the showroom . . . they will continue a business relationship . . . with schools, there is never any guarantee of continued business.

One of the smaller specialist booksellers and library suppliers claims that the 'glory years' came around the mid 1980s, when only 10% discount (maximum) was given to schools on purchase of non-net books and nil on net books – including library titles, of course. When the new Primary and Secondary School Licence came into being, 10% discount had to be given to schools on all net library books and this was crippling for many of the smaller suppliers. Suddenly discounts of 12–13 per cent became the norm on non-net books and even 15% was quoted by a few of the larger schools' suppliers. It became impossible to compete with the giants of the trade who were receiving a greater discount from the publishers.

For library suppliers the effect of the move towards more paperback publishing has been the very significant issue of unit cost. The unit cost is kept low, particularly with children's paperbacks, inevitably affecting profitability: far more paperbacks have to be processed to achieve the profit possible from hardbacks, but the handling cost of a paperback may be higher. A particular issue is where there is simultaneous publication of a hardback and a paperback edition, at a price of £3.99 for paperback; £8.99 for hardback: the choice for hard-pressed librarians is clear!

From the specialist bookseller's and library supplier's viewpoint, direct marketing to schools by publishers is seen as potentially disastrous; they, as the expert middleman, may be cut out completely. Discounts greater than the bookseller themselves get may be offered by the publisher direct to the school, in this competitive market. This has forced library suppliers and booksellers to rethink *their* marketing. It is noticeable that a number are now working closely with teachers and librarians, offering training courses and producing more informative and focused guides to bookstock, often targeted at parents or teachers.

A number of library suppliers have reshaped their catalogues, in line with elements of the National Curriculum, for example Peters Library Service produces GCSE Fact File and National Curriculum Focus, to help librarians keep up to date with developments, and a regular magazine, *Update* intended to review new developments and projects within Peters and the trade. Peters Library Service also currently sponsors the Library Association Carnegie and Kate Greenaway Awards, producing posters and publicity material for the award as well as the major press launch and shortlist party. From its early days, Peters has commissioned sets of posters about children's books and libraries and now has a gallery of free posters, of both its own commissions and posters from publishers, available for librarians or teachers.

Books for Students publish *Radical reading: books for teenagers*, their monthly *Promotions news* listing new promotions and new titles, and a CD-ROM service which allows customers to try out facilities at the showroom. They also provide *National Curriculum ideas cards*, linking the CD-ROM to National Curriculum topics and activities, cross-curricular, with each suitable disc. All kinds of other tasters, in the form of free posters, bookmarks, etc., are also on offer.

Library suppliers remain cautious about carrying stocks of CD-ROM products. While recognizing that schools are beginning to demand reference CD-ROMs, access and use in most schools is still very limited unless the CD-ROMs are networked or there are more machines or CD-ROM towers. Price is an issue, too, for the supplier as, unlike most books, CD-ROMS are reducing in price, making stockholding unwise unless the supplier wishes to sell at a lower price than originally paid! CD-ROMS cannot be a loss-leader, as paperbacks are that already.

Bookclubs and mail order

The recent accent on literacy and the controversy over whether standards of reading have improved or declined over the years, has generally helped the purchase of books. The increased parental interest in books and reading has led to an expansion of outlets for book sales direct to children and to parents, at home and at school. There has been a significant growth of children's book clubs aimed at home buyers, offering a selection of the best titles at discount prices, for example Books for Children, Red House, Children's Book of the Month Club, as well as school bookshops and mail order bookclubs run in schools by teachers, such as The Puffin Book Club and the Scholastic Bookclubs. Book fairs set up in schools and run by outside suppliers have similarly raised awareness and enhanced sales.

A number of publishers commend these initiatives as having a huge impact in increasing the sales of fiction and picture books to schools *and* in helping to sell backlist titles, particularly poetry, anthologies, picture books:

> Once heavily dependent on buoyant library and school markets that supported a strong and traditional output of both fiction and information hardbacks, children's publishing has adjusted to a new climate dominated by book clubs and school book fairs. The book clubs vary in operation, but the principle remains the same: they are reaching new markets, and much of the demand is for a different kind of book. Parents, the main purchasers through book clubs, want good books, but they also want value for money. Where a librarian would go for the durability of a hardback, a parent prefers the affordability of a paperback. Price is critical. (Eccleshare, 1995, p.20)

Attenborough, as long ago as 1989, was noting: 'The school bookshop movement and the growth of children's book clubs both in school and at home have made enormous strides in bringing books directly into the hands of readers. They've created an appetite, an audience' (Attenborough, 1989) and continuing this message in 1994:

> The selling of books, through schools – through school bookshops, book clubs, book fairs – has grown dramatically in recent years, simply because the alternative of a wide

range of the right books in the high street has not been there, with some advice and help. The selecting by specialists, the clarity of purpose, the likelihood of somebody in that school environment having knowledge and interest and an ability to guide, make that method extraordinarily potent. The carefully targeted and limited range selected by chains such as the Early Learning Centres gives that same imprimatur, too. (Attenborough, 1994, p.24)

However, an article in *The Bookseller* in 1995, while commending the initiatives of the book clubs, drew attention to the increased competition among them. It noted that there are ten clubs specializing in children's books, selling through schools or individual membership, some operating with mailings, some based on fairs, book parties or a mixture of these. The publishers Puffin and Usborne run their own bookclubs. They have recently been joined by Dorling Kindersley, who run their own book parties, through agents. Numbers of members are impressive: the very specialist multicultural and non-sexist Letterbox Library with 15,000; Books for Children (owned by Time-Life) with 150,000; Red House has 400,000 family members. The competition appears to be stiffest in the school book club field, where the two largest school book operators are Books For Students with their Wise Owls Club and Scholastic. Scholastic has four clubs, aimed at specific age groups between 2 and 14 and has 30,000 active clubs within schools. Heffer's 'Bookworm Club' has around 5000 group members in over 3000 schools. All are noticing that there is more competition and that teachers have less time to spend on extra-curricular activities: 'One of the biggest difficulties is the motivation of the teacher and the time needed to run a club' (*The Bookseller*, 1995b).

Concern to raise awareness of gender, race and class issues resulted in the setting up some ten years ago by a women's cooperative of a mail order bookclub, The Letterbox Library:

> Books are an important avenue through which children learn what is expected of them. Many children's books present their readers with a narrow range of options, by showing girls and boys in stereotyped ways . . . The images of family life often ignore the fact that many mothers go out to work, some children live with one parent, and not all families are white and middle-class. Men are rarely shown sharing domestic tasks or caring for children . . . We select books which show boys and girls as independent, resourceful, caring and emotional. We look for books which show children living in a variety of different settings, and which reflect our multi-ethnic society. (The Letterbox Library, 1993)

The increased parental interest in books and reading also led to the rapid expansion of the Early Learning chain stores now found in many high streets and to books being sold in supermarkets. Walker Books started this trend when they began supplying children's books to Sainsbury's in 1985. Since then this trend has been followed by Marks and Spencer, Tesco and Safeway, each selling specific ranges of children's books. This trend is welcomed by many:

A new set of traditions in children's bookselling has been formed by the likes of Tesco, Asda, Woolworth's, Toys R Us, ELC and Children's World which thankfully has resulted in books being taken away from their elitist position in the marketplace, and affording them a chance to compete for the gift or pocket-money pound alongside toys, games, audio and video. (Somerville, 1994, p.25)

The growth of the above 'specials' market has considerably changed the editorial and marketing attitudes of many publishers. Walker Books, Kingfisher and HarperCollins have editorial teams developing projects specifically for the specials market.

All publishers are looking for innovative ways of ensuring that they retain their market share, with things like dumpbins in libraries, newsletters, direct mailing to librarians. It is clear, looking through current publishers' catalogues and lists, that the needs of children, particularly their educational needs, are seen as paramount. In addition to standard catalogues of new releases and/or backlists, publishers are targeting specific areas of the National Curriculum or particular identifiable groups, e.g. parents, teachers, librarians.

Examples of this are *National Curriculum for English: books for Key Stages 1 and 2 Reading* (Cooling, 1995), an extensive list of Penguin books for specific stages in the National Curriculum, chosen and annotated by critic Wendy Cooling. Such publications are an enormous help for the busy teacher and much to be commended, provided that teachers remember that this is only a selection of *Penguin* books. Puffin also produce *Children's books: a parent's guide* (Puffin, 1995), a similarly useful and accessible guide to help parents chose the right books for their children. It includes over 200 Penguin titles, arranged in six age groups and with a thematic index. It sold 28,000 copies in its first six months.

Publishers are finding that teachers are expecting more books to be labelled, graded and coded for their perceived needs. Parents, too, are concerned to be told precisely what to give their children to read at each stage and as one publisher says: 'if teachers are not going to have enough book knowledge (which they frequently don't) and libraries are going to lose their specialists, and booksellers are as hopeless as ever at providing advice, then we publishers will have to take on that advice role in a more forceful way.'

Net Book Agreement

The Net Book Agreement (1957) has been abandoned. It was a simple and approved agreement between most significant publishers which was designed to improve the availability and sale of books to the public by encouraging booksellers to stock and sell a wide range of books. It provided a marketing system for books which brought different and complex demands from consumers, booksellers and publishers together. Consumers wanted well stocked bookshops near their homes, offering both the new and the established, and able to meet their needs at every level. Booksellers needed to be able to offer the range of stock required to meet this demand. Publishers needed to get their titles on to the bookshelves in the bookshop, so that they were displayed and had a chance of selling in a high risk market. The Net Book Agreement encouraged the stocking of books by enabling – but not requiring – a publisher to impose a condition that a book should not be sold to the public at less than a minimum price determined – the net price (The Publishers Association, 1991).

With certain exceptions, publishers had remained in support of the Agreement until the middle of 1995. It is too early to predict the effect on children's book publishing and the supply of children's books to public libraries and school libraries and sales to the general public. It is generally anticipated that abolition will reduce the price of best sellers, with heavy discounting, at least initially, of high volume, mass market books. It is also anticipated that, at the same time, the price of more specialist, less popular books will rise.

A promotional leaflet about the NBA, with quotes from well-known authors, produced by the Society of Authors in 1992, highlighted some of the contentious issues surrounding the NBA:

> The Net Book Agreement encourages the publication and promotion of a wide variety of books to cater for all aspects of public interest. We at the Society of Authors believe that the abolition of the NBA would be a threat to the publication of many first novels, as well as to poetry and academic works. (Penelope Lively, 1992)

> Innovation, experimentation, risk-taking are the lifeblood of books. They are the qualities needed alike by writers, publishers, booksellers and readers; for those qualities to flourish it is essential the NBA be retained. (Sally Beauman, 1992)

> Books are nutty, eccentric things, which have a cultural importance which far exceeds their commercial worth. The NBA seems to be a conservationist device, allowing literary wildlife at least to survive, if not flourish, in all its diversity. It ensures the mass market books indirectly subsidize the commercially crazy projects that keep the world of ideas spinning. (Martin Waddell, 1992)

It is too early to say whether any of these predictions may be correct. It is widely assumed that smaller libraries are less likely to be able to attract large discounts from suppliers and that there will be a reduction in the quality of service from suppliers following their need to compete on price (much of the servicing currently on offer is essentially hidden discount). Thus the demise of the Net Book Agreement might lead to schools and libraries getting a *lower* discount and thus paying more. Some libraries and schools have very difficult and costly servicing requirements; realistic servicing charges may have to be introduced.

Christmas 1995 was less successful in terms of sales than was predicted. The majority of publishers are still publishing net books but there are signs that prices are rising by one or two pounds, to allow some flexibility to give extra discounts.

In other words, the pattern appears to be higher prices all around to allow a more obvious discount. It is possible that libraries may end up slightly better off, because they will be able to negotiate discount on all books they are purchasing, rather than purely the high profile best sellers. The library supply picture is very confused and confused further by the creation of new library authorities, following local government reorganization. It is to be hoped that the demise of the Net Book Agreement does not foreshadow the end of specialist children's book supply.

INTERNATIONAL MARKET

As long ago as 1985, the late Sebastian Walker, dubbed The King of the Co-Edition, was celebrating six years as a publisher and looking forward to the ensuing, albeit difficult years, in terms of doing even more to increase the 'world's awareness of the educational potency and the sheer fun of children's literature . . . Co-editions only happen if you've got frightfully good books of the highest possible quality' (Powling, 1985).

Chester Fisher highlights the influence of the international market, in terms of what a publisher considers viable for publication:

> Publishers must now consider the requirements of the international rights market, particularly in colour illustrated books where the origination costs are very high. British publishers, due to their small home market, have always had to look beyond their own country for sales to spread origination costs over more copies. The British contingent at international book fairs, such as Frankfurt and Bologna, is usually the largest after the home countries . . . The largest market for such books has traditionally been the United States. It is possible that Europe, particularly France and Germany, will become of equal importance. The developments in Eastern Europe also offer new horizons for publishers as does the Far East and possibly South America. (Fisher, 1994, pp.33–4).

The most successful companies in this market appear to be Walker Books in picture books and Dorling Kindersley in non-fiction, because their books, in addition to being of excellent quality and cleverly marketed, have a wide appeal in international markets. Over 18 million copies of the Dorling Kindersley's Eyewitness Guides have been sold in 39 countries (Peters Library Service, 1995). There are also considerable opportunities in an international market for multimedia products. Again this is a market which Dorling Kindersley are exploiting very effectively.

Exports represent a significant proportion of overall educational publishing but because of the market specificity of books produced specifically for the National Curriculum, the scale and growth of the international market offers few benefits of scale to publishing which reflects the needs of UK schools.

In mainstream children's book publishing, as opposed to educational publishing, Klaus Flugge, of Andersen Press, bemoans the insular nature of the British, particularly with regard to translations of children's books:

> The British have more or less turned their backs on foreign books for children . . . there is a lack of interest in this country in anything foreign . . . Translation is the heart of literature . . . It is through literature that we most intimately enter the hearts and minds and spirits of other people . . . we become a thousand different people and yet still remain ourselves. At the moment, the British are becoming more insular, less connected to others, less able to appreciate what other people produce and think and envision than they ever were. (Flugge, 1994, pp.209–10)

Conglomerates

Overall the volatility of the school book market has led to a decline in the number of publishers serving it. There are now little more than a dozen major school publishers whereas fifteen years ago there would have been two or three times that number. The continual fluctuation of funding in the market makes it very difficult to plan for reasonable growth and development of a business. This leads to problems of cashflow, mergers and takeovers.

In many cases this has led to the consolidation of schoolbook publishers, through acquisition of smaller companies, amalgamation or restructuring. There has been a growth in publishing conglomerates, with Octopus owning Heinemann and Methuen; Penguin owning Viking, Puffin, Hamish Hamilton; Random Century owning Collins, Bodley Head, Cape, Hutchinson, Julia MacRae Books: 'Jobs and working practices have been radically altered as companies have restructured to transform their internal function in a very different environment. This has caused upheavals in many houses, as staff struggle to deal with the speed of change and its impact on themselves and their colleagues' (Kahn, 1992, p.258).

Chester Fisher expresses concern that the strict cost controls which have been adopted in all aspects of the publishing operation have led to less risk-taking and concentration on the few tried and tested names. This has been paralleled by a radical restructuring and realignment of publishing companies, with smaller companies disappearing or being absorbed into larger conglomerates, many owned by American, French and German companies. The result is a concentration of imprints, the results of which have yet to be seen: 'Some believe that it will reduce editorial creativity and expertise . . . The occasional outstanding newcomer may well come from the smaller imprints' (Fisher, 1994, p.34).

CONCLUSION

In summary, the last 20 years has seen an enormous period of change in the market for children's books, in the changing school and public library markets and in the retail trade, particularly through direct marketing. The effects of educational reform, local government reorganization and local expenditure cuts have had a profound effect on publishing for the children's book market. For all of the reasons outlined in other chapters, access to a wide range of books for children is an essential part of the individual child's growth. The future of the publishing, bookselling and library supply industries is a critical part of this, if the quality and range of books and other media for children are to be maintained into the next century.

Notes

1   I am indebted to the many publishers, booksellers and library suppliers who responded to my request for information. As a number of individuals asked for confidentiality to be maintained, some quotations are not attributed and some companies are not named. I am also indebted to John Davies of the Educational Publishers Association for his help.

2   I am also indebted to the library suppliers and booksellers who responded to my request for information. As a number of individuals, for commercial reasons, asked for confidentiality to be maintained, their contributions are anonymous, unless information is already in the public domain.

REFERENCES

Attenborough, E. (1989), 'Low status, low sales – the debilitating equation in children's bookselling', *The Bookseller*, 27 January 1989, 262.

Attenborough, E. (1994), 'If I were a children's bookseller', *The* Bookseller, 5 August 1994, 24.

Beauman, S. (1992), *What price reading? the truth behind the myth of cut price books.* Society of Authors leaflet.

Book Trust (1992), *Books in schools*, a report from the Book Trust in association with the Educational Publishers Association and funded by BNB Research Fund Report 60. Book Trust.

The Bookseller (1995a), 'OUP finds a buzz in paperbacks', *The Bookseller*, 17 February 1995, 90.

The Bookseller (1995b), 'No complacency in the clubs', *The Bookseller*, 3 March 1995, 33.

The Bookseller (1995c), 'Schools can't afford books for revised national curriculum, says EPC', *The Bookseller*, 21 April 1995, 6.

Coleman, J. (1993), 'Ringbinder rules', *Books for keeps*, no.79, March 1993, 24.

Cooling, W. (1995), *National Curriculum for English: books for key stages 1 and 2 Reading.* A Penguin Children's Booklist. London, Penguin.

Davies, J. (1994), 'The Dearing review: where next for educational publishers'. Personal communication from John Davies, Director, Educational Publishers Council, the Publishers Association.

Davies, J. (1995a), Personal communication from John Davies, Director, Educational Publishers Council, The Publishers Association.

Davies, J. (1995b), Presentation by the Educational Publishers Council to the Minister of State for Education: summary of key points.

Davies, J. (1995c), *The Dearing review.*

Dearing, Sir R. (1993), *The National Curriculum and its assessment: final report.* School Curriculum and Assessment Authority.

Department of Education and Science (1975), *A language for life.* (The Bullock Report). London, HMSO.

Department for Education (1995), *The National Curriculum.* London, HMSO.

Eccleshare, J. (1985), Introduction to *Children's books of the year 1985,* 1. London, National Book League.

Eccleshare, J. (1986), Introduction to *Children's books of the year 1986,* 1–2. London, National Book League.

Eccleshare, J. (1987), Introduction to *Children's books of the year 1987,* 1. London, Book Trust, 1.

Eccleshare, J. (1988), Introduction to *Children's books of the year 1988,* 1. London, Andersen Press.

Eccleshare, J. (1989), Introduction to *Children's books of the year 1989,* 1. London, Andersen Press.

Eccleshare, J. (1990), Introduction to *Children's books of the year 1990,* 6. London, Andersen Press.

Eccleshare, J. (1992), Introduction to *Children's books of the year 1992,* 5–6. London, Andersen Press.

Eccleshare, J. (1993), Introduction to *Children's books of the year 1993,* 5–6. London: Andersen Press, 5–6.

Eccleshare, J. (1995), 'Children's books – a market in flux', *The Bookseller,* 3 March 1995, 20.

Edwards, V. (1995), 'Books and bi-lingual pupils', *Books for keeps,* no. 91, March 1995, 24–5.

Educational Publishers Council (1971), *Books in school.* London, EPC.

Elkin, J. (1994), *A multicultural guide to children's books 0–12.* Researched and compiled by Judith Elkin, ed. Rosemary Stones. London, *Books for keeps.*

Fisher, C. (1994), 'Publishing and bookselling – an overview' in *Skills for life?: the meaning and value of literacy. Proceedings of the Youth Libraries Group Conference, 1992,* Keith Barker and Ray Lonsdale (eds.), 31–6. London, Taylor-Graham.

Flugge, K. (1994), 'Crossing the divide: publishing children's books in the European context', *Signal 75,* September 1994, 209–10.

Girling, B. (1989), 'Children's books: letter', *The Bookseller,* 3 February 1989, 401.

Girling, B. (1990), 'Room for growth – the UK children's book market', *The Bookseller,* 11 May 1990, 1526–8.

Gotch, C. (1992), 'Are we being served? What booksellers and publishers want from each other': highlights of the Children's Book Circle Conference, 1992.

Guardian (1993), Letter in *The Guardian,* 19 May, 1993.

Hill, R. (1991), *The Books for keeps green guide to children's books.* Richard Hill (ed.). London, *Books for keeps.*

Hoffman, M. (1995), 'Judging a book by its format', *The Bookseller*, 3 March 1995, 26.

Kahn, P. (1992), 'Educated stress', *The Bookseller*, 31 January 1992, 258.

Letterbox Library (1993), *Newsletter and booklist* no. 38, New Year, 1993. The Letterbox Library, Unit 2D, Leroy House, 436 Essex Road, London N1 3QP.

Lively, P. (1992), *What price reading? the truth behind the myth of cut price books*. Society of Authors leaflet.

Lloyd, D. (1994), 'If I were a children's bookseller', *The Bookseller*, 5 August 1994, 28.

Moss, E. (1973), Introduction to *Children's books of the year 1973*, 9. London, The National Book League.

Moss, E. (1974), Introduction to *Children's books of the year 1974*, 7. London, The National Book League.

Moss, E. (1975), Introduction to *Children's books of the year 1975*, 12. London, The National Book League.

Moss, E. (1976), Introduction to *Children's books of the year 1976*, 5. London, Hamish Hamilton in association with The National Book League and The British Council.

Moss, E. (1977), Introduction to *Children's books of the year 1977*, 5. London, Hamish Hamilton in association with The National Book League and The British Council.

Moss, E. (1978), Introduction to *Children's books of the year 1978*, 5. London, Hamish Hamilton in association with The National Book League.

Moss, E. (1979), Introduction to *Children's books of the year 1979*, 5–6. London, Julia MacRae Books in association with The National Book League.

Naidoo, B. (1994) 'Challenging ways of seeing?' *A multicultural guide to children's books 0–12*. Researched and compiled by Judith Elkin; Ed. Rosemary Stones, 11. *Books for keeps*.

Nettell, S. (1995), 'Backlist v frontlist', *The Bookseller*, 3 March 1995, 25.

Peters Library Service (1995), *The publishers' supplement 1995*. Peters Library Service, 120 Bromsgrove Street, Birmingham B5 6RL.

Powling, C. (1985), 'What makes Walker run?', *Books for keeps* no. 30, January 1985, 14.

Powling, C. (1995), 'The Return of Common Sense', *Books for keeps*, no. 90, January 1995, 3.

The Publishers Association (1991), *The Net Book Agreement*. London, The Publishers Association.

Puffin (1995), *Children's books: a parent's guide*. London, Penguin Books Ltd.

Randles, H. (1995), 'W H Smith – fewer titles, more sales', *Books for keeps*, 17 February 1995, 90.

Rosen, M. (1993), 'On the importance of books in schools', *Books for keeps*, no. 79, March 1993, 4–7.

Rough, S. (1984), *Children's books and the chocolate factory: a report on the children's book conference*. Children's Book Circle of the Booksellers Association, 14 February 1984.

Sherrard-Smith, B. (1981), Introduction to *Children's books of the year 1981*, 5. London, Julia MacRae Books in association with The National Book League.

Sherrard-Smith, B. (1982), Introduction to *Children's books of the year 1982*, 7. London, Julia MacRae Books in association with The National Book League.

Somerville, C. (1994), 'If I were a children's bookseller', *The Bookseller*, 5 August 1994, 25.

Stones, R. (1994), 'I din do nuttin . . . to Gregory Cool', *Books for keeps*. no.88, September 1994, 4–5.

Tapissier, M. (1994), 'If I were a children's bookseller', *The Bookseller*, 5 August 1994, 26.

Taylor, J. (1988), 'Children's books – are they earning their keep?', *The Bookseller*, 11 March 1988, 995.

Thomson, P. (1992), 'Disability in modern children's fiction: novels for 9–16 year olds', *Books for keeps*, no.75, July 1992, 24.

Tucker, N. (1994), 'Encyclopaedias in the age of the ringbinder', *Books For Keeps*, no. 86, May 1994, 22–3.

UNESCO (1982), 'UNESCO London Declaration', *Library Association record*, 84 (6), June 1982.

Waddell, M. (1992), *What price reading? the truth behind the myth of cut price books*. Society of Authors leaflet.

Wood, A. (1993), Introduction to The Federation of Children's Book Groups Silver Jubilee Conference, Stratford-upon-Avon, 1993.

6

Collection development

Ray Lonsdale

INTRODUCTION

Arguably one of the most important responsibilities of the librarian (indeed, among the greatest arts that librarians possess), is that of planning, building, maintaining and promoting a dynamic and pertinent collection. Collection development, the generic term used to denote this process, comprises a series of complex procedures which we will explore in this chapter. We shall begin by defining the term 'collection', and consider a new concept, the 'virtual library'. Selection and acquisition, collection evaluation and review – elements of collection development – will be examined in some depth, and the contribution of a collection development policy document and its structure will be discussed. The range of bibliographical sources and services used to support the varied activities of collection development will be analysed, and the chapter concludes with a brief examination of issues associated with the organization and promotion of stock.

Before we embark on our exploration of collection development, a word about terminology. There is sometimes confusion about the meaning of certain terms used to describe the various activities which make up collection development. This is particularly evident when reading the British and the North American literature. Indeed, the term 'collection management' which was formerly used to describe one discrete activity of collection development, i.e. one 'designed to optimize the use of existing information and fiscal resources to assure the most effective collection development' (Dewe, Lonsdale and Jones, 1995, p.7), is increasingly used as a synonym for collection development. Where discrepancies occur, these will be elucidated.

THE COLLECTION

The term 'collection' which is at the heart of the management process under consideration, has undergone changes in meaning during the last 20 years. There has been a move away from the narrow interpretation of the 'collection' as simply embracing resources held within the confines of the public library. A 'collection' now encompasses human and material resources available within the community as well as information and materials held in other library and information systems. It is no coincidence that the term 'stock', which has been favoured in the UK for many years (hence 'stock selection', 'stock management'), is slowly being replaced by the term 'collection'.

The concept of the 'virtual library' or the 'electronic library' has also arrived with the advent of the new technologies, in particular networking systems. The following extracts offer an insight into the notion of a 'virtual library'.

> The term 'virtual library' has been floating through the ether for some time. It surfaced again recently in a report on the formation of a coalition of librarians and computer professionals to help organize information on national computer networks. The goal of the coalition is to 'put a 'virtual library' into scholars' hands'. . .
>
> University libraries are rapidly becoming accessible to anyone with a personal computer and the means to connect to library computer systems. On the local level, that connectivity can take the form of a modem and a local telephone call.
>
> Typically, the user searches the library's online catalogue, a database that contains bibliographic records for books and journals. Electronic access is normally possible, however, only for materials represented by machine-readable (MARC) records . . .
>
> One agenda item is for all types of libraries to provide online access to their collections by completing the retrospective conversion of their card catalogues.
>
> Telecommunications access to library databases eliminates the distinction between local and remote users, but this access creates new policy dilemmas. Who should have access or priority for access? What security is needed, especially for local files? What standards are necessary for making a variety of files available? (Mitchell and Saunders, 1991, p.8)
>
> The Electronic Library is a teaching, learning and study environment for higher education in which information is held primarily in electronic form. It is not restricted to a physical locale. Users may access it from anywhere and it will give access to information held in many places. It will contain text, still and moving images, and sound. It will be intimately linked with the publishing and bookselling industry.
>
> This statement articulates the belief that conventional library services can only provide a partial answer to the needs of higher education in the future. It states clearly that there will be a fundamental shift in the balance of resources from print sources to electronic sourced information. It implies that the proportion of resources expended on acquiring and maintaining collections will steadily reduce. (Arnold, Collier and Ramsden, 1993, p.3)

As these two excerpts imply, the concept of the virtual collection is developing most noticeably in higher education. There is growing evidence in North America and Australia that public libraries are exploring its potential too, as are school libraries. With the development of networking systems in the UK public library sector, should children and children's librarians not be permitted similar access to national, even international collections and databases? This question is no longer theoretical, and children's librarians should revaluate their concept of the collection and investigate the possibilities and implications of the 'virtual library'.

THE NATURE AND SCOPE OF COLLECTION DEVELOPMENT

In his seminal work on the subject, Edward Evans offers the following definition which highlights the nature and significance of collection development. It is, he remarks: 'the process of making certain that the information needs of the people are met in a timely and economic manner, using information resources produced both inside and outside the organisation' (Evans, 1987, p.65).

Central to this interpretation is the belief that the collection is not to be developed for the self-satisfaction of the librarian but it is ultimately to serve the information requirements of the clientele. Also implicit is the need for us to think beyond our immediate physical collection to those human and information resources held within our community and within other institutions – the 'virtual library'.

But what of the scope of collection development? If the literature is scanned, or if one discusses the subject with colleagues, different interpretations exist as to what it constitutes. A common myth is that it is limited to the process of selecting new stock, and it is not uncommon for some children's libraries to create stock selection policies which masquerade as collection development policies. However, it is much more extensive than that, embracing the following elements:

- evaluation and selection of new materials for purchase;
- evaluation and selection of new materials available as gifts;
- production of in-house material for the library collection;
- evaluation of the existing collection (sometimes referred to as stock editing);
- weeding, repair and replacement of items already in stock;
- relegation of material;
- supplementing the collection by cooperative systems and interlibrary loans;
- preservation and conservation;
- promotional activities.

For these procedures to be undertaken effectively, management must ensure that they are carried out:

- continuously, i.e. assuming that, regardless of the scale of the operation, collection development is a full-time activity. Even when budgets have shrunk, the scope, condition and use of the collection must be monitored;
- consistently, i.e. according to agreed and known policies and principles;
- by the most appropriate people available;
- in a coordinated manner.

It has become increasingly apparent that a systematic programme for collection development needs to be instigated if the various activities outlined above are to be successfully executed. An effective programme depends on the formulation, circulation and use of a written policy, an agreed policy to which people are committed, and one which is known to exist by all concerned, including the users. We will explore the elements of collection development in some detail later within the context and structure of a policy document.

A COLLECTION DEVELOPMENT POLICY

Children's librarians have been especially conscientious about developing policies for their services. With ever dwindling funds for materials, it becomes even more important to ensure that the processes of collection development are effective and efficient, i.e. that the limited money is spent as carefully and critically as possible. A policy can help ensure the effective spending of the library budget.

Meeting users' needs and expectations and cultivating the collection's strengths are facilitated through a policy. Similarly, it can help avoid unprofitable arguments and unpleasantness due to uncertainty and inconsistency, and library staff can be consistent in the activities which are being undertaken. A policy can also serve as a useful political tool if challenged on an item which has been selected or when seeking support for funding or new developments.

When selection or evaluation involves individuals from other sections or libraries, coordination can be more easily facilitated, and continuity can be achieved when new staff take responsibility for collection development.

Finally, and perhaps most fundamentally, a policy can provide the basis of future planning for the children's service.

The case for having a *written* policy should not be overlooked. If it is written down then the policy is likely to be more clearly thought out and more effectively communicated to its potential users. Some libraries do see dangers in having a written document, usually for political reasons; however, the prevalent trend is to have a written statement. The recent guidelines for developing children's libraries published by The Library Association reaffirm this point (Library Association, 1991, pp.23–8).

Convincing arguments have been put forward by theorists and practitioners alike to support the need for a written policy. Yet when UK children's libraries are scrutinized there is a perception that written policies are not as evident as they are in the USA or Australia. In a study of audiovisual and computer materials provision in UK children's libraries and schools library services, only 12.9% of authorities had created a formal policy for *all* materials (Lonsdale and Wheatley, 1991, pp.31–55). Just over half had informal policies and almost one third no policy at all. More detailed analysis by format revealed that a third of authorities had a formal policy for books as compared with 16% for audiovisual materials and 8% for computer software. The practical difficulties of formulating policies was cited as the most common reason for the dearth but optimistically half of authorities indicated their intentions to create a policy. A more recent study revealed little improvement, with a significant number of authorities still without a written policy (Lonsdale and Everitt, 1996).

Before examining the content of such policies there are several considerations which must be borne in mind. First, collections are dynamic, and consequently policies need to be revised periodically so that they reflect or anticipate changes in society, in the community, and in national and local priorities. If the components of the policy are not modified accordingly then the policy will become superseded and redundant. At the outset a procedure for reviewing individual sections of the policy should be established. Some libraries undertake this annually or biennially.

Second, policies are most usefully seen as guidelines rather than mechanically applied directives. Finally, there should be a policy not only for the whole system but also for specific services (e.g. young people, school library services).

Components of a policy

The first point to note is that many different models exist. In North America, the American Library Association has established guidelines for libraries to use (Perkins, 1979). At first glance these may appear too comprehensive and perhaps too idealistic. However, they do afford a useful structure which incorporates the various elements of collection development mentioned earlier, and which can be adapted by children's librarians for their policy statement. What is offered below is a set of components which are found in a collection policy.

Collection policy components:

(i)   Introduction
The function of the introduction is to set out the status of the document(s) within the institution, and to establish the uses to which it may be put. In this respect, there may be a statement about the reasons for developing a policy, how it was developed and by whom; a list specifying the audience; a definition of the scope of the policy and an indication as to revision.

(ii)   Basic philosophy and goals of the Institution and the collection
The objectives of the collection need to be created not in isolation but in terms of the parent body's goals (usually embodied in the authority's mission statement). Sometimes these can appear too idealistic or too broad, e.g. 'to enrich the lives of all children in the community'. But useful things can be said in terms of achievable and measurable goals, e.g. 'to support the recreational reading of children', or 'the professional needs of the library staff' or 'to support visual and computer

literacy' – if these are encompassed by the philosophy of the institution. Some policies assign priorities indicating the most critical objectives which need to be met.

The following statement taken from a policy document from one of Britain's largest public library authorities is fairly typical:

> The library service aims to serve the informational recreational, educational and cultural needs of all children and young people in the community. This readership, ranging from babies to teenagers, will include the gifted reader, the able, the less able, the handicapped, and the minority language speaker. All libraries should continue to provide a selection of attractive and accessible material which will:- provide enjoyment, enlarge the mind and the imagination, contribute towards the intellectual, emotional, psychological and social development of the individual, encourage an appreciation of beauty and human achievement and aspiration, reflect individual, local and national values and experiences in the context of multi-cultural Britain and the wider world, introduce children to their cultural heritage, provide a vicarious experience of life in terms of time, place and culture, offer experience in the creative and scientific inquiry process, enable the reader to acquire and develop a critical awareness of knowledge, values and attitudes, develop the use and understanding of language, provide for children's information needs, including support for both formal and continuing education.

(iii)   The communities to be served

This section will be closely allied to the overall goals of the institution and should delineate, in some detail, the various communities to be served by the collection. If necessary it will highlight groups within that community who may have specific needs, e.g. the deaf, the visually impaired, the dyslexic child. Frequently, reference to these will be made when setting out the types of materials to be included in the collection (see scope of the collection below).

A constant review is necessitated since communities will be liable to change. In formulating this section, the librarian needs to be cognisant of not only existing communities but also *potential* communities which have hitherto been excluded. Once again, given funding and resource constraints, policies usually accord priorities to communities.

(iv)   Scope of the collection

This usually constitutes one of the most comprehensive elements in the policy document, setting out the following in terms of inclusion and *exclusion*:

(a)   subject fields – if a broad range then they may be indicated generally by reference to Dewey Decimal Classification or other classification notation. Special fields such as materials for parents or professional literature will also be listed in this section;

(b) formats – e.g. computer software, paperbacks, videos, multimedia;
(c) languages and translations;
(d) multiple copies – stating the areas where duplicate copies are permissible and the formulae for purchase;
(e) other exclusions – what other materials are excluded and the factors responsible for their exclusion. An example taken from recent policies concerns the exclusion of certain forms of 'do-it-yourself adventure novels' (the horror content) and 'Sindy tie-ins' (the poor quality of the writing).
(f) special collections

(v)   Controversial materials and political correctness
This has become an increasingly important consideration in UK children's librarianship in recent years. The policy should set out the conclusions reached by the library (or institution) regarding issues such as sexuality in literature, political and religious bias, violence, sex-role and gender stereotyping. A clear statement will serve to substantiate any defence which the librarian may be called to make. This will usually comprise a reference to appropriate statements issued by professional bodies and legislation. Some libraries also provide a complaints procedure (including proforma letters) which staff can use when dealing with complaints.

(vi)   Gifts and donations
Although most common in academic libraries, some public libraries may be offered gifts and donations for the general collection or as the basis for special collections. This may be a problem area and libraries usually set out the conditions under which they will accept gifts and donations.

A collection development policy may contain detailed statements about essential procedures such as selection and acquisition, collection evaluation, collection review and promotion. Given their complex nature these may constitute separate documents. Some observers (Gorman and Kennedy, 1992) maintain that these procedural documents are not 'policy' statements and should not be integrated within a collection development policy. However, others argue that it is not easy to disassociate policy from such procedures. Since these processes are an essential part of the process of developing and managing the collection and embrace wide-ranging issues they will be dealt with individually below.

Implementation and evaluation of the policy

Every effort must be made to familiarize the staff with the content, use and role of the policy. This will include *all* staff involved in the selection and acquisition of library materials for whom acceptance and implementation should pose no problems. All the other staff members who handle, process and use the collection should also be made familiar with the policy. Libraries will frequently achieve this by holding informal meetings or by integrating sessions on collection development within the in-service training programme.

Once a policy has been implemented there is a view that it should also be disseminated more widely within the institution and even to the community outside. Some children's librarians have provided policy statements for perusal by senior educational personnel within the authority and to bodies such as the Parent Teacher Association. As Gorman and Kennedy remark: 'if the policy statement profiles the library, why not give it a high profile?' (Gorman and Kennedy, 1992, p.84).

Policies in children's libraries

While there is general acknowledgment within the professional literature that an effective and pragmatic development policy is critical for the successful development of the collection, this is not necessarily reflected in practice. Two recent pieces of research into UK children's libraries revealed that approximately one third of authorities have no formal written policy (Lonsdale and Wheatley, 1991 and Lonsdale and Everitt, 1996). While a respectably high proportion of authorities have created informal and formal policies these are primarily concerned with books and the more established audiovisual materials. Almost half have no policy for computer, multimedia and other IT applications, and other specialist areas of the stock such as European language materials are often not represented. If collections and services are to respond to the new multimedia developments in education and society at large, and to specialist demands,then it is surely imperative that comprehensive policies are drawn up.

SELECTION AND ACQUISITION PROCEDURES

Janet Hill, in one of the earliest works devoted to children's book selection, saw the process as the 'cornerstone of librarianship' (Hill, 1969, p.8). She emphasized the need for selection to be based on a positive policy which is related to the real reading needs of children. Many other librarians and educationalists have since echoed this sentiment. Jean Bird maintains that young adults who read voluntarily and successfully are usually confident in the choice of material and 'such confidence can be actively encouraged, firstly through judicious selection and organization of the bookstock and, secondly, by paying greater attention to the process of choice undertaken by most children and the forms of guidance they seem to want and benefit from' (Bird, 1982, p.69).

Implicit in these statements is that the user is the central focus of selection. However, how do we best serve the user? Gorman and Kennedy succinctly summarize a potential dilemma especially critical in the context of work with children:

... one librarian may argue quite legitimately that the selection of library materials should aim at providing the users with exactly what they want. Another librarian, though, may argue with equal fervour that the library, as a socially responsible institution, should qualify this approach by selecting the best material available that meets the users' demands. A third librarian may go further, stating that the library should select simply the best there is without worrying about demand. (Gorman and Kennedy, 1992, p.69)

To help resolve the issue of need versus want and to achieve effective selection a statement of agreed procedures and criteria is required.

Procedures

The central questions are: who should select, what information is required, where do librarians get that information from and how should the process be managed? We will consider each of these in turn.

Selection responsibility

Who should select books/materials for children and young adults? There is a consensus which suggests that the specialist professional children's librarians should be primarily responsible because of their intimate knowledge of the target group and the literature, achieved through specialist education and training. However, this notion is being challenged in some quarters. We are witnessing the increasing use of non-professional and para-professional staff as selectors. Authorities such as Sheffield have incorporated these staff into the selection team because of the great experience gained in working closely with children and their parents. However, some librarians would feel this diminishes their professionalism.

The degree to which young people should engage in selection constitutes a second issue which confronts some libraries. The potential contributions of the child have been strongly advocated by some authorities, but here close consideration must be given to the management of their selection.

Information requirements

Anne Everall, in a perceptive article on book selection for children, sets out a comprehensive list of information needs which must be fulfilled if effective selection is to be facilitated. These comprise such elements as:

- the child community, its nature, size, racial composition, age groupings;
- the adult communities concerned with children;
- the reading needs of the child;
- cultural, social and recreational influences;
- feedback from users;

- the library environment, i.e. prevailing ideologies, policies and practices;
- publishing and bibliographical data about the books and materials;
- performance of the stock (Everall, 1993, pp.5–10).

The selection and acquisition process

It is usual to develop a policy for the selection of new materials which will ensure that procedures are carried out in a coordinated manner. A selection policy is also important to ensure the consistency, variety and balance of stock. It can help in selecting materials which may be problematic e.g. controversial titles and lesser known works. A policy should enable the librarian to explore the thorny issue of whether to respond to the needs of the child or whether to extend the child's reading habits. Publishers too may benefit from the selection policy, an issue to which we will return later.

With regard to the components, it is evident that there will be some overlap with the components listed in the collection development policy, e.g. aims and objectives of the organization/children's department. This is inevitable, since selection policies often constitute separate documents. Criteria constitute another element and this topic is discussed below. Finally, the policy should provide guidance on how the process of selection and acquisition should operate, delineating how selection decisions are implemented, how responsibilities are apportioned and specific acquisition procedures.

The process of selection and acquisition is well documented in the literature (Griffiths, 1983; Yates, 1987; Eyre and Rippingale, 1994; McLeod, D. 1994; and Sarah Blenkin and Helen Lewins (1990) offer a unique set of case studies illustrating the different selection procedures employed in children's libraries).

Two issues which are largely ignored in the literature should be raised. The first concerns what some regard as the undemocratic nature of pre-selection (i.e. a team or individual pre-selects from booklists or approvals and draws up a core listing for scrutiny by other, usually, decentralized libraries) and the problems associated with the dissemination of selection decisions throughout the system. In some cases decisions are not made known to librarians in the branches and this causes friction.

Second, a closer rapport is developing between UK children's publishers and children's librarians. Publishers have asked to attend selection meetings in order to understand how decisions are reached, to listen to criticisms of their publications, perceive the reading habits and needs of young people and identify gaps in the market. Conversely, librarians are being asked to act as readers for new manuscripts, and publishers have acknowledged that they should provide more information about new authors, illustrators and trends in publishing to support the promotion of the collection.

Criteria

As Vivien Griffiths intimates in her work on stock selection, if the selection of specific items for the collection is to be carried out systematically, then it is necessary to base that selection on sound evaluation, employing a set of agreed criteria (Griffiths, 1983, pp.5–10). This is particularly the case where a number of people undertake selection as a team, perhaps meeting occasionally but working separately.

Ideally the aim is to provide guidelines rather than to dictate choice and many libraries produce their own in-house criteria for children's materials. The basic questions one asks in selection are:

(i)   What is the item attempting to do?
(ii) Is this aim relevant to the needs of our users?
(iii) Is there evidence to suggest that the item is likely to succeed in its aim?

There has been a recent revival of interest in establishing and employing criteria. Reduced funds for purchase of materials means that there is a need to buy 'the best available', to buy one item in an interest area where formerly a range of items was bought. Libraries are also now concerned to offer a range of media, and although there is much expertise in the selection of books, many librarians have less assurance when selecting from a range of sound recordings, video programmes, multi-format kits, CD-ROMs – to say nothing about realia!

Selection criteria are concerned with matters like scope and level of treatment, of up-to-dateness, authority of author or other producer, and so forth, but they should be applied in the light of the objectives of the library, our understanding of the needs of the users, and the nature and condition of the existing collection. It is nigh impossible to create a definitive set of criteria, since beyond the elements cited there is great scope for interpretation. Many library authorities have created their own in-house lists which indicate the different interpretations of selection criteria for children's fiction and non-fiction and non-book materials as perceived by UK practitioners in the field.

One of the most difficult issues concerns criteria for the new technologies. While there is a rich literature about criteria for children's books and the more established audiovisual materials, little has been published about the specialist criteria for selecting multimedia and other new electronic media such as the Internet. There are some useful guidelines available, however. Perhaps the most detailed and pertinent are those emanating from research into the use of multimedia (Harry and Oppenheim, 1993; Nordgren, 1993). Unfortunately, these are published in the more academic research journals and there is an urgent need to draw out the conclusions of this work and to disseminate them to the practitioner via professional journals and in training courses. The Youth Libraries Group of

The Library Association is currently planning to publish a set of criteria for the new technologies.

EVALUATING THE COLLECTION

It is increasingly important that there should be systematic and continuous feedback on the use and effectiveness of the collection we have provided. Financial restrictions have concentrated librarians' minds powerfully in all sectors of librarianship, not least in children's libraries, bringing an urgent need to identify and eliminate wasteful provision. The overriding concern when monitoring provision is 'does the collection reflect the library and information needs of the 'community' to be served, both in terms of what *is* available and what is *not?'*

To support collection evaluation the library may establish a policy designed to inform staff of the methods employed to evaluate stock, and to offer guidance on how to implement these methods, how to analyse the results of evaluation and the procedures for acting upon those results, i.e. relegation of materials, ordering of new titles, transfer of stock to different libraries.

Methods of collection evaluation

A variety of evaluation methods may be employed which can be classified into two broad categories, user-oriented and collection-based. There is a rich general literature pertaining to both categories which offers practical guidance in applying these methods, although little has been written specifically on the evaluation of children's collections.

User-oriented methods

User-oriented techniques are employed to analyse the use made of the collection by young people, parents, carers and other adults concerned with children. They include circulation studies based upon analyses of data from the circulation system. Loan statistics can offer useful insights into such areas as subject category use, use of formats, gender use, incidence of loan.

To complement data about loans, it may be necessary to investigate the use of material within the library. Sometimes referred to as 'in-house' studies, information may be collected about the use made of magazines, reference materials, audiovisual and computer software which is not available for loan. A variety of techniques may be employed, including counts of reference titles when shelving, borrowing registers for computer and audiovisual materials, data from slips which children initial after reading particular magazines.

User surveys constitute a particularly valuable method of discovering users' needs, expectations and responses to the collection. They may be both quantitative and qualitative in approach and may present crucial insights which will not be forthcoming from circulation and in-house studies. Conducting surveys, especially of children, is not without its problems, and training in data collection and analysis is usually required if valid results are to be obtained. A further limitation of this approach is that only a partial picture of user perceptions may be created since the survey may ignore that section of the clientele who are not using the service at the time of the survey and will preclude non-users.

Usually, measurement is primarily concerned with user satisfaction. One other form of measurement seeks to go beyond this and evaluate the *benefit* of providing a service or particular item of the collection. Evaluation of *benefit* is usually related to *cost* of provision (hence '*cost-benefit* analysis'). While it is possible to assess benefits arising from the provision of some types of material (most obviously industrial libraries), in the terms of measurable benefit to the parent organization, benefit arising from some other types of provision is either unknowable or not the business of the librarian. Children's librarians in the UK are beginning to address this question, and are currently exploring appropriate methodologies.

Collection-oriented methods

These methods are primarily concerned with evaluating the range, nature and status of the materials held within the collection. With the absence of British national collection standards for children's libraries, one approach is to compare, systematically, elements of the collection (e.g. subject fields, genres, types of material) with the specialist bibliographical and reviewing sources. This will enable the children's librarian to ascertain the percentage of 'standard' or 'recommended' titles held in stock, and to identify potential gaps in coverage. The danger in this approach is to assume that such bibliographical lists necessarily reflect the library's (or authority's) precise requirements.

A traditional and sometimes effective approach is to undertake a physical examination of the collection. This requires the librarian to be fully conversant with all areas of the collection (and children's publishing) in order to evaluate the collection's range and depth in relation to the prescribed aims of the collection policy. Any procedure must take into account the fact that, at any one time, a percentage of the collection will not be on the shelves. A knowledge of what is on loan or at binding is essential to complement the physical evaluation.

Some libraries use comparative statistics as a basis of evaluation, comparing the size of the collection (or elements of the collection), and the degree of expenditure on material with other library authorities serving similar populations. National analyses of collections such as that produced by LISU at the University of Loughborough can provide the basis for such comparative investigations (Creaser, 1995).

Continuous and systematic monitoring of collection provision, leading to adjustment of policies or systems, used to be the exception rather than the rule. This is changing in children's libraries, and while the most appropriate methods will vary according to the particular circumstances, a planned system with assigned responsibilities is increasingly being incorporated into collection development policy documents.

COLLECTION REVIEW

Collection review comprises the procedures of weeding (removal of items from the shelves), replacement of stock, preservation (binding, repair, removal to environmentally controlled storage, conversion to an alternative format, e.g. CD-ROM), and relegation. Of all the aspects of collection development that we have considered, it is perhaps collection review which is least likely to be undertaken conscientiously and in a systematic fashion. And yet there are discernible benefits to be derived from establishing a pragmatic schema or policy. Ridding the collection of redundant stock ensures greater accessibility, and can result in greater user satisfaction, leading ultimately to an increased use of the stock.

A significant amount has been written about the methods used to undertake collection review although little is specifically concerned with children's libraries. Gorman and Kennedy (1992) and Slote (1989) are two of the most comprehensive guides.

BIBLIOGRAPHICAL AND REVIEWING SOURCES AND SERVICES

Fundamental to the success of a programme is the availability of a range of bibliographical and reviewing sources which will support the processes of selection, evaluation and relegation. There exists in the UK, as in most other countries, a large and diverse range of such sources although there has been little attempt to investigate the use made of these by librarians. We know little about why a specific bibliography or bibliographical service is preferred and no attempt has been made to examine the cost effectiveness of these bibliographical sources. The area is ripe for research.

This section seeks to explore the nature and range of these sources and to comment on the issues they present. In the absence of any up-to-date and comprehensive consideration of sources and services for children's librarians in the UK, a detailed analysis is offered.

Published bibliographies

These constitute one of the largest and most familiar of sources and comprise three broad groups:

(i) Trade bibliographies

A systematic range of trade bibliographies exists in the UK and in many other countries. The British publisher Whitaker has, for many years, produced a 'family' of listings which, although originally designed for the publishing and book trade, are widely used by librarians when managing the collection. Their structure enables them to play specific roles in the various processes of collection development. To select new titles in advance of publication two works of special relevance are available, the Spring and Autumn issues of *The Bookseller* and the monthly *Books of the month and books to come*. The former title appears twice a year and offers information about projected titles during the next six months, allowing the librarian sufficient time to place an order before publication. There are two attractive features which have particular pertinence for children's librarians. First, the subject arrangement which, unlike other issues of *The Bookseller*, delineates categories of children's books: Children's Fiction (hardback), Children's Fiction (paperback), Children's Non-fiction (hardback) Children's Non-fiction (paperback), Children's Picture Books (hardback), Children's Picture Books (paperback). This allows quick access to a specific type of book which is not facilitated by the weekly listings.

The second feature is the short publisher's blurbs which are offered in addition to the listing of new titles. These provide commentary on the content of the new titles and also on new developments within publishing houses, e.g. the appearance of a new series, the decision to publish a multi-format work, etc. Thus, an important insight into trends in the publishing of children's books is offered.

The Autumn and Spring numbers of *The Bookseller* are popular with librarians abroad since the six months advance notice can help overcome the significant time lag between the selection of a new title and its appearance on the shelves. Caution must be taken, however, since a small percentage of titles projected for publication may not appear, or may appear late or with a changed title.

Books of the month and books to come offers two months advance notice and may be used as a check on orders. However, the lack of good subject access and the absence of divisions dedicated to children's books does limit its usefulness.

The weekly *Bookseller* can be used as a final check for new publications but only if author and title are known.

To support the replacement of materials as a consequence of weeding or relegation, Whitaker offer, in addition to their general in-print bibliography *British books in print*, the specialized and useful *Children's books in print*. The strengths of this tool are its comprehensive subject arrangement, the age and reading interest indicators, and the miscellany of information about children's literature and the book publishing world. The only drawback is that this work appears only annually which means that it is not a definitive statement as to what is in print.

Despite the availability of the *CD-ROM Bookbank* which permits enhanced access, the trade bibliographies offered by Whitaker do not play such an important role as one might have expected. Why is this the case?

One reason concerns the limited array of materials included in the bibliographies. Non-book material, for example, is excluded, with the exception of some simultaneous publications, making the work irrelevant for those responsible for developing multimedia collections. Little foreign language material is included and local publications together with some categories of ephemeral material are largely excluded. Finally, with the exception of the Spring and Autumn numbers of *The Bookseller* no evaluative information is offered to support the selection of material.

Recently the supremacy of Whitaker has been challenged by the appearance of an exciting new British trade bibliography published by BookData, *Bookfind-CD-ROM*. Four versions are available, the most comprehensive of which is called the World Edition. The annual subscription is high which means that only large library services such as university and the larger public libraries will be able to subscribe. There is a second version called the Compact World Edition and a standard edition which is largely British and European in scope. In response to a demand from school libraries and children's libraries, a fourth version, known as *TES BookFind* has also been produced. Currently this costs £400 + VAT to commercial bodies but only £175 + VAT for schools, which makes it very attractive.

From the outset, BookData recognized the need to provide not only bibliographic information, but some sort of descriptive or evaluative data that can help those undertaking selection.

Publishers' blurbs are incorporated as part of the short entries. Although they are brief, terse and subjective, they offer an idea of what an ambiguous or amorphous title may encompass. For the majority of non-fiction publications, there is also a longer listing of data which contains statements taken from the work itself, often from the contents page. This is quite considerable descriptive information which may be useful when making essential selection choices. A recent innovation, restricted to *TES BookFind*, is the linking of its bibliographic sources with reviewing sources. A reference from items cited within the main database to reviews of these items in professional journals is given. The reviews are produced verbatim, and BookData has established agreements with a number of major reviewing journals within that field and obtained copyright clearance to publish the reviews as part of the bibliography. This is an exciting and important additional dimension for a trade bibliography.

TES-BookFind offers impressive search facilities using Boolean, facilitating comprehensive subject searching. All the data can be downloaded, and there is facility for downloading and transferring a MARC format, which can then be incorporated into an OPAC. School libraries are already using the data as the basis of their catalogue entries. It is also possible to use the data for ordering purposes, and a useful database of publishers is supplied.

Some libraries are starting to use the descriptive annotations not only for collection development purposes, but to compile bibliographies, in-house bibliographies which they give to their clientele. A library can download and create its own bibliographical listing for use as an SDI service or as a promotional tool. Although the information remains the copyright of BookData, permission is granted for libraries, publishers and booksellers to use this for normal working conditions.

As CD-ROM facilities develop in British public libraries both *Bookfind-CD-ROM* and *TES-Bookfind* would appear to have an assured future.

(ii)   British National Bibliography
Traditionally this major bibliography has not featured greatly in the management of children's collections, except in the largest of public libraries. However, if access to the bibliography is facilitated, its potential contribution should be explored. The comprehensive and sophisticated indexes can be used to check if there are any gaps in the collection, and the availability of Cataloguing In Publication (CIP) entries have attracted some librarians who use it to identify forthcoming publications. Be warned, however, for although children's fiction is categorized and easily identifiable, non-fiction for young people is integrated within the main sequence and does take some finding.

(iii)   Subject and special format bibliographies
A vast array of bibliographies has been published covering subjects, user groups (e.g. children with special needs) and particular forms of materials (e.g. audio cassettes, computer software). Bodies such as the Youth Libraries Group of the Library Association, The Young Book Trust, the School Library Association as well as commercial publishers have been responsible for the publication of bibliographical lists which are characterized by their ad hoc nature. Some may contain simple bibliographical details while others offer useful critical annotations. These works can support the process of stock evaluation when the librarian is developing particular areas of the collection and they can also be valuable aids when weeding and considering the replacement of copies.

One problem with many of these works is that they do tend to date quickly, and because of their ad hoc nature (few reappear as new editions) they have only a retrospective value. For new titles the librarian has to explore the range of reviewing journals which are discussed below.

A second problem is the subjective nature of these listings. Many attempt to be objective but some by their very nature are overtly subjective and must be used with care.

Library Suppliers

Although there is little empirical research, a great amount of informal evidence is available suggesting the role played by national library suppliers in the various processes of collection development is of great importance. Suppliers vary according to size and emphasis, with companies such as Peters, JMLS, Books for Students and Baker Books specializing in the area of work with young people. The services which are offered will vary in specific terms from supplier to supplier but they can be summarized as follows:

(i)   Forthcoming and in-print listings

These are generally non-evaluative and provide essential bibliographical information. A recent innovation has been the appearance of specialist listings on particular fields of children's fiction and non-fiction publishing. Books for Students is one supplier who has produced such listings and has tailored specialist lists to suit the specific needs of clients, e.g. books for teenage readers. These can provide useful guidance when developing and evaluating areas of the collection. Some suppliers now include interesting and pertinent narrative information about authors or trends in publishing as part of these bibliographical sources. Librarians have found the biographical details about new authors particularly beneficial when organizing promotional events.

(ii)   Approvals

Approvals are consignments of publications which are supplied to libraries for short periods by the suppliers and which permit the physical evaluation of material, so essential in the selection of children's books. This service is heavily used throughout the UK and to many librarians needs no further explanation. Some recent trends concern the availability of pre-publication titles instead of newly published titles which helps to overcome the traditional problem of time lag, thus enhancing the acquisition process. Suppliers also make available sets of approvals within discrete subject fields.

A recent initiative which is causing some consternation among children's librarians is the decision by several suppliers to replace their approvals collections by a CD-ROM disc which provides title pages of the books together with bibliographical information. This has been developed initially for adult materials, and many children's librarians feel that it will prove inadequate for selection purposes since it offers no substitute for physically evaluating the text and illustrations.

(iii)   Exhibitions

Virtually all suppliers have permanent exhibitions of materials available for sale which are enthusiastically visited by librarians, usually at the end of the financial year when the realization dawns that there is money left in the resources fund.

This approach permits the librarian to view a comprehensive selection of material but unless well planned it can be a most unscientific exercise.

(iv)   Bibliographical information services
Some of the larger suppliers will, for a fee, undertake comprehensive bibliographical searches of their own and other national and international databases. This service is particularly relevant for the specialist librarian in academic libraries, but is seen as being increasingly useful to librarians working with young people when compiling in-house bibliographies for staff, parents or children.

(v)   Processing of material
This has proved an important service for many librarians especially those operating alone or with limited staff. The delegation of responsibility for cataloguing, classification and physical processing of the book to the supplier can result in great economies in terms of time for the librarian.

It is clear that library suppliers do offer a pertinent range of services to support, and informal evidence suggests that they are heavily patronized. However, there are limitations which should not go unnoticed. Suppliers do handle a limited range of publishers, and even if an authority uses several suppliers, publications from minority and small presses such as Gay Men's Press and Virago may be excluded. The majority of suppliers offer only a limited array of non-book material. T. C. Farries has developed a reputation for this aspect of collection development but librarians concerned to develop a multimedia collection must use other bibliographical sources. Foreign language publications, too, are available from the general suppliers only on a limited scale, and libraries must have recourse to specialist suppliers such as Roy Yates and Albany Books Ltd. Finally, the cost of subscriptions may outweigh the potential advantage of the service.

Bookshops and bookdealers

National and local bookshops can provide an important service for children's librarians. In areas where there might be difficulties in using library suppliers, librarians have developed a close rapport with the local bookshop and visit it to physically examine new (and old) titles. Specialist shops have a unique role for certain categories of material, especially foreign language publications, computer software, audio cassettes, etc. Occasionally, secondhand dealers may be used when replacing out-of-print titles. Recently one library authority was completing its collection of Carnegie award winners, and had recourse to using antiquarian dealers who specialize in children's books to obtain copies of early titles.

Publishers and producers

Research undertaken in the field on audiovisual and computer provision reveals the indisputable dominance of publishers' and producers' listings as the basis of selection (Lonsdale and Wheatley, 1991). The same is probably true for other areas of highly specialist materials, e.g. foreign language publications, special format materials for children with special needs, etc. The dearth of coverage of non-book materials in the bibliographical sources considered so far is the obvious reason for this. However, managing a collection of specialist producers' catalogues is fraught with difficulty. This is owing to the lack of a proper publishing infrastructure, and also a lack of awareness on the part of many suppliers as to the information needs of the library (in contrast to book publishers). Frequently listings will be mailed out irregularly and producers' catalogues usually lack the indexing, arrangement and annotations found in book publishers' catalogues.

The lists and flyers produced by book publishers do have a special appeal to some librarians and teachers. The colourful formats and attractive presentation of information tend to seduce the user into believing that these sources are beyond criticism. The danger of subjectivity does need to be comprehended, since they are primarily marketing devices.

Another potential pitfall is to base selection on a very limited range of publishers. Teachers, in particular, tend to select from educational publishers' lists because they are the most familiar. The consequence is that important fiction and information books from non-educational presses are missed, and the collection becomes a very narrow representation of what is available.

Journals

Journals have a particular contribution to make in the selection of non-book material for children, and combine with publishers lists to form the major selection aids in these areas. For the librarian concerned with developing a professional collection for colleagues, journals offer an important, sometimes unique, source for grey literature, i.e. research documents, reports, conference proceedings about children's librarianship and literature.

Informal sources of information

Frequently word-of-mouth plays a significant role in disseminating information about projected publications. Readers and staff are likely to pick up from the media references to books which are in the process of being written or which publishers are contemplating, and this long before details appear in the published bibliographical sources. It is equally true for professional literature on librarianship and information science and for research reports which may not be published commercially. Such information is often gained in informal discussions at conferences and exhibitions and can be fed back to the library.

Reviewing journals

Let us first dispel a myth. Reviews of books and other materials are not used solely for the selection of new materials. They can also be used when evaluating the effectiveness of the collection and when undertaking collection review and relegating materials. The ever-decreasing budgets and the widening publishing base of children's material has resulted in an increased use of reviews to support evaluation. It behoves the librarian to become acquainted with the strengths and weaknesses of the major reviewing sources in the field, including those which publish review articles – so useful for collection evaluation. The major British professional reviewing journals are:

- *Books for keeps* (Magazine of the School Bookshop Association, British Council).
- *Carousel* (Federation of Children's Book Groups).
- *Dragons teeth* (National Committee on Racism in Children's Books).
- *Junior bookshelf* (Marsh Hall).
- *The school librarian* (School Library Association).

In addition, the weekly and daily newspapers are other valuable reviewing sources especially the *Times Educational Supplement*, which is particularly good for reviews of non-book materials. A range of educational journals are also available and the discerning librarian will not miss publications of non-library bodies such as *Under Five Contact*, the official journal of the Pre-school Learning Alliance (formerly the Pre-school Playgroup Association), which offers interesting reviews written by parents and teachers of material for the young child.

Inevitably there are constraints which need to be borne in mind. Time lag is an obvious one, although there is a fair degree of anecdotal evidence to suggest that, for certain categories of children's materials, librarians and teachers would rather sacrifice speed for an accurate assessment of a title. One recent trend concerns the appearance of the early warning review – reviews which are based on advance page proofs and pre-publication copies. Subjectivity is another factor to contend with, although the majority of the journals mentioned tend not to display overt subjectivity.

Acquaintance with the reviewers and their peccadillos is essential. Finally, there is the vexed question of where to locate a review of a specific work. For retrospective use (i.e. in stock evaluation) *Children's book review index* is a useful tool. Despite its North American orientation, the coverage of UK literature is reasonably wide and since no UK equivalent exists it is a useful source.

PROMOTING THE COLLECTION

Earlier in this chapter we mentioned that the collection policy document may contain a statement about promotion. Whatever the mode of promotion, a considered, comprehensive and pragmatic written strategy is called for, setting out the rationale, and linking it to the collection.

Marketing and promotion constitute the substance of Chapters 7 and 8. However, it is reasonable to argue that the promotion of the stock does not begin with a programme of activities, rather it starts with the physical organization and arrangement of the collection and the attitude of staff. We are going to explore this issue in more detail.

Categorization of stock

A cardinal rule, but one often overlooked, is that the arrangement of the collection should accurately reflect the needs of the user and not the perception which the librarian may have of those needs. Research in North America has revealed that collections are frequently librarian-oriented, and that young people and adults choose materials with little information and guidance. The process is often haphazard and readers find materials despite the arrangement and not because of it. One example concerns collections of audiovisual and computer materials. Nearly a quarter of UK authorities holding media collections for young people do not site them in the children's department but in the adult or music library (Lonsdale and Wheatley, 1991). This can impose barriers, especially for the young child, which should be dismantled if the young are going to derive maximum benefit from the libraries holdings.

One way of helping to ensure that the collection reflects the child's needs is to categorize stock, to move away from the traditional arrangements by author and classification. A number of British library authorities currently practise categorization, each system having developed its own pattern, reflecting the prevailing ideologies of the authority or institution.

In summary, the advantages of categorization include: improving access to materials; making browsing easier and more fruitful; promoting little used materials; increasing self-help (East Sussex and Cheshire county libraries are but two authorities who have established that categorization enhanced the readers' ability to procure relevant materials for themselves); and acting as a catalyst to the weeding of the collection, retaining only those titles which are sought after.

Categorization may take different forms. It may involve the replacement of the classification system with a series of subject headings based on the user's perception of the subjects. Some libraries follow the structure of the classification scheme while others have constructed their own sequence. Alphabetical fiction sequences may be replaced by arrangement according to different genres, e.g. adventure, poetry, or thematic divisions, e.g. tie-ins, award winners, humour. Age divisions (e.g. beginner reader, teenage) for both fiction and non-fiction are also common forms of categorization. Elizabeth Hibbs and Lucy Love's account of developing categorization in the children's section of the public library offers useful insights into these and other approaches (Hibbs and Love, 1992).

Categorization has not been without its critics in the UK who suggest that it fosters laziness among readers, encourages 'spoon-feeding', constrains reading habits and panders to popular taste. Despite these claims, there does appear to be a significant and increasing body of evidence to indicate the success of categorization in terms of the high satisfaction and preference on the part of the user.

Other modes of arrangement of stock

Categorization is but one mode of alternative arrangement. There are other aspects of collection organization which for some years have formed the subject of current debate. Briefly these include: the integration or partial integration of single- and multi-volume encyclopedias within the non-fiction lending sequence; the establishment of a paperback section; the amalgamation of young adult and adult fiction; the establishment of adult collections of books on subjects such as parenting, reading and child development for parents and carers with young children in the children's library, and the integration of non-book materials within the book collection. With regard to the last issue, authorities are divided on the value of integration, with over half having separate media collections (Lonsdale and Wheatley, 1991). This may seem to fly in the face of the traditionally held advantages of integration, yet internationally, we are witnessing the development of hyper-libraries for young people. Physically separate, these Star Trek-like capsules are located in, or proximate to, the children's collection. Usually they comprise banks of personal computers and other hardware at which children can access data in a multitude of formats. Conventional audiovisual materials are generally integrated within the bookstock.

OPACs and access

The mode of information retrieval used is another important element in promoting the collection. *Investing in children* (Department of National Heritage, 1995) welcomed the growing increase in the provision of OPACs for young people. However, irrespective of the physical nature of the catalogue, only 28% of authorities holding AVC materials which are potentially available to young people actually list them in the Young People's Services catalogue (Lonsdale and Wheatley, 1991). This finding does beg the question as to whether young people are able to retrieve effectively information pertaining to different media, especially where the materials are scattered across several different departments.

While OPACs are being made available to the young (and certainly children appear to have no difficulties using them), are conventional OPACs necessarily the best way of accessing material? There is at least one specialist OPAC designed for children, the *Kids catalog* which has explored the use of icons in addition to conventional text. Interactive multimedia systems created to help young people select books and promote reading, such as the innovative Book Wizard (Lonsdale, 1995), could well act as an inspiration in the future design of OPACs. Indeed, more imaginative ways of helping children choose materials are being investigated, especially in North America, and a recent international conference in the United States will undoubtedly prompt greater recognition of OPACs for children in the near future.

CONCLUSION

Collection development constitutes a major responsibility for the children's librarian, indeed, it is at the very heart of our professional remit. To facilitate maximum development, there is a strong argument for each library authority to adopt a comprehensive, pragmatic and dynamic policy. Unfortunately, there has been a reluctance on the part of many UK libraries to acknowledge their full responsibilities in this respect. Children's librarians have, to some degree, been the exception, and have recognized the importance of establishing selection policies. But this is only part of the equation, and as this chapter has sought to demonstrate, our responsibilities go beyond the selection and acquisition of materials and embrace collection evaluation, review and promotion.

Implicit in this stance is the need to ensure that staff are adequately trained in the many dimensions of collection management, an issue currently being attended to by the Youth Libraries Group. There is also a necessity to ensure that due attention is paid to the field of collection development in the library and information science curriculum, and that academics and practitioners are encouraged to resolve the longstanding problem of the dearth of professional literature on the subject.

REFERENCES

Arnold, K., Collier, M. and Ramsden, A. (1993), 'ELINOR: the electronic library project at De Montfort University, Milton Keynes', *Aslib proceedings*, **45** (1), 3–6.

Bird, J. (1982), 'Young teenage reading habits'. London, British Library.

Blenkin, S. and Lewins, H. (1990), 'Collection management in British children's libraries: a report of five case studies', *Collection management*, **13** (4), 77–87.

Creaser, C. (1995), *A survey of library services to schools and children in the UK 1994–1995*. Loughborough, Library and Information Statistics Unit, Department of Information and Library Studies, Loughborough University.

Department of National Heritage (1995), *Investing in children: the future of library services for children and young people*. London, Library and Information Services Council (England), Working Party on Library Services for Children and Young People. London, HMSO.

Dewe, M., Lonsdale, R. and Jones, P. H. (1995), *Collection management*. Aberystwyth, Open Learning Unit, Department of Information and Library Studies University of Wales Aberystwyth.

Evans, G E. (1987), *Developing library and information centre collections*. 2nd edn. Littleton, Colorado, Libraries Unlimited Inc.

Everall, A. (1993), 'Book selection for children: the critical questions', *Youth library review*, **16**, Autumn, 5–10.

Eyre, G. and Rippingale, R. (1994), 'Managing stock for young people in Derbyshire', *Youth library review*, **17**, Autumn, 8–12.

Gorman, G. E. and Kennedy, J. (1992), *Collection development in Australian libraries*, 2nd edn. Wagga Wagga, NSW, Charley Sturt University, Centre for Information Studies.

Griffiths, V. (1983), *Buying books: is a book selection policy really necessary?*, Buying books: practical guides. London, Youth Libraries Group.

Harry, V. and Oppenheim, C. (1993), 'Evaluation of electronic databases – Part 1: criteria for testing CD-ROM products', *Online and CD-ROM review*, **17** (4), 211–22.

Hibbs, E. et al (1992), 'The case for categorization: an investigation of children's selection methods', *Youth library review*, **14**, Autumn, 16–19.

Hill, J. (1969), *Book selection for children*. London, Library Association.

Library Association (1991), *Children and young people: Library Association guidelines for public library services*. London, Library Association Publishing, Chapter 4, 23–8.

Lonsdale, R. (1994), 'Enter the Book Wizard: new directions in IT and reading', *Youth library review*, **18**, 5–13.

Lonsdale, R. and Everitt, J. (1996), 'Breaking down the barriers: the provision of modern foreign language material to young people in public libraries in the UK', *Journal of librarianship and information science*, **28** (2), June, 71–81.

Lonsdale, R. and Wheatley, A. (1991), 'The provision of audiovisual and computer services to young people by British public libraries: collection management and promotion of services', *International review of children's literature and librarianship*, **6** (1), 31–55.

McLeod, D. (1994), 'Children, videos and libraries: bringing it all together', *Acquisitions librarian*, **11**, 73–9.

Mitchell, M. and Saunders, L M. (1991), 'The virtual library: an agenda for the 1990s', *Computers in libraries*, **11** (4), 8–11.

Nordgren, L. (1993), 'Evaluating multimedia CD–ROM Discware: of bells, whistles and VALUE', *CD–ROM professional*, **6** (1), 99–105.

Perkins, D. L (ed). (1979), *Guidelines for collection development*. Chicago: American Library Association.

Slote, S. (1989), *Weeding library collections: library weeding methods*. 3rd edn. Englewood, Libraries Unlimited.

Spiller, D. (1991), *Book selection: an introduction to principles and practice*. 5th edn. London, Library Association.

Van Orden, P. J. (1985), *The collection program in high schools*. Littleton, Colorado, Libraries Unlimited.

Yates, J. (1987), 'Books selection for young people in the public library: a survey', *Assistant Librarian*, **80** (4), 55–62.

7

Meeting their needs: marketing and library services

Margaret Kinnell

INTRODUCTION

Serving the library and information needs of children, apparently such an easily identifiable sector in society, might seem to present fewer problems than serving other groups in the population. The 'market' of children and young people can be targeted according to age, and also by their stages of education: pre-school, primary, secondary, tertiary. However, there are some dangers in such a simplistic approach to defining the categories of those being served by library services – which in public libraries today means children from young babyhood through to adolescence and adulthood. For example, even babies differ markedly from three months to six months in their developmental needs. Toy manufacturers understand this very well and adopt a strategy which ensures that toys are designed for various stages, from birth onwards. Age can be a complex variable, as the Ford Motor Company, too, discovered when they designed an inexpensive and sporty car specifically for young people. They actually found that people of all ages were buying it: the psychologically young, rather than the chronologically young were, in reality, their target market (Kotler, 1988). Similar problems to those of manufacturers are experienced by library managers when designing services for children and young people. Categorizing users presents operational problems as well as offering apparent solutions. Age or level of education are only two of several relevant variables. Gender differences in reading habits and leisure pursuits require consideration, as do cultural issues in a multicultural society. Specific questions also arise:

- How should children's needs be separated from and linked to those of adults?
- What place is there for teenage collections and services, separate from both children's and adult library services?
- What are the complex information needs as well as the reading developmental needs of children and young people, and to what extent do these differ from those of adults?

A more focused, marketing led approach to library services may facilitate insight into such essential questions about the relevant library and information needs of children and young people, and indeed all sectors of the population being served by libraries. Marketing has more and more become an essential management tool for librarians. There are several issues which have brought marketing increasingly to the fore. First, defining, providing and promoting services which accurately match needs – and which fall within the objectives of the public library service – are now more pressing than ever, given financial constraints. Second, accountability for every aspect of public library service has become a key issue following the Citizen's Charter initiative (Cabinet Office, 1991) and the subsequent development of charters by many public libraries. In the consumer-conscious 1990s the community has come to expect a high level of service from its publicly funded bodies. Third, and in response to this, managers have accepted the need to develop improved quality in service delivery and to implement monitoring systems as part of quality assurance. The introduction of Audit Commission performance indicators has further focused professional attention on measuring and assessing performance across the range of services.

It is notable that, in her Parliamentary Answer in response to the Aslib *Review of the public library service in England and Wales* (Aslib, 1995), the Secretary of State continued this theme of high expectation and the importance of clear deliverables. She linked children's with adult service functions and indicated the need to be specific in service delivery. Implicit in her statement was the need for librarians to target their resources more effectively on these core functions, which she defined as:

(i) providing reading for pleasure
(ii) enlightening children and developing lifelong reading skills and habits in adults
(iii) encouraging lifelong learning and study
(iv) providing reference material including public information about local and national government and EU publications, current affairs, and business information
(v) providing materials for the study of local history and the local environment (Hansard, 1995).

In this chapter, these issues of the definition, provision and promotion of children's and young people's library services to meet identifiable needs will be considered using marketing principles as the focus for analysis. The Department of National Heritage's seminal report, *Investing in children*, has already drawn attention to users' needs. They considered that 'recognition of these needs should inform and determine the aims and objectives of all libraries that serve this client group' (Department of National Heritage, 1995). However, they also found perturbing gaps in our understanding of children's reading habits and the impact of wider library and information use on children's lives. Developing clear priorities and objectives for library services was also of concern. Their recommendations can be grouped into three categories which repay further consideration, using a marketing perspective:

1. the need for a more strategic focus in the planning of services;
2. the development of more effective functional approaches, especially in understanding users, designing services, linking to other service sectors (adult and schools services), monitoring and evaluation;
3. better tactical communication with users and with relevant professionals and opinion formers.

In many ways the report's analysis of the issues facing library services for children differs little from that of other service sectors – in the commercial as well as the public sector, which reinforces the value of using marketing ideas to support good management practice. Quite simply, old ways of doing things are no longer acceptable. Changes in expectation, government regulation and technological innovation have created a new environment for delivering services. People, both users and staff, are now recognized to be part of the service and relationships with them need to be managed. Quality control is seen to be difficult, with services 'consumed' as soon as they are produced. This, too, requires skilful management. Maintaining the right level of service to meet demand and to time constraints is a continuing problem, and the means of distributing the service (especially to adolescents who have particular needs) has to be more carefully considered (Lovelock, 1992).

In this chapter, a marketing approach which has been applied across the service sectors will be used to assess these and other issues facing children's and young people's services. While links to marketing in the manufacturing sector will also be traced, a well-developed literature now exists for the marketing of services, and this will provide most of the insights into the strategic, functional and tactical aspects surrounding the marketing of library services.

STRATEGIC PLANNING

The story of children's and young people's library services in the UK has been, until recent years, one of a clear commitment to the educational and leisure reading needs of the community. Of all the services provided by public libraries, children's services have enjoyed perhaps the most commitment from their staff and commensurate high levels of support from users. There is still evidence of this in the continuing high issue figures for children's books, which rose from 82 million in 1990–1 to 101 million in 1992–3 (Department of National Heritage, 1995, p.15). Initially, though, children's services took some time to become a significant part of the public library. They only really took hold following the establishment of county libraries in the early years of the twentieth century and through the commitment to providing services to schools (seen at first in some areas as one means of preventing schools from demanding textbook provision through the public library service) (Heeks, 1996). By the 1960s children's services were highly developed, if piecemeal, and included a range of services to teenagers (Ellis, 1971). Developments then and since show no evidence, though, of a coherent, strategic approach to children's library work, in line with theories of strategic management and marketing.

Classically, these theories describe marketing strategy as an explicit set of decisions, often with analogies to military strategies (Kotler & Singh, 1981; Trout & Ries, 1985). Such decisions take a wide, long-term view of the organization's place within its operating environment, including the placing of a marketing strategy in relation to the wider goals of the organization. As it has been recognized, definitions of 'strategy' have proliferated in the management literature and there needs to be some caution when using the term to assess the success or failure of an organization in developing this wider view of itself in relation to its market. Nevertheless, strategic theory has considerable relevance for decision makers in public libraries (Wensley, 1987). Two key areas have been identified, 'allocating resources' and 'defining the activity'.

Allocating resources

A marketing strategy will indicate the direction of the business in terms of its products (or services) and those markets that will be emphasized. For library services this means defining those activities which are core to the objectives of the organization and those segments of the target market most in need of services. This has been a problem for public libraries, which have a statutory duty to provide the 'comprehensive' service demanded by the 1964 Act and have expanded their range of services dramatically in recent years. When children's library services, in common with other service areas, developed rapidly during the 1960s and 1970s there was little national coordination of policy, other than the lead provided by the Library Association's Youth Libraries Group through selection aids and short courses and the general guidance offered by the Department of Education and Science and the Office of Arts and Libraries on the possibility of joint school/children's libraries. Experiments on this model were tried and discounted. Children's library accommodation to meet the perceived needs of the population was generally provided in separate buildings in some authorities and in the same building as adult services in others (Ellis, 1971, p.123). And even within a local authority there remained specific problems, for example, how to continue the services to children living in rural areas during the long school holidays. Both nationally and locally there was a lack of strategic planning to deal with such issues. The Library Association's *Guidelines*, published in 1991, have been an important recent addition to the debate (Library Association, 1991) and offer evidence of good practice which can be a useful benchmark for authorities. However, they are not a substitute for local planning and are most useful in the context of a public library's strategic plan when decisions on service priorities to meet the needs of its community have been set.

A study of the marketing strategies of public libraries and leisure services in 1994 found that this lack of a strategic view of the role of the library service remained a problem. It was found that public libraries needed to agree what 'business' they were in. Leisure, educational, cultural and social reasons for providing a library service needed to be reconciled. Only 3% of library services in the study had actually formulated a marketing strategy to address this (Kinnell & MacDougall, 1994). As both the Comedia Report, *Borrowed time* (Comedia, 1993), and the Aslib *Review* for the Department of National Heritage have found, deciding the core activities of public libraries continues to be problematic. The Secretary of State's interpretation of their primary objectives has clarified the picture, but each library authority will wish to interpret this statement in relation to its particular circumstances. *Investing in children* has stressed the importance of an 'integrated strategy for delivery of library services for children and young people through individual school libraries, the schools library service, and the public library . . . ' (Department of National Heritage, 1995, 5.2). However, their view that this integrated strategy should be owned by the local authority may be overlooking the very real difficulty that grant maintained status, Local Management of Schools and the new business footing on which many schools library services now have to operate (Heeks & Kinnell, 1992; Coopers & Lybrand, 1994) has set public library services apart from rather than closer to other services for children. Schools are increasingly operating outwith the local authority and the present government has established policy to continue this trend. A marketing strategy for a children's and young people's service in a public library authority will indicate direction over the long term, bearing all of the above in mind. However, in the current climate, the core objectives of the public library service are likely to be paramount in the thinking of members and senior library managers. Identifying those services and target markets for their community which will be particularly emphasized in their planning may not assist the collaborative ideal proposed in *Investing in children*.

Defining the activity

Rather than deploying resources widely across a range of activities, a marketing strategy is concerned to allocate funding for service development, staffing levels, and promotion, across the prioritized areas. Building a sustainable competitive advantage will be a major theme. It is often argued that libraries, as a public service, are not in competition. However, libraries do compete for that most valuable of all resources: their users' time and patronage. Children and young people now spend much of their time playing computer games or watching television in preference to reading (Children's Literature Research Centre, 1994). They now expect a library service to provide information via the computer, as well as through books, and that computers and associated software should be available in their libraries for homework, games playing and wider personal information needs. The Internet is beginning to transform young people's lives at school and in the home, and public libraries need to provide guided access to its resources. A recent study found that 'the full spectrum of recreational needs' using technology was, however, not being exploited by libraries (Lonsdale & Wheatley, 1992) and, as the Aslib *Review* reported, there is a view amongst teenage users of libraries that 'procedures are old-fashioned' (Aslib, 1995, p.144). The *Review* team felt that the importance of libraries for children was likely to increase given the demands of the National Curriculum on text books, the increasing deprivation of children in society and their frequent isolation as full-time parenting in the home has largely disappeared. Convincing young people that the public library is relevant to their life-styles and needs is therefore necessary. Developing a marketing strategy which takes account of the changes in the service environment for young people will be essential to achieve this.

While theory on marketing strategy emphasizes the need to plan and to conceive new approaches to tackling the issues facing an organization, there is also need, though, to ensure that planning does not become an end in itself. Strategy has to degenerate into action. 'The nature of strategic action or "being strategic" involves responding to the balance between analysis and action because we have to recognize that many of the market uncertainties can only be resolved, even partially, by action itself' (Wensley, 1987, p.46).

MARKETING FUNCTIONS

There is, therefore, some encouragement from theorists in this emphasis on strategic actions: for, where marketing is at present being practised in libraries, it appears to be largely functional rather than strategic in character. Inevitably, there are also disadvantages as well as some advantages associated with a mostly functional approach to marketing in libraries. Strategic thinking is often uncomfortable, or it should be. Ensuring that difficult questions are asked and that the unthinkable is considered is the role of the strategist. While there is evidence of some strategic market planning under way in library authorities, this probing of assumptions which has been the hallmark of successful business marketers has been largely absent. As was noted above, there are significant questions to be asked about library services to children and young people, questions about the role of the public library, its relationship to other services and how it should be delivered. The present book-based service, which has largely failed to capture the imagination of adolescents has been shown to require fundamental reappraisal.

A dearth of such challenges is largely owing to the peripheral role of marketing in public libraries. Most public library managers do not perceive marketing as a key management function (Kinnell & MacDougall, 1994). The uptake of marketing overall is still patchy, despite the existence of a substantial literature on libraries marketing (see, e.g. Cronin, 1992).

Nevertheless, it has been found that a measure of marketing activity is not always dependent on a dedicated marketing function in a library authority; in some authorities simply the impetus from the range of services available has generated marketing activities. For example, targeting of customers, especially children and young people, and pricing policies with regard to fines levels for different categories of users (children and old people), have been commonly applied. Promotional activities have also been instigated as a result of the wide range of services being provided by libraries. A relationship between targeting, pricing, promotion and the range of services offered has been found to exist (Doherty, Saker & Smith, 1995). This indicates that the rational, prescriptive approach to public libraries marketing which emanates from the private sector (see, e.g. Yorke, 1984a) is not the only model being applied, and that alternatives using more incremental approaches are possible. While such activities could become unbalanced so that, for example, promotion is seen as the overriding element in marketing, in a context where financial and human resources are limited such piecemeal marketing is often the only practicable way means of implementing some marketing activity.

From the 1994 study of public libraries marketing strategies it was clear that public librarians have been developing marketing functions, largely using the traditional four 'Ps' of marketing: product (service), place, price, promotion. While a strategic approach to marketing is limited, some functional aspects, even where unevenly applied, are reflecting operational realities (Kinnell & MacDougall, 1994).

Product/service

After defining its broad objectives and targets in the strategy statement, a library service will wish to clarify its identification of the groups it seeks to attract, in order to design services appropriately. In the case of services to children and young people this seems at first sight self-evident. However, as was noted in the Introduction, segmenting the target market is not achieved effectively using only a few variables. Target segments need to be accurately defined. For public libraries, which have a duty to serve the whole community, there is little choice but to meet as many needs as possible given the limited resources, but this duty does not obviate the absolute imperative of determining priorities and clustering segments, both to achieve economies of scale and to attract a wider customer base, especially of adolescents, who are the group least attracted at present to libraries and reading.

Many local authorities have stated policies on those groups in their community deserving of special support, which impact on all service areas. Edinburgh District Council, for example, 'have a stated policy on targeting special groups – people with disabilities, minority ethnic groups, women, and so of course that has to be reflected in everything we do . . . The political philosophy filters down through everything' (Kinnell & MacDougall, 1994, p.96). Even given the statutory duty to provide a service to all members of their community and with local political influences such as these in evidence, library services do have some flexibility. There are lessons to be learned from local authority leisure services. They, too, are operating in a competitive environment in which young people have increased calls on their leisure time and more choice than ever before. Leisure services therefore have to identify the specific interests of their targets and how these may best be met. They also work within a local authority culture which may set a political agenda. However, lifestyle analysis can provide a useful means of segmenting and clustering many of the variables in the Introduction. In one study of the leisure market six market segments were found to exist, using such an analysis:

- The passive homebody
- The active sports enthusiast
- The inner-directed self-sufficient
- The culture patron
- The active homebody
- The socially active (Andreasen and Belk, 1980, 112).

Market research was undertaken, with informal interviews and focus groups used to gain insights into motivation, attitude and behaviour. Based on this, the researcher could then prepare a more formal questionnaire which was administered to a sample of service consumers to collect data on their attitudes to the services, service use patterns, awareness of services, as well as personal and behavioural details of the sample. This type of market research, which is concerned with identifying the life-styles of its patrons is, as yet, rarely undertaken by library services, but will be increasingly valuable for ensuring facilities meet the changing needs and expectations of clients (Yorke, 1984a).

Market research to refine segments and their needs will therefore not only reflect the reading habits of children and young people – the area of most research in recent years – but also those wider leisure and information needs of young people that should be met through library services. As the Department of National Heritage Report found, current market research undertaken by or for library services has focused on existing users, rather than non-users, for whom libraries have no relevance as they are at present designed and promoted (Department of National Heritage, 1995, 2.2). There is scope for targeting more groups among non-users and to seek models of marketing research from other service areas to help in redesigning services which will satisfy a wider customer base.

For example, the Marriott hotel chain used consultants to conduct a large-scale consumer study among business and non-business travellers, randomly sampled, and aimed to establish an optimal hotel design. The results of this study provided specific guidelines for selecting target market segments, positioning the hotel within the market and designing an improved facility in terms of layout and services (Wind, Green, Shifflet & Scarbrough, 1992). Such a study would have value for identifying those features of a library service of real relevance to young people, to augment the kinds of quantitative and qualitative user satisfaction measures suggested in the American Library Association's invaluable document on *Output measures for public library service to children* (Walter, 1992). This includes measures such as library visits per child, building use, furniture and equipment use, circulation of material, turnover rate, 'fill' rate (percentages of searches for materials that are successful), and information transactions.

As part of the redesigning of services to meet changing needs, it will also be necessary for libraries to assess their present portfolio of services. Other than new facilities, most library managers will be dealing with long established ongoing services which have grown haphazardly over the years. Cronin has illustrated the wide range of this existing library 'product mix', a range which will need to be reassessed in light of cultural and consumer changes in order to provide the necessary depth as well as breadth which will result in a top quality, relevant service (Cronin, 1984a). Information technology has made the most considerable impact on what is being offered and the temptation for librarians has been simply to continue adding services and facilities as new technology has arrived. However, the product/service portfolio has to be managed, not only to ensure its continuing relevance, but also to maximize resources. Decisions have to be reached on: assessing and improving the overall mix of services, assessing and improving individual services, improving services over their life cycles (Kotler & Andreasen, 1991). This last point is vital. Library services have traditionally taken too long to jettison services which have outlived their usefulness (newspaper reading rooms continued in many libraries, for example, well into the 1960s). There is also a danger, though, in developing new services which may just be part of a transient 'fad'. Skateboarding parks, provided by many leisure authorities in the late 1970s but which then lost their interest for young people as fashions changed, offer a salutary lesson.

An element in the service offering which should receive particular attention is, of course, the staff. Specialist children's librarians are an essential component in the service. The emphasis in studies of children's and school libraries has tended to lie with the amount being spent on materials: the most recent Library and Information Statistics Unit survey showed that only 17 out of 124 library authorities met the Department of National Heritage recommended target for spending on children's stock in 1994–5. While this is worrying, even more so is the fact that staffing provision has fallen dramatically in some areas: by 30% in London, 18.5% in Wales and 60% in Northern Ireland. Even where numbers have risen, as in the Shire counties, this is from a shockingly low base. There are a mere 691 professional children's librarians being employed in 128 library authorities across the UK, usually responsible for all of the target groups, from children through to adolescents (Creaser, 1995). In the United States there has been concern for much longer over the issue of staffing to meet clients group needs and specialist posts for young adult services are more common than in the UK (National Center for Education Statistics, 1988). Education and training for such staff is essential, given the lack of specialist courses in children's work within Schools of Information and Library Studies, and presents real problems for individual library services which may be able to employ only a few professional specialists. However, paraprofessional staff are also important and training needs to take account of their significance as the front-line employees dealing with children.

Place

Decisions on place are also fundamental to the delivery and accessibility of library services and demand especial care. The young and the elderly are particularly vulnerable to poor decisions, and difficulties in serving rural populations continue to be a problem. Outreach activities of various kinds have been the response of most library services, with librarians also 'moving into the age of deinstitutionalized information retailing' (Cronin, 1984b). Bookbuses and holiday mobiles have been successful in many authorities, especially in supplementing core services during holiday periods. Services for travellers' children, ethnic minorities and children in hospital all require particular delivery systems, including appropriate staffing.

However effective technology can be in providing electronic links to information providers, there will always be the need for excellent book and non-book materials collections for children and young people, conveniently sited and well organized for ease of use. This was demonstrated in the success of Renfrew's establishment of JILL, in 1983, as a specialist teenage library to support young people in the Johnstone area. The library received an urban aid grant, in recognition of their particular problems of high youth unemployment (Hendry, 1986). A study of the kinds of clients being served revealed that they needed a service quite different from that for adults and for children. They wanted a separate space where their needs were paramount. JILL operates from such a base, with a specialist librarian who selects materials and trains other staff in dealing with this client group. The results, as compared with information provision in the traditional library setting, have shown that awareness of libraries and library membership is significantly higher than elsewhere (Neill & Johnson, 1991). Another successful initiative, along similar lines, but with more emphasis on the multicultural aspects of services to adolescents, was that of Bradford's Xchange, a service for teenagers in the Central Library (Wilkes, 1986). A study of new concepts of developing library services for young adults in Germany is exploring further possibilities, many of which have also been tested already in the UK, including the role of computers in libraries for young people (Glashoff, 1995).

As teenage library provision, in particular, has shown, young people are particularly sensitive to the 'atmospherics' of the library. The look and feel of a building send messages and can radically affect the behaviour of users. It has been noted that 'customers make judgments about the quality of the service they are receiving on the basis of items such as the state of the building, the furniture and fittings . . . Banks have understood this and are changing their "physical evidence" away from "marbled mausoleums" to warmer financial service shops' (Smith & Saker, 1992). Equally, the setting within which library services for children and young people are delivered demands a high level of quality in design, equipment, furniture and decor. In some library services teenagers themselves have been involved in planning their accommodation. Hertfordshire, for example, attempted, with a measure of success, to produce a new design using a leading furniture supplier's computer-aided design facilities and the input of local teenagers (Department of National Heritage, 1995, 5.6.7).

Price

The pricing of services for children and young people is rather more emotive, given the tradition of a freely provided core library service. However, the reality is that many 'non-core' (i.e. non book-lending) services are being charged for in library authorities, even to children, more in the English counties than elsewhere. These include charges for talking books, recorded music, videos, software, toys and games, magazines and comics. Charges are also frequently levied on requested items and for overdue books and other materials (Creaser, 1995, p.40). There has been little investigation in local authorities of the impact of what are, in effect, pricing policies on the use of services, although more work has been undertaken in leisure services which charge for virtually all of their services to young people. A popular scheme in some leisure services is a discount card offering significant reductions on a range of recreational facilities, which has been seen to encourage the use of facilities (Kinnell & MacDougall, 1994, p.136). Potential for partnerships with other service providers – including leisure and youth services – and with commercial organizations, for example in providing promotional activities may be the means of enhancing funding of those services where revenue generation is both possible and acceptable.

Public library services often have a special relationship with their 'customers' quite different from that of a manufacturer or even services in the commercial sector. Public library customers are also usually members of their service, and the desire on the part of library staff is to create a long-term relationship with them. This is especially important with regard to child and adolescent membership, which is developing future library use and supporting the habit of life-long reading. In considering how to develop a pricing policy for elements of their children's services, library managers may see the practice in other service areas which have developed a membership relationship as particularly relevant. Discounted rates for members are common, as are advance notification and priority reservations. Some membership services offer rental of equipment for a base fee and then make charges for each separate transaction above a defined minimum (Lovelock, 1983). However, it is also important for library services to keep their stated aims and objectives in mind, as a too commercially oriented service may create conflicts. Library services for children and young people have as their primary aim the promotion of reading and use of libraries. Anything which detracts from this will endanger the fulfilment of the library's mission. A balance has to be struck between revenue generation to pay for existing services and the development of new ones, the creation of value in the minds of library users by some charging element, and assuring open access to books and other materials.

Promotion

Often felt by librarians to be the most important element of marketing, to the extent that the two words are frequently used synonymously, this has been found to be one of the best developed areas of library marketing (Doherty, Saker & Smith, 1995). There has been a problem though, with many not-for-profit organizations, like libraries, who have over-emphasized promotion to the deteriment of other aspects of the marketing mix. 'They have regularly used advertising, personal selling, sales promotion, and publicity – often very aggressively and effectively – to communicate with both their contributors and their clients. However, these organizations have not integrated their promotional mix into a total marketing program' (Stanton, Etzel & Walker, 1991, pp.518–9). The use of promotional tools by library services is very wide and has often been particularly focused on children's services, and the range of promotion activities and approaches is elucidated in the following chapter.

MARKETING TACTICS

The aims of the tactical level of marketing are to communicate the benefits of the service to the target groups and to ensure that the organization's objectives and the library needs of children and young people are continually being addressed. Promotion is inevitably included in this, but effective communication is about much more than a series of promotional messages to the target groups. It also includes developing relationships with key opinion formers who have a stake in the services.

While this is essential at the local level, the overall environment in which individual library services are operating is substantially influenced by national policy development. Input to tactical marketing at national level, through participation in professional organizations such as the Library Association, the Youth Libraries Group and the Association of Senior Children's and Education Librarians, and in working parties, is therefore needed. The Working Party on Library Services for Children and Young People of the Library and Information Services Council (LISC(E)), with seven senior librarians as its members, produced the important Report *Investing in* children for the Department of National Heritage in 1995, and exemplifies such significant input to national policy making. Membership of regional and national committees of the Youth Libraries Group and other organizations, such as the Federation of Children's Book Groups, also enables professionals at all stages in their careers to participate in the shaping of the environment for their library service.

CONCLUSION

While meeting the needs of children and young people through effective library services is inevitably dependent on adequate resourcing of services, marketing enables those resources that are available to be most effectively deployed. At all levels – strategic, functional and tactical – a marketing approach to service development and delivery can produce considerable benefits to libraries. Moreover, a critical and analytical use of marketing principles enables library managers to plan a coherent service which is seen as part of a wider whole.

From the evidence of recent studies of libraries' marketing there is marketing activity under way in many library authorities. However, much of it is piecemeal and lacking in strategic focus. There remains much to be learned from experience in other sectors. Now that communication of the benefits of services has been so successfully articulated in *Investing in children*, there is an opportunity to follow through with more targeted marketing approaches in public library authorities. Increasing the range of marketing functions is indicated, especially more sophisticated marketing research to target children and young people more effectively, together with service design and management of the service/product mix. Most important of all, marketing activities will need to be seen as part of a strategic and visionary approach to service development so that they are integrated fully with the management of the service as a whole.

REFERENCES

Andreasen, A. R. and Belk, R. W. (1980), 'Predictors of attendance at the performing arts', *Journal of consumer research*, September, 112–20.

Aslib (1995), *Review of the public library service in England and Wales for the Department of National Heritage*. London, Aslib.

Cabinet Office (1991), *The citizen's charter*. London, HMSO.

Children's Literature Research Centre (1994), *Contemporary juvenile reading habits: a study of young people's reading at the end of the century*. Roehampton, Roehampton Institute Children's Literature Research Centre.

Comedia (1993), *Borrowed time*. Stroud, Comedia.

Coopers and Lybrand (1994), *Schools library services and financial delegation to schools*. London, HMSO (Library Information Series 21).

Creaser, C. A. (1995), *A survey of library services to schools and children in the UK 1994–95*. Loughborough, Loughborough University Library and Information Statistics Unit.

Cronin, B. (1984), 'The marketing of public library services in the UK – the rationale for a marketing approach', *European journal of marketing*, **18** (2), 37.

Cronin, B. (1984b), 'The marketing of public libraries in the UK – practical applications', *European journal of marketing*, **18** (2), 45–55.

Cronin, B. (ed.) (1992), *The marketing of library and information services 2*. London, Aslib.

Department of National Heritage (1995), *Investing in children: the future of library services for children and young* people. London, Library and Information Services Council (England), Working Party on Library Services for Children and Young People, London, HMSO.

Doherty, N. F., Saker, J. and Smith, I. G. (1995), 'Marketing development in the public library sector: an empirical analysis', *Journal of information science*, **21** (6), 449–58.

Ellis, A. (1971), *Library services for young people in England and Wales, 1830–1970*. Oxford, Pergamon Press.

Glashoff, I. (1995), 'The development and testing of new concepts for library services for young adults: description of a project in Germany', *The new review of children's literature and librarianship*, Vol.1, 1–12.

Hansard Parliamentary answer (1995), *Hansard*, Vol. 268, column 852–4, 18th December. London, HMSO.

Heeks, P., 'Services to schools' in: M. Kinnell and P. Sturges (eds.) (1996) *Continuity* and *innovation in the public library: the development of a social institution*. London, Library Association Publishing. Chapter 7.

Heeks, P. and Kinnell, M. (1992). *Managing change for school library services*. London, British Library. (Library and Information Research Report 89).

Hendry, J. (1986), 'JILL's pure brill', *Library Association record*, **88** (2), February, 78.

Kinnell, M. and MacDougall, J. (1994), *Meeting the marketing challenge: strategies for public libraries and leisure services*. London, Taylor Graham. Chapter 3.

Kotler, P. (1988), *Marketing management: analysis, planning, implementation and control*. 6th edn. Englewood Cliffs, N. J., Prentice Hall.

Kotler, P. and Andreasen, A. (1991), *Strategic marketing for non-profit organisations*. 4th ed. Englewood Cliffs, N.J., Prentice-Hall.

Kotler, P. and Singh, R. (1981), 'Marketing warfare in the 1980s', *Journal of business strategy*, **1**, 30–41.

Library Association (1991), *Children and young people: Library Association guidelines for public library services*. London, Library Association Publishing.

Lonsdale, R. and Wheatley, A. (1992), 'The provision of computer material and services to young people by British public libraries', *Journal of librarianship and information science*, **24** (2), June. 87–98.

Lovelock, C. H. (1983), 'Classifying services to gain strategic marketing insights', *Journal of marketing*, **47**, Summer, 9–20.

Lovelock, C. H. (1992), *Managing services: marketing, operations and human resources*. 2nd edn. Englewood Cliffs, N. J., Prentice Hall, 1–8.

National Centre for Education Statistics (1988), *Library human resources: a study in supply and demand*. Chicago, American Library Association.

Neill, L. and Johnson, I. M. (1991), 'Information for unemployed teenagers', *International review of children's literature and librarianship*, **6** (2), 95–117.

Smith, G. and Saker, J. (1992), 'Developing marketing strategy in the not-for-profit sector', *Library management*, **13** (4), 10.

Stanton, W. J., Etzel, M. J. and Walker, B. J. (1991), *Fundamentals of marketing*. 9th edn. New York, McGraw-Hill.

Trout, J. and Ries, A. (1985), *Marketing warfare*. London, McGraw-Hill.

Walter, V. A. (1992), *Output measures for public library service to children: a manual of standardized procedures*. Chicago and London, Association for Library Service to Children, Public Library Association, American Library Association.

Wensley, R. (1987), 'Marketing strategy' in M J. Barker (ed.), *The marketing book*. London, Heinemann, 29–47.

Wilkes, B. (1986), 'Library services for city children: a case study of Bradford, England', *International review of children's literature and librarianship*, **1** (2), 12–26.

Wind, J., Green, P. E., Shifflet, D. and Scarbrough, M. (1992), 'Courtyard by Marriott: designing a hotel facility with consumer-based marketing models' in Lovelock, C. H., *Managing services: marketing, operations and human resources*. 2nd edn. Englewood Cliffs, N. J., Prentice-Hall. 118–37.

Yorke, D. (1984), 'Marketing and non-profit making organisations', *European journal of marketing*, **18** (2), 17–22.

Yorke, D. A. (1984b), 'The definition of market segments for leisure centre services: theory and practice', *European journal of marketing*, **18** (2), 100–13.

8

Promoting libraries and literature for young people

Gayner Eyre

INTRODUCTION

Public relations and promotion has played a central part in services to children and young people for many years, receiving prominence in the 1960s and 1970s as evidenced by Janet Hill's *Children are people* (Hill, 1973). In many ways this period was very much a golden age when public expenditure allowed for initiatives and developments. Local authority reorganization in 1974 brought with it a wave of expansion which forced librarians to re-think all service provision and to include promotional strategies as part of the fundamental service. Since then, promotion, as all aspects of library service provision, has undergone a number of sea-changes which relate directly to the ideologies of the day and the circumstances surrounding the parent organization. It may be argued that in today's climate promoting library services to young people is more important than ever.

> The 1990s will be a critical phase in the history of the public library service. In addition to social and technological developments, libraries will face major political changes ... It is undoubtedly true that the public library service will have to galvanize itself into action if it is to avoid being smothered by the embrace of those who wish to privatise it. (Fisher, 1989, pp.ii–iii)

PR and promotion of library services generally and to children in particular has always been important, but with the gradual erosion of services as a result of diminishing public expenditure over the past decade promotion and PR take on a new urgency. Ironically, in times of constrained resources, funding for effective PR and promotion is often given low status and is one of the first areas to be cut. Yet it is arguably even more essential that the value and role of libraries of all kinds are communicated effectively to actual and potential users, those who have control of budgets and politicians at all levels.

POLITICAL FRAMEWORK

As noted in earlier chapters two very important national documents have been published which highlight the importance of services to children and young people. *Investing in children: the future of library services for children and young people*

(Department of National Heritage, 1995) provides a very valuable and comprehensive insight into the needs of young people and also offers guidance to public librarians on providing adequate services. *The review of public library services in England and Wales*, commissioned by the Department of National Heritage (Aslib, 1995) stresses the crucial role that libraries have to play in the development of the individual: services to children are placed as one of the central functions of public libraries. Both reports, coupled with the articles in the professional press and discussion they have generated have done much, in themselves, to raise the profile of library services for young people. Both documents were initiated and financed through government departments. In parallel to these initiatives, there has been discussion and legislation concerning educational issues. The National Curriculum has been implemented and revised (Dearing, 1993). There has been great debate over literacy and reading standards (Department of Education and Science, 1992) and there have been great leaps forward in the use of technology in schools.

Within the profession generally, debate has been taking place on literacy, its meaning, role and function and the pivotal role it plays in all library service provision, particularly to young people. In 1992 the Youth Libraries Group of the Library Association devoted the annual weekend school to the topic.

Taking all this into consideration it would appear that the needs of children and young people have received a good deal of attention of late. It would also be natural to assume that the source of some of the attention, i.e. government departments, would mean that guidelines and recommendations would have been translated into action. This, sadly, has been negated by the current economic and political situation. The philosophies engendered by the politics of the new right over the past two decades have paid lip-service to accountability to customers through legislation such as the Citizen's Charter (Cabinet Office, 1991). In fact, when seen in the light of the gradual erosion of services enforced by the severe cuts in government expenditure within the public sector over the last two decades, this accountability must be treated with caution. These philosophies and constraints have given rise to a preoccupation by library services, often through expediency, with implementing more right-wing philosophies, which to some extent negate the important initiatives outlined above. Cuts in staffing, material funds and general budgets have forced libraries in the public sector – and school libraries are included here – to concentrate on issues such as management information, performance indicators and cost effectiveness rather than the more traditionally based service philosophies. Not that these do not have their place and indeed must be embraced to ensure the survival of services.

Where promotion of library services is concerned, emphasis has shifted to the adoption of marketing strategies and strategies borrowed from the world of business and commerce, rather than the outreach approach pioneered by Janet Hill in her seminal work of two decades ago (Hill, 1973). Because of the thinking of the current age this approach cannot be ignored, but there is still a place for considering the needs of children as individuals and their right to the provision that library services can make for them. With this in mind, this chapter aims to take a child-centred approach to considering the promotion of libraries and literature for young people.

SERVICE PHILOSOPHY AND PROMOTION

A child-centred approach

It is with the needs of the individual child that service philosophy and promotion should begin. Provision and promotion of services presupposes a knowledge and understanding of the world within which today's children live on a global, national and local basis. It is worth noting that the gradual trend away from children's specialist to generalist posts in many public libraries has made this more difficult. This understanding has always been, and still is, important in providing any service to young people but in these days of cut-backs it is even more important to understand these needs in order to create the most relevant service and target scarce resources effectively.

Children are often seen as an homogenous group, but of course the varieties of background for each child, be it ethnic origin, socioeconomic, regional, cultural, familial, is infinitely various, as are issues such as experience and ability. Every child is unique and each has his/her own special needs (Spink, 1989). However, children do share similar experiences: all for example are required by law to attend school (or receive some form of approved education at home) until the age of 16. There are common strands of interests and children may be perceived as an identifiable market as evidenced by literature, films and those commercial products which are produced specifically for children. But before any discussion of promotion takes place it must be understood that the world of the child is complex, yet an understanding of it is fundamental to any service promotion. It is only within this context that his/her needs are determined.

Having gained an understanding of the needs of the child, the second most important factor is an understanding and belief in the role library resources can play in the life of a child, and allied to this, is a knowledge of the services and materials available. At this point it is possible to work out the strategies to make services and resources as accessible as possible to every child.

The role of libraries

Tony Benn, in his address to The Library Association UmbrelLA Conference in 1992, described libraries as the 'cornerstones of democracy'. Living in a democratic society requires skills and knowledge and suggests that individuals within that society have entitlements, at least of access to such skills and knowledge. Benn goes on to state that librarians are the gatekeepers to the world of information and knowledge. This is also endorsed by others:

> Good libraries empower. Using their resources can unfetter our imaginations; disclose hitherto unrealized worlds; promote knowledge; induce pleasure; make us laugh; impart insights; challenge our misconceptions; assuage fears; prick our conscience; inflame our sensibilities; and provide professional refreshment. What we learn from good books and other resources becomes part of us. (Kinnell, 1992, p.5)

Children may gain from libraries, first and foremost, enjoyment of story experience, of language, of associated art (Library Association, 1991, p.29). The resources of a library may foster knowledge of the wider world and an understanding of other people as regards behaviour, culture, or situations. A child can gain self-knowledge through relating to situations, events and characters. The library can provide for children's information needs. Good services may help to engender confidence, in the acquisition of vocabulary, speech and language skills and provide support for reading skills. Libraries may present opportunities for shared experiences between adult and child. Central to the philosophy of library provision for young people is to support formal and informal education.

Access underpins all services, both to materials and literature and to the greater library network. This access is enhanced by the assistance and guidance of knowledgeable and trained staff with an expertise which is unparalleled elsewhere. The library is a neutral ground on which the individual child may grow through independent and unhindered discovery. It is a place to learn and practise information skills (Library Association, 1991, p.29). Libraries provide for children's leisure, educational, emotional and intellectual needs. They provide a 'uniquely objective source of information for young people, enabling them to discover and use the power of access that information skills can bring in the society of today and tomorrow' (Library Association, 1991, p.9).

Why promote libraries and literature to young people?

The above pointers demonstrate the value of libraries, materials and library services to young people. The fact that all these exist and are available is of little use, however, to the individual who is unaware of them.

The Library Association guidelines, *Children and young people*, states: 'Promotion is a vital and integral part of service delivery and is not something to be added on. Promotional strategies should, therefore, be built into service development at the planning stage' (Library Association, 1991, p.29).

At a time when senior managers and local politicians are now being forced to streamline services, promotional activities may be regarded as extraneous to core activities and consequently vulnerable to cuts. It therefore becomes essential to have a clear idea of the aims of promotion and to be able to justify this to those who have budgetary and decision-making powers. Usherwood argues that public relations should be seen as an integral part of the management of any organization and that it is erroneous to treat promotion as a separate entity (Usherwood, 1981, p.6).

Aims of promotion

At this point it may be useful to consider what is meant by promotion and PR. A number of authors on the subject have tried to give definitions. It may be described as the gaining of public support for an activity, cause, movement or institution. The following by Mildred Knight Laughton gives a reasonable summary: 'a planned, continuous communication effort designed to gain support by developing mutual understanding and co-operation between an organization and its publics' (Huws and Eyre, 1994, p.7). Promotion may also: 'offer everyone a lifetime library and information entitlement, a right to our highest quality of service, through improved diffusion and our best practice across all organizational sectors.'

If libraries do empower and if it is agreed that every child has the right of access to that empowerment regardless of background or origin, then promotion becomes perhaps the most important aspect of service. The power of libraries is available only to those with access to and knowledge of all those facilities offered by a good library. Not all young people are equal in this. Some will have far more advantages than others, resulting from factors such as background, education, literacy and proximity to adequate library facilities. To redress the imbalance it is therefore necessary for any good library to incorporate public relations and promotions strategies into the infrastructure of the library's policies and practices. It is arguably especially true where children and young people are concerned as access to such facilities may help to create the foundation for a fulfilled life.

Rationale

This rationale may be refined to illustrate the importance of promotion:

- 'Catching them young' fosters library use. The Library Association guidelines state that surveys have shown that most habitual adult library users were library users as children (Library Association, 1991, p.10).
- Children from all backgrounds and cultures have an equal right of access to all the benefits listed above. If every child is a potential user then it is the duty of children's librarians to make sure that every child has knowledge of what is available. Not all children and young people are fortunate enough to have parents or carers who will introduce them to literature, libraries and information sources. It could be argued that particular care should be taken

to ensure that those who have the least advantages in this respect are targeted.

- Knowledge is power. Access to that knowledge can provide a foundation-stone for life. As children are at the beginning of life, they have the right to know what is available to them, either directly or through the adults who care for them, whether parent or teacher.

The main aims of promotion of library services to users must begin with the rights and needs of children, but there are also sub-objectives to promotion.

Sub-objectives

- Promotion of services may increase awareness of the library in general, raise the profile of the library and enhance its image. It may be used to advertise a new service or service-point to promote services to particular groups such as teenagers.
- Promotion is required to exploit literature in the widest sense of the word. Covering fiction and non-fiction, and various formats including machine-readable formats, this will help to encourage reading, foster literacy and provide enjoyment. It may help also to draw attention to important issues such as the environment or health-related topics or to current and topical themes.
- Increased awareness of facilities may help to enhance formal and informal education. Children and adults will be introduced to the library and its services and stock and, through library instruction, the use of library materials.
- The library may be promoted as a community facility, a meeting place or information point, and to act as an outlet for promoting community activities. It may also be used as a facility to promote the arts, new technologies and new methods of communication such as the Internet.

Framework for promotion

Promoting services to children and young people cannot exist in a vacuum. Bob Usherwood states: 'Most things that take place in a library and some that do not have a public relations effect. The . . . librarian, like any other manager must always seriously consider the PR and public relations aspects that he and she takes' (Usherwood, 1981, p.3).

The first step is to provide a relevant and comprehensive service tailored to the needs of the children served. It has been mentioned earlier that an understanding of the world of children is central to providing and promoting literature and services. It is this knowledge which should shape the service and materials offered. All too often this is an ideal rather than a reality and many library services to children are provided through tradition or habit rather than by taking account of changes and new demands affecting young people. A good example of this is seen in many rigid selection policies which do not take account of the increasing demand for new formats of materials. Many libraries for example will not stock any materials produced in computer formats. Contracting materials funds are often given as the excuse, but if libraries are to remain relevant and sustain any attraction for young people then this is surely false economy.

Unless there is a relevant and attractive service then there is nothing worthwhile to promote. Indeed promotion may be dangerous as it raises expectations. This may seem obvious but is worth stating as this mistake is sometimes made. Imagine the consequences, for example of creating an interest in a new CD-ROM collection if there are only a couple of titles available. How many library services have drawn up charters and promoted them only to find that they cannot fulfil the promises contained therein?

Promotion is therefore not merely about advertising or undertaking promotional activities, but an intrinsic part of the service. As such it must be thought out and properly planned.

To whom is promotion aimed?

Promoting libraries and literature for young people is not only aimed at young people themselves but at a variety of potential target groups. One of the significant issues of the world of children is that it is inhabited by a variety of adults, many of whom will play a part in the shaping of children's lives. It is worth remembering that adults play a large part in shaping and censoring the production of literature for young people (Library Association, 1991, p.10). As well as keeping in mind children of all ages and abilities, from a wide range of cultural backgrounds, when planning promotion it is neccesary to consider parents and carers, particularly for the younger age group.

It is therefore as important to promote literature and libraries to adults as to children:

- Teachers are also in the business of promoting literature and education, and raising awareness among teachers and working alongside them may reinforce the message libraries are trying to give.
- It may be necessary to promote literature and services to young people to other staff, including management. It is important to raise the profile of children's services, for example for the purposes of budget allocation. This is particularly pertinent in a school environment in the present economic climate.

- One area which is often forgotten when staff are under increased pressure is informing the profession. Not only does this raise the profile of the particular service point but also provides incentive and ideas for others.
- It is vitally important to raise the profile of library services to children and young people with local officials and those who have influence on expenditure or resourcing such as councillors, education officials and school governors.

Margaret Marshall in her *World of children's books* (Marshall, 1982, pp.155–6) provides an exhaustive listing of possible target groups: 'Each of these offer different promotional opportunities which need to be thought through.'

The library environment

The library building and environment, the quality and state of stock, access to that stock and other services, the attitude of the staff and the quality of service received are all potent factors in determining whether or not children and adults will use the library.

To take these issues singly, the building will create the first impact on any user. The situation of the library should be such that it offers maximum accessibility to all potential users including very young children, parents with prams, children with disabilities and any other individual with possible mobility problems. Large windows with attractive displays or alternatively where children can be seen reading or working will also encourage use. The environment should be conducive to the function of the library. Are there areas where pupil's can work quietly for example, where they can browse or use different media? Readers are directed to Michael Dewe's excellent work for further reading on this subject (Dewe, 1995).

The library in question may not be a static service point but a vehicle, a book bus or mobile library for example. The Library Association guidelines (Library Association, 1991, p.30) advocate a bright, colourful exterior design to enhance their appeal to children. Inside, the same principles apply as to a fixed service-point. Vehicles have the advantage of mobility and can be used in major events or to target client groups not near library buildings.

The architectural structure and design of a building will often be beyond the control of the librarian unless he or she is involved in planning a new library. The environment may still be made welcoming and attractive to young people; appropriate furnishings; bright colour; attractive displays and exhibitions including children's own work, mobiles, posters, toys, plants. Many children's libraries now have 'feature furniture' as a focal point, such as shelving in the shape of cars, trains or dragons on which children can play. Many publishers and suppliers now produce posters and mobiles, stickers and dump bins advertising books and authors, many available free of charge. These may be used to brighten up the library and are particularly useful if money is short. The Library Association guidelines say that for children 'visual impact is all important'.

Stock

The quality and state of the stock has already been mentioned but is worth re-iterating. If there is nothing there of interest to a child, he/she is not encouraged to use the library again. The more often children are disappointed when seeking a specific item or materials for a given topic, the less likely they are to return. Similarly, if stock is disintegrating it is unlikely to be very attractive and in days of constraint this is something which must be given careful thought.

The way stock is displayed is also important in the promotion of literature to young people. Traditional methods of arranging and displaying materials may be off-putting to all age groups. 'A cardinal rule – but often one overlooked – is that the arrangement of the collection should accurately reflect the needs of the user . . . Research in America has revealed that collections are frequently librarian oriented, and that young people and adults choose materials with little information and guidance' (Lonsdale, 1995).

With the user in mind, various forms of alternative arrangement such as categorization of stock may be considered. Imaginative display of materials may also be used whether in the form of face-on display or the use of paperback spinners or dump-bins as in retail outlets.

Access

Gaining access to the library and its materials and services is very important for all. First, is the library signposted: can it be found without too much trouble? Is there access for children and adults with disabilities? Once inside the library how easy is it for children to gain access to materials and information? It is very important to have adequate guiding and attractive and accessible arrangement of materials. Although it is now recognized by educational psychologists that all individual children have special needs, those for whom English is a second language, those with reading difficulties, aural or visual impairment or dyslexia, among others, may have particular problems when using the library. In good systems such as Birmingham, much thought has gone into making library facilities accessible to these groups. Although their needs are desperate, quite often the solution may suffice, for example most groups (except children who have visual problems) require very clear, simple guiding with unambiguous visual symbols. In addition the layout of the library should be logical, material shelved at the right height for the age group and any indexes and catalogues should be easy enough to use for the appropriate age group. Children are easily daunted by not being able to find what they require on their own.

Staffing

Investing in children (Department of National Heritage, 1995) and the Library Association guidelines (Library Association, 1991) both stress the need for well trained and informed children's specialists. Without them promotion is impaired. The attitude of the staff can enthuse and encourage children and it can also put them off for life. This applies not only to the staff specifically responsible for children's services, but for all those who may come into contact with young people and relevant adults. Customer care is one of the major concerns of most library services and is seen as being an important determinant in the image of the library.

Promoting in the community

There is growing recognition that 'the library' is not a building but a service which extends beyond the confines of the library walls. Outreach activities have to some extent fallen out of favour due to lack of resources in both financial terms and in terms of staff time. However if the objectives of promoting library service to young people are to be truly achieved then such activities must be considered. One of the functions of outreach may be to extend provision of library service and materials into various centres and establishments within the community.

Particular client groups have forced librarians to re-think the parameters of the library service

- It is widely accepted that library use falls when children reach mid-teens and youth centres have been a popular target for deposit collections. Unfortunately constraints are now forcing library services to retract such services.
- The purpose of promoting in the community may be to target traditional non-users of library services and resources, e.g. pre-school children in an inner city area where parents do not see the library as a priority.
- Promotion may take place in the community when trying to encourage new library members. Schools and nurseries provide a captive audience conveniently brought together.
- Several authorities, believing in the 'catching them young' theory now target new and expectant mothers in maternity hospitals with book displays, leaflets and even enrolment forms in 'new mothers' packs'.
- When new service points are opened, often temporary enrolment desks are set up in focal points for the community such as shopping precincts or community buildings.
- Outreach activities may also be applied to a school library where the school is the immediate community. Making contracts in the staff room, attending head of department meetings, parents evenings, visiting feeder schools are all elements of outreach.

The important point is that working out in the community ensures that non-users of the library are targeted. For greater impact, major events may take place in the wider community as in the case of Bookweek in Northern Ireland for major initiatives events and activities may literally be held anywhere. Usually key factors are adequate space and reaching as wide an audience as possible.

Despite economic constraints promotion and PR should ideally be proactive. This means going into the community to promote libraries and literature rather than waiting for members of the community to come through the door.

Promotional activities and publicity

Promotional activities and publicity through the media are often seen as the centre of promotion but are in fact more or less the end product of a continuum of service provision. It is recognized that all promotional activities should have stated objectives. There should be a defined purpose for every activity, leaflet, or community visit. At this point therefore decisions must be made on what is being promoted, why it is being promoted and to whom.

Methods of promotion are many and various. The target audience, the reason for promoting and the resources available will dictate the nature of the activity. If a new service point has opened and there has been a decision to advertise the fact to the local community more 'gimmicky' tactics may be employed, e.g. the use of children's entertainers or a party. The objective here is to attract the community through the doors and to break down any barriers between the staff and the community. On the other hand, if the objective is to promote an area of stock, for example poetry, then the approach would be completely different and activities may include poetry reading, a poetry workshop run by a local poet, or the use of drama to focus on one or two specific poems. Activities may fulfil several functions, but the key point is that the methodology should fulfil the objectives.

There is not enough space within this chapter to list all the possibilities for promotion. However, many may be categorized and some of the categories are listed below together with examples:

Printed materials

Printed materials are many and various. Publicity packs, leaflets, posters, as well as local media coverage for special events, particularly holiday activities, are fairly standard forms of publicity, although the quality of these varies enormously from authority to authority. Most authorities produce introductory leaflets, explaining what the library has to offer and 'joining packs' for children which include information for children themselves and their carers. Other examples are: **Camden's** *Let's read: how you can help your child*, aimed at the value of reading and sharing with children and *Beginning with books* exploring books for the very young. **Lambeth's** introduction for children is in pop-up, pull-out format. **Hampshire** offer an early years pack including advice to parents, leaflets and posters when babies are enrolled and **Croydon** have an attractive folder for under fives.

Annual reports are not what are traditionally thought of as promotional material but, of course, are important documents in that they inform the policy-makers and budget holders of what is happening. Annual reports and reviews can be deadly dull, full of statistics, meaningful to the initiated but giving little feel to the quality and range of services. Bolton used their annual report for 1994/95 to detail their first large-scale survey of library users and consider development in children's library services. **Camden's** fairly informal annual report gives a clear perspective of the range of activities for children in libraries, while **North Tyneside's** *Review of the year for 1994/95* is produced in a lively magazine format, with pictures, and gives a real feel for the wide range of activities being undertaken. **Redbridge** produce a very simple, attractive, colourful single folded sheet highlighting their achievements in *Another successful* year. Pictures and captions give a snappy summary of events during the year, including the results of their survey which showed that 9 out of 10 library users were 'highly satisfied' with Redbridge's library service: worth celebrating!

Booklists are a traditional way of promoting literature for young people. **Hertfordshire** produce a range of small folded sheets around all themes and genres, for all age groups. Some examples include *Special books for special children*, *Cuddle up with a book*, and *One voice, many voices: poetry*. Other examples include **Staffordshire's** *Books for toddlers* and *Books for babies*, eye-catching A4 sheets and **Hampshire's** booklists and author bookmarks which include *Just for a laugh* and *Creepies*. **Norfolk** have an attractive chart of the top-scoring books for teenagers.

Leicestershire produce high standard publicity materials with guides such as *Help at hand: a selection of books to help children deal with special situations* and *Open books open minds: fiction to support religious education*. Of similarly high standard are **Lambeth's** lists with such titles as *Black poetry* and *Black women writers*. Other printed items may include magazines such as **Rotherham's** *Freewheeler* which includes jokes, poetry and best books. **Gwent** also have a regular magazine, *Bookworm*, for young people.

Wolverhampton explored the European year of older people and solidarity between generations through a project called 'Reading through the years'. This led to the publication of *Reading through the years: favourite books of childhood as recollected by local people* (beginning with the Lord Mayor) and a booklist of children's books with an intergenerational theme. This idea of using library members is taken up by **Redbridge** in *Desert island books*, chosen by library members, in this case children, and by **West Sussex** with *On-line: smart reads, hot sounds, the facts*, chosen by young people and produced in an attractive pop magazine format. Linking local history, reminiscence and user's literary skills was used to good effect in **Cornwall's** centenary celebration for Camborne Library, with a published collection of poetry, *Camborne reflected*, inspired by Camborne Town and written by schoolchildren.

A number of authorities have a reader's passport, which children have stamped every time they read a book by a particular author. Looking very much like a real passport, this is a clear encouragement for children to read more. Examples are **Ealing** and **Camden**.

Promotional talks

Promotional talks are a popular and traditional method of getting the message across. These may be of a general nature or be used to target specific age groups, on particular themes or to exploit areas of stock. One advantage of such talks is that they offer the opportunity for immediate feedback.

User education, both formal or informal, may be employed by both public and school libraries. It can perform a number of functions such as introducing young people to using the library as a whole, help in understanding particular issues such as classification or categorization, or may be used to exploit sections of stock or even the contents of individual sources.

Some library authorities and schools have extremely well developed user education programmes which encompass a number of of the functions given above. Students are introduced to information retrieval and the use of various formats of materials from archives to the Internet, perhaps beginning at a very basic and general level. More advanced level activities may include a very detailed examination of materials geared to a particular subject and include training in the use of both primary and secondary sources.

Displays and exhibitions

This is another time-honoured way of exploiting literature and enhancing the attractiveness of the library. Such displays may be within the library itself or in any venue, be it a traditional venue such as a school or in more innovative settings such as shop windows and dentists' waiting rooms. They may be used to highlight a category of stock and, in fact, are often an adjunct to categorized collections. They may be on any theme from the colour blue to Carnegie and Kate Greenaway winners. Topical issues such as the environment or health are often favourite topics.

Displays may exhibit fiction and non-fiction, poetry and prose or may not include stock at all. The use of artefacts and imaginitive use of posters, photographs, etc., often enhance such displays.

Of course a library may wish to promote itself as a community resource by housing displays and exhibitions by other agencies, maybe the work of local schoolchildren. The library may wish to reinforce its cultural role by hosting travelling art exhibitions or historical displays.

Events, activities and initiatives

Activities and events have been a staple part of the children's librarian's diet for at least the past three decades and cover a range from regular activity sessions in the local library to large-scale, county-wide, or in the case of Northern Ireland country-wide events. A survey recently undertaken by the School of Information Studies, University of Central England, reveals that despite the many financial problems currently faced by local authorities, the majority are still able to offer an 'impressive range of storytelling and activity sessions'. One example quoted is **Leicestershire** which enjoys a national reputation for innovatory work with children and young people. The regular programme includes: summer activities; lively performance storytelling and use of puppets to promote books and reading; 'booktalking' with older children to extend awareness of what books are available and to encourage them to borrow and read; programmes of user education to help children develop their information-handling skills and make purposive use of the library; extensive work with the under-fives including work with parents and carers (on Nursery Nurse Diploma courses or Preschool Playgroup Association courses) and older pupils (in schools), helping them develop their own skills in choosing and using books with children.

Some initiatives were felt to be worth noting for their originality, innovation and the quality of publicity materials. **Mid Glamorgan** produced a particularly attractive range of posters, a variety of reading games and trails. A number of reading games and trails were also noted such as **Leicestershire's** Robin Hood Reading Game, **North Shields** and **Tyneside** ran a Robert Westall trail, **West Sussex** a Monster Magic Reading Game and on a more general theme **South Glamorgan's** Book Quest and **Kirklee's** Habitat Hunt (an environmental information skills game).

On a larger scale a number of authorities host children's book festivals, often with sponsorship from publishers, suppliers, local arts councils or others. Included in these are **Salford's** *Booksplash* and The Northern Children's Book Festival in **Newcastle**. In 1995 many of these were timed to coincide with the Library Power Campaign. Examples here include South East Wales Children's Book Festival run by **South Glamorgan**. All these initiatives are major promotional opportunities for libraries and an opportunity for young people to come face to face with well-known authors.

Television, radio, local and national newspapers may be used in a variety of ways to promote both libraries and literature. Local radio for example may be used to promote specific activities or to host a whole programme devoted to children's books. Berlie Doherty, the award-winning children's author, for a number of years hosted a review programme on Radio Sheffield, where a group of young people discussed books they had read.

It is worth mentioning here that there is a growing trend for merchandizing bearing the logo of the library authority and/or promoting particular events. Again the list of possibilities is too long to include but examples of such items may be mugs, T-shirts, pens and even umbrellas.

Cultural role

One of the great advantages that libraries enjoy is that they are placed within communities. As such they are well placed to fulfil a role as cultural centres. They are the natural place for the promotion of literature including poetry, prose and drama. This may be literature created by the local young people as well as that produced by mainstream publishers. Writers in residence have been appointed in many authorities, for example, to encourage writing by children as well as adults. Libraries also offer a venue for visual and performing arts and music.

In addition they are cultural centres in the true sense of the word, highlighting local culture and able to highlight the cultures of children representing the various groups within the community. This may be by offering activities such as Eid parties, celebrations for Chinese New Year, etc.

A library may fulfil a community function by making space and buildings available for other organizations or groups, for example the local playgroup may meet there, or by acting as an outlet for services offered by others, e.g. an outlet for a local toy library.

Working with others

This subject has been discussed elsewhere but it is worth mentioning here as working with others in promotion is often of mutual benefit to libraries and to other agencies and individuals. There are a number of advantages which may include forging links with groups and organizations whose objectives complement those of the library: maximizing resources including finance, human resources, space and communication channels: creating greater opportunities in applying for grants, awards and sponsorship. There is often a secondary advantage and that is it opens up channels of communication to provide feedback on stock and services and establish a useful network of contacts.

Within the local community librarians may wish to work with such groups as schools, playgroups, mother and toddler groups and youth centres, either to raise the profile of the library with these groups or to provide joint ventures such as activities – book fairs, bookweeks in schools and open days. Groups may be invited to support a library initiative or library staff may take advantage of promotion opportunities opened by events held by others, in providing talks, displays or other support. Paying the fees and expenses of authors or theatre groups may be diluted by 'sharing'. It may be that the library joins in local community events such as pageants and festivals.

The library may jointly produce publications such as a magazine for teenagers with the local youth centre. If the library provides a newsletter, community groups may be asked to contribute and vice versa. Many under fives groups produce local news-sheets and many communities produce publications. They are often very grateful for contributions and offer a tremendous opportunity for free publicity in the form of articles, annotated booklists, details of library services, etc.

On a wider basis the central offices or umbrella organizations of many of the groups mentioned are useful when coordinating large-scale events as they often have their own communication networks. Local newspapers and media are very good allies if they are involved from the planning stage. **Norfolk's** 'Treasure Island' initiative was sponsored by the local newspaper and there was the added advantage of extra publicity. The possibilities are endless. Cooperation may also be with large stores, local bookshops, theatres, cinemas, other council departments, centres for the disabled, and many others.

Sponsorship

There is increasing demand for sponsorship and cooperative ventures with the commercial sector. It is noticeable that such opportunities are becoming more difficult to obtains as competition increases. Sponsorship of a financial nature may be to sponsor events, publicity or outreach to special needs groups. Appeal may be made to commercial organizations or to fund-raising initiatives such as the BBC's Children in Need Appeal.

Sponsorship may not be through direct payment. Publishers often wish to promote their own authors. Publishers will often seek venues through journals such as the *Bookseller* and libraries have the opportunity of hosting these. Most publishers have publicity departments whom librarians may contact to discuss author visits, hire of costumes and obtaining biographical and promotional material about authors and their books. Suppliers may also sponsor or at least provide contacts for such events although there is a growing tendency for suppliers to host their own author evenings. However, they may be able to lend support in other ways such as providing contacts, helping with printing, or giving the benefit of their marketing expertise.

Working with others usually means that more spectacular and far-reaching events may be staged than by a librarian working in isolation. Valuable contacts are made and above all it is often more fun! A word of advice is to involve any outside agency as soon as possible in the planning cycle, preferably at the planning stage. This ensures that both sides have the opportunity to consider and discuss the ideas which will afford maximum benefit to all organizations involved.

Managing promotion

Any promotional strategy must be set within the context of the philosophy of the parent body, if it is to achieve credibility with local powers and hence to succeed and to be relevant. For example an authority may have the objective of 'helping the individual to achieve his/her rights within a democratic society.' To meet this objective it is important to make sure that every individual from a very young age, or his/her carer knows

- that the library exists;
- what it can offer;
- how to gain access to the service points;
- how to exploit facilities and information sources.

Library promotion should:

- meet clear objectives;
- be targeted to defined audiences;
- convey a clear message;
- be cost-effective in the use of funds, materials and staff time;
- use the most effective and appropriate medium, bearing in mind the agreed objectives and intended audience;
- be professional in its appearance or delivery;
- be adequately financed from a defined budget.

In addition printed materials should:

- use clear, appropriate and jargon-free language;
- take account of the value of a common house style.

Increasingly libraries and sections of libraries are required to produce business plans, although they may be known under other guises such as forward planning documents. Today these have to be shown to be realistic and it is essential that issues are thought through. The planning and organization of promotion begins here and must be juxtaposed with all other aspects of service provision. It is essential to:

- set priorities;
- state aims and objectives;
- formulate realistic strategies;
- identify and allocate resources and supply costings;
- ensure that there is some method of evaluation.

Setting priorities is most important as there is never the time or resources to do everything. Formulating aims and objectives helps to focus ideas and hone down grandiose schemes to manageable and realistic proportions and also helps to pinpoint the target groups. Aims and objectives also make the planner distill what is to be achieved by the whole process.

It is important to identify and allocate resources at an early stage, as it is that which establishes whether or not plans are feasible. Allocating resources is not just a matter of finance, but all resources must be taken into consideration including human resources, equipment and facilities and time. It is at this stage that a decision as to any other people or services such as printers or caterers, etc., must be made.

CONCLUSION

Over the last ten years or so, promotion of library services for all, including children, has gained respectability. In the 1980s the Publicity and Public Relations Group of the Library Association came into being as did the LA/T. C. Farries Awards. The messages given about the importance of library services to young people by the *Investing in children* and the *Review of the public library service* are encouraging. We must hope that the financial constraints imposed on many schools and local authorities will not negate these more positive aspects.

REFERENCES

Aslib (1995), *Review of the public library service in England and Wales for the Department of National Heritage*. London, Aslib.

Cabinet Office (1991), *The citizen's charter*. London, HMSO.

Dearing, R. (1993), *The National Curriculum and its assessment: final report,* London, School Curriculum and Assessment Authority.

Department of Education and Science (1992), *The teaching and learning of reading in primary schools 1991: a report by HMI Stanmore*. Department of Education and Science. London, HMSO.

Department of National Heritage (1995), *Investing in children: the future of library services for children and young people*. Library and Information Services Council (England), Working Party on Library Services for Children and Young People. London, HMSO.

Dewe, M. (1995), *Planning and designing libraries for children and young people*. London, Library Association Publishing.

Fisher, M. (1989), in King, I., *Promote! The handbook of public library promotion*. Leicester, Public Libraries Group of the Library Association.

Hill, J. (1973), *Children are people: the librarian in the community*. London, Hamish Hamilton.

Huws, G. & Eyre. G. (1994), In Eyre G., *Making quality happen: a practical guide to promoting your library*. Exeter, Youth Libraries Group of the Library Association.

Kinnell, M. (1992), *Learning resources in schools: Library Association guidelines for school libraries*. London, Library Association Publishing.

Library Association (1991), *Children and young people. Library Association guidelines for public libraries*. London, Library Association Publishing.

Lonsdale, R. (1995), *Focus on the child*. (Module developed for the Distance Learning Programme, Department of Information and Library Studies). Aberystwyth, University of Wales.

Marshall, M. (1982), *An Introduction to the world of children's books*. Aldershot, Gower.

Spink, J. (1989), *Children as readers; a study*. London, Bingley.

Usherwood, R. (1981), *The visible library: practical public relations for public librarians*. London, Library Association Publishing.

9

Children's libraries: current practice in action

Judith Elkin

I'm still happier in a library than anywhere else. For me, it's like the moment in a swimming pool when you finally slip under, the water closes over your head, and a feeling of absolute peace and privacy comes over you. In my novel, *The Granny Project*, Natasha says that, if the public library did not exist, she would not want to exist either. That's how I feel, still, after all these years. (Fine, 1993, p.23)

When *Jane Eyre* gave me nightmares someone locked the bookcase, and got me a children's ticket at a branch library . . . It took me a long time to get the hang of books that I could understand, and that long ago librarian knew just what to do with me, easing me from Tolstoy to *Puck of Pook's Hill*, and from Ruskin to *The Hobbit*. By and by I discovered the possibilities of fun reading. (Walsh, 1993, p.23)

INTRODUCTION

Two authors, Jill Paton Walsh and Anne Fine capture the essence of the public library in terms of their own development as children: hugely influential to themselves as individuals and for future children who have revelled in their writing. Previous chapters have explored the value of literature and literacy to the individual child and the essential role of libraries in ensuring equal access for all children to the widest range of literature. The current political and economic climate within which libraries operate has also been examined, alongside current reports, guidelines, standards and exploration of management and marketing practice.

Descriptions of current practice are diffuse in the literature. This chapter provides the opportunity to bring together a feel for current practice nationwide. The changes brought about by local government reorganization make the picture rather fluid but the chapter captures elements of current practice which are transferable to newly formed, unchanged or restructured authorities, as either examples of good practice or stimulus for change.

PROFESSIONAL PROFILE

The 1980s saw a growing awareness among public librarians in general of the responsibility for children matched by a more proactive and professional approach among children's librarians themselves. This was rewarded by the movement of a number of senior children's librarians into senior general management posts. To many children's librarians this was unsurprising. Children's librarians had developed management skills to a high level: they tended to have a very clear view of what they were doing and why: they respected their clients, children and their carers; they were knowledgeable about children's books, child development and educational issues; they understood children's information needs and the value of information-handling skills at various stages of their development. In most library authorities it was the children's library service that had published selection criteria and multicultural policies way ahead of their colleagues in adult services. Most had a strategic view, although rarely published as such.

Yet there was also confusion, in terms of the perceived 'professional image'. The explosion of activities in children's libraries, with book weeks, author visits, book buses, book boats, family reading groups, storyhours, activities, under fives groups and development of specialist services for teenagers was wonderful to behold. The pages of the *Library Association record* were full of children's librarians dressed up as Spot the Dog or Postman Pat. This was very positive but also professionally problematic, as children's librarianship became perceived as marginalized, oddball, not very serious, compared with 'quality' professional work being done elsewhere. Little attempt was made publicly to justify such work: how did it contribute to the individual child's development or imaginative stimulation? It was very colourful and great fun, but not viewed as meaningful and certainly not seen as requiring high-level professional skills.

Such work appeared to have little sense of direction or strategy and led to library services for children being viewed as something separate, rather precious but second-rate, suitable for the less adequate and more delicate professional. Yet, in reality both then and nowadays, no other specialist has such a wide range of abilities and interests to meet among clients, across the whole spectrum from the bright pre-school child to the semi-literate teenager as well as to their intermediaries: parents, carers, teachers, childminders, playgroup leaders, social workers, community workers, youth leaders, religious leaders.

A much more professional management approach has developed during the 1990s, largely as a result of economic restraints which have caused children's and school libraries to be under threat of closure or reduction in services and changes following the Education Reform Act and Local Management of Schools which have forced libraries to cost out school library services. Services have been forced to justify their existence and develop aims, objectives and business plans. This has been followed by mission, policy and strategy statements and charters for children. These are discussed below.

CURRENT PRACTICE

Policy statements

The rest of this chapter considers current developments in the management and delivery of children's library services and considers evidence of good practice. It looks at mission and policy statements, charters, standards and some key specialist services. Information was gathered through a survey carried out by the author during 1995 and from information provided by ASCEL.[1]

A number of the key recommendations of *Investing in children* (Department of National Heritage, 1995) were concerned with the need to have published charters, mission statement and policy guidelines, although in reality in a number of authorities these already exist. A large number of authorities already have policy guidelines, some purely for stock selection, some specifically aimed at various sectors of children, for example the under-fives (**Essex, Hertfordshire, Norfolk, Birmingham**); primary and secondary age (**Hertfordshire**), teenagers (**Wiltshire**); children with special needs (**Hertfordshire, Essex**); equal access or anti-racist policies (**Wolverhampton, Liverpool, Bradford**).

A number also already have charters (**Birmingham, Hampshire, Norfolk, Gwent, Mid Glamorgan, Hertfordshire, Leicestershire**); mission statements (**Norfolk, Wolverhampton**) or promises (**Croydon**); statements of aims and objectives (**North Yorkshire, Croydon, Nottinghamshire**); performance indicators (**Nottinghamshire**); service specifications (**Gwent, Hertfordshire, Cambridgeshire**); customer care statements (**Gwent, Wiltshire, Kirklees**); business plans and stated strategies (**Cambridgeshire, Hertfordshire, Bolton, Gwent, Cynon Valley**); information strategies (**Hertfordshire** for 14–19 years olds). Some of these are detailed below.

A useful chart of all library authorities, listing those with school library services, children's library services, business plans, charters, costing for SLSs, publicity, training and youth libraries has recently been compiled by ASCEL and is available as part of membership of ASCEL.

Mission statements

Two mission statements set the scene:

> This service is founded on the firm belief that libraries make a major contribution to children's and young people's development and can help them achieve their full potential. Their quality of life and learning can be significantly enhanced through the ideas and information contained in books and other media. The needs of children and young people are at the heart of the library service. The goal is to provide a high quality service for all children and young people in North Tyneside, regardless of gender, disability, ethnic, cultural or religious background (**North Tyneside**).

We exist to develop enquiring minds, encourage a love of reading and stimulate the imagination of young people to ensure that libraries are for life (**Hertfordshire**).

This is within the framework of the County Libraries' vision of 'Becoming so central to life in society that business, industry and government compete to fund our services' (**Hertfordshire**).

Charters

Charters have become rather fashionable in recent years, with the government publishing customer charters for schools, further and higher education, railways and the health service, among others. Inevitably, perhaps, local authorities and libraries as part of these have followed suit. Public libraries are among the most highly regarded and heavily used of local public services but often in a situation where the general public have no clear view of what they can expect of the local public library. The Library Association, in recognition of this, has published a model charter. This is intended to help individual library authorities to develop their own customized local users' charters for public libraries (Library Association, 1993). Many authorities have indeed done this, or produced their own more targeted charter.

Some charters include children implicitly in all-embracing phrases such as:

Birmingham Library Services exists to provide, promote and encourage access to information and imagination through books, print and other forms of communication . . . We will welcome anyone of any age to use libraries or become a member (**Birmingham**).

We give everyone access to books, information and works of creative imagination which will encourage them to take part in cultural, democratic and economic activities; educate them, either formally or informally; help them make good use of their free time; promote reading as a basic skill for life; and make them aware of the value of information and encourage them to use it (**Norfolk**).

Others, such as **Gwent** have a general customer charter which includes a section on services to young people. This emphasizes the library's responsibility to all local children, not just its current users:

- children from all backgrounds and cultures will have equal right of access to library services in Gwent;
- all libraries will be child friendly with consideration being given to accessibility for children with special needs: children will have safe access to all areas of the library;
- all libraries will have a range of resources available for each customer group between the ages of 0–16 years. There will be clearly guided areas for these customer groups;

- all staff will welcome children and their adult carers and promote the full range of services available;
- all libraries will offer a range of activities to promote reading, the enjoyment of libraries and resources;
- advisory services about children's literature, reading and libraries will be provided for children and adult carers (**Gwent**).

The **South Eastern Education and Library Board of Northern Ireland** has moved a stage closer to children themselves, with a 'promise to children' which states:

We promise . . .
- to listen to what you have to say about your library;
- to explain how the library works and how to use it;
- to help you find the books and information you need;
- to provide the best books for you to enjoy;
- to encourage you to read as widely and as often as possible;

We will do our best to make your library a . . .
- safe,
- attractive,
- friendly,
  . . . place for you and your family to visit.

The Promise is also incorporated into a leaflet for parents, *Your child and the library* which sets out the responsibilities of the Library:

- to ensure that the library is a safe, attractive and welcoming place for you and your child;
- to be fair but firm in dealing with children who disturb or upset other library users;
- to take reasonable care of all children on our premises. Your pre-school child must be accompanied by an adult or a responsible older brother or sister;
- to ensure that all our children's activities are well organized and properly supervised;
- to help your child to understand and use the library and obtain the resources or information she/he needs;
- to provide a varied and balanced stock carefully selected by well trained staff.

Croydon Libraries also have a promise to children:

We promise:

- to be friendly and welcoming;
- to provide a pleasant, attractive place for you to visit;
- to help you find the books and information you need;
- to encourage you to find books;
- to listen to what you have to say about your library.

In return, please:

- look after everything that you have borrowed from the library and make sure it is brought back on time;
- look after your library ticket and remember to bring it to the library with you.

The above promise is displayed in all libraries in Croydon as a full colour, illustrated A3 laminated poster which was launched during Library Power Week in May 1995.

Standards

Some authorities have a published set of standards specifically for children's library services. More common is a set of general standards which incorporate standards for children, often based on the LA guidelines for children and young people.

Norfolk's Standards of Customer Service states that: 'The library and information service provides access to knowledge to enable Norfolk people to enjoy learning, leisure and thinking in a safe and welcoming environment.'

The Library Association has drawn up a model *Statement of standards* which supports the *Charter for public libraries* (Library Association, 1993). It contains recommendations on what constitutes a high quality library service, based on existing good practice, identifying a realistic number of key standards and providing benchmarks to assist local authorities to develop their own local statement of standards. While all of the standards can be viewed as relevant to children's library services, the proposals with specific reference state that:

- all libraries will provide facilities for children in line with the Library Association Guidelines: *Children and young people*;
- each library authority will adopt a comprehensive stock management policy;
- each library authority will ensure that there will be a range of staff available with specialist knowledge, for example children/young people.

Business plans, service specifications, objectives, policy documents

There is considerable overlap between service specifications, policy and strategy statements in published documents. Many authorities are in the process of preparing business plans, and this has been speeded up with respect to schools library services by Local Management of Schools and the pressures of financial delegation to schools. Business Plans in the children's library area are still relatively uncommon, although some elements may be included elsewhere in published policy statements. Some commendable examples follow:

Hertfordshire has a business plan for its young people's services. This is an impressive document which spells out the aims and objectives, customer profile, organization and management, communication and service strategy. The business plan is seen as a working document which will 'grow, develop and change over coming months and years'. Overall strategy documents have been written for each aspect of the service – for under-fives, junior services, teenage, special needs, activities, marketing – to ensure that everyone is aware of the total service. Action plans for each service are revised annually.

Hertfordshire's service specification requires each library to provide a service to meet the aims and objectives of the young people's service. The service targets are:

- completion and annual revision of community profile;
- number of children who are members should be within 25–40% of children in catchment area;
- number of children who are members who have used the library within the past year;
- one fifth of library space should be made available to provide a service to children;
- completion and annual revision of stock profile.

The last target is specified tightly, with stock on loan as percentage of holding, stock turnover per annum and stock as percentage of library total, for picture books, fiction, non-fiction, spoken word and teenage. Libraries not conforming are allowed two years to work their stocks to the specified levels. Each library is expected to formulate a development policy for their children's library as part of their business plan which is reviewed with team leaders annually. It is expected that the budget for young people's libraries will be in line with usage and population statistics, i.e. normally about 20%. The recommended breakdown is: 30% picture books; 5% beginning to read; 15% younger readers; 20% fiction; 20% non-fiction; 9% older picture books, special collections; 1% parents collection plus additional stock from the adult library.

Each library is expected to provide outreach, with at least three activities for children and/or their carers each year, in addition to summer activities programmes and annual contacts with each playgroup, educational institution and all childminders.

The service specification spells out the skills which staff working in the children's library should have or develop:

- an understanding of child development;
- detailed knowledge of children's books and related materials;
- knowledge of education trends;
- knowledge of and ability to work with child related groups;
- familiarity with contemporary child culture;
- storytelling and other performance skills;
- presentation skills;
- understanding of parents' expectations;
- personal qualities including empathy with children and young people.

Somerset's *Children's library service: policy review* (January 1994) explores in considerable detail the why, who, what, where, how and when of services to children at the current time. It considers the characteristics of a public library children's service that distinguish it from related operations (School library services, bookshops, bookclubs, school libraries) and give it a particular identity that should be recognized and developed. The possible characteristics noted include:

- a broad user base
  - children of all ages, needs and tastes;
  - parents, carers, educators;
- a wide stock and information network
  - children have access to whole range of library provision, including reference service;
  - stock selections not solely linked to curriculum, or what will 'sell' best;
- regular literature promotion and user education
  - quality is the focus (without vested interest)
  - user education can include *all* aspects of a library;
- service free at the point of delivery;
- all library service points are staffed throughout opening hours, which include some outside school hours;

whilst recognizing some less positive characteristics:

- facilities unequal across service points as regards shelfstock, opening hours, space, staffing. Also, mobile library schedules don't favour school-age children at many stops.
- The service can't provide the tailored range and volume of stock for school needs, which for example the schools library service or school libraries can.

The review is being used as the basis for an agreed strategy and action plan for improving and developing the service, along the lines identified.

Gwent has a business plan for 1995/96 which clearly lays out the description of the business, with aims and objectives, a SWOT analysis, stating honestly their strengths, weaknesses, opportunities and threats and the plan for the year, divided into accommodation, stock, staff and services.

Leicestershire's *Objectives and outline strategies* (1990) outline the scope of the service to be provided for children and young people: Leicestershire Libraries and Information Services will:

- select, organize and display books and other materials and encourage their use;
- give advice to help adults and children make best use of the range of materials available;
- encourage and develop use through activities in libraries, play schemes, cooperation with schools, talks to groups and other appropriate activities.

Essex have separate policy statements covering their schools library services and children's library services matrices. The latter states quite clearly the client group served (children aged 0–16, including teenagers, parents and carers, volunteer community groups and other support agencies and schools), distinguishing these from the services provided to schools through the schools library service, i.e. the public library provides loans to teachers and pupils as individuals, display facilities for pupils' work, in-library user education, visits by staff to schools for the purpose of promoting libraries and reading and loan collections to community groups such as playgroups, mother and toddler groups but not special loan facilities, bulk loans, advice on setting up or maintaining the school library (the province of SLS). There is also a statement on library services for children with special needs and a statement on library services in multicultural Essex.

Hampshire's set of policy guidelines for children's library services lays out the following long-term objectives in relation to the children's library service:

> To provide library services to assist children to the means of self-development by books and related materials, and to encourage the use of the library's services to further this end by:

- promoting an awareness of the value of reading;
- assisting language and literacy development;
- promoting an understanding of libraries and books as a fundamental means of acquiring information skills and awareness.

The majority of the rest of Hampshire's policy relates to the provision and selection of materials for children, and in many ways parallels Hertfordshire's service specification. The policies are clearly and strategically stated. They look at the value of fiction and information books for children and criteria for their evaluation; stock selection and stock revision, with recommended proportions of stock as follows: a minimum of 40% and a maximum of 60% of the book fund to be spent on stock revision; no more than 40% shelf stock to be information books; maximum of 10% of the fiction budget should be spent on lightweight fiction; maximum of 5% total book fund on story cassettes, with the recommendation that 35–50% of children's stock should be on issue at census time. The recommended composition of fiction stock is 30–40% books for babies, picture books, beginning readers, younger information books; 20–30% younger readers; 25–30% junior fiction and picture books for older readers; 5–15% stock for aged 11 up, with a minimum of 25% fiction shelf stock to be paperback moving to a minimum of 70% aged 11 up.

Hampshire also has a very clear statement about class visits to libraries, spelling out the aims of such visits, emphasizing the role of the public library in promoting a wide range of books to improve reading standards and giving clear guidelines to staff on organizing class visits, aiming to make visits as productive as possible and ensuring high standards across the county.

North Tyneside's policy guidelines for children and young people's (CYP) library service are founded on the North Tyneside Libraries document *Key activity areas* (1993), which places the CYP service at the start of a continuum of library provision for the whole community and aims to:

- provide specialist training and support to all library staff and others;
- provide a library stock relevant to children's needs;
- provide a child-friendly environment in our libraries;
- support and encourage children's learning from the earliest age;
- support and stimulate community development in partnership with other agencies;
- provide effective access to information sources;
- enable children to make full use of library resources;
- promote and encourage reading and the enjoyment of books with children and their adult carers.

Stock selection policies

Stock selection policies are widespread and usually incorporate or are accompanied by a carefully constructed set of criteria for assessing children's books. A number of stock selection policies are prefaced with a justification for the need for careful selection and highlight the importance of reading and access to books and other materials. The four areas of child development requiring access to library materials, highlighted in the LA guidelines are often quoted: intellectual and emotional development; language development; social development; educational development.

Some library authorities publish separate selection guidelines for non-book materials, e.g. **Norfolk** have separate guidelines for selecting fiction; non-fiction; poetry cassettes and language tapes, the latter considering issues such as quality of narration, suitability of narrator, dialect, quality of production.

Bradford prefaces its checklist of what to look for when choosing books for a multicultural society with a clear statement:

> Racism is a highly charged and important issue. Generally speaking publishers of material for children are much more aware than they used to be of the need to be sensitive to issues of race, gender and disability. However we still need to be vigilant. It is simply not good enough to say: It doesn't do any harm, children don't notice. The whole point about racist imagery is the subconscious conditioning which goes on and which can have far-reaching consequences in a child's mind. This is not just a negative response – in libraries what we are seeking to do is not just to root out the bad, but even more importantly to bring in the good. We need books which relate to the lives of children living in the 1990s, and which offer good positive images.

Conflicting roles of public and school libraries

The emphasis on the role of the public library in its own right, rather than as a support for the inadequacies of school libraries and the demise of school library services, was well spelt out in *Investing in children*, as highlighted previously. This is supported by responses from individual library authorities, which acknowledge the undoubted increase in attempts by schools and teachers to use the public library to support the curriculum. Several of them lay down very carefully in writing the different services that can be expected by schools from the public library and the schools library service. Leicestershire have clear guidelines for staff on services which are available to schools through the public library, e.g. public library user education; in-service training; local studies materials; booktalks; storytelling; bookfairs; displays/exhibitions in libraries; childcare talks; talks to parents groups, etc.; loans to nurseries.

The London Borough of Redbridge has a policy statement on the use of the public library service to children and the schools resource service, which begins:

> Until recently there has been no conflict of interests between the Public Library Service for children and the Schools Resource Service – the first aiming to serve children, their parents and carers, the second serving teachers, advisors and home tutors within the Borough. From April 1995, following financial delegation to schools, schools will be able to choose to buy in to the Council's Schools Resource Service on a cost recovery basis, ie staffing, resources, overheads for a service previously provided free.

Bradford Libraries published guidelines in 1994 for working with schools and with the Education Library Service (ELS), which specify quite straightforwardly what the *free* public library service might be expected to offer compared with the delegated ELS; it begins with the general principle:

> Our role in public libraries is entirely in the area of encouraging children to use libraries and enjoy books. Sometimes this logically means working closely with schools, but when this happens it is always in relation to the ultimate aim of promoting public library use and literacy . . . and promoting books.

It encourages public library staff to go into schools for promotional talks to children or parents and carers about the value of the public library or to promote specific events, to liaise with teachers about library visits.

Wiltshire are quite adamant about this: 'The public library should not offer any service to a school that is already available from Wiltshire Learning Resources', and publishes a guide to what can be expected from the public library, which largely coincides with the policies of the previous two authorities described above, and what can be expected from Wiltshire Learning Resources.

Evidently most authorities are becoming increasingly aware of the need to have clear distinctions. This of course is not a new issue, because public libraries for years have freely supported inadequate school libraries and often substituted for non-existent or inadequate schools library services, with little or no support from the education authority and, sadly, with little public recognition. Local Management of Schools and increased pressure to support the National Curriculum, has merely focused attention on this issue and forced it into the open: all services above and beyond the standard personal loan and access to books and information, as spelt out above, have now to be paid for by schools.

Schools library services

While this chapter concentrates on children's library services, it is worth briefly commenting on the professional approach clearly evident in a number of schools library services, particularly with respect to their written policies and publications promoting their services. These generally cover services such as loan service, project collections, advisory and consultation work, in-service training and perhaps purchase schemes.

The mission statement issued by the **American Library Association** as a model for school library media programs is a useful starting point for individual schools in the UK:

- to ensure that students and staff are effective users of ideas and information. This mission is accomplished:

- by providing intellectual and physical access to materials in all formats;

- by providing instruction to foster competence and stimulate interest in reading, viewing, and using information and ideas;
- by working with other educators to design learning strategies to meet the needs of individual students (American Library Association, 1988, p.1).

A few good examples from the UK are:

Hertfordshire has a well-formulated business plan and separate guides to the service for nursery, special, primary and secondary schools, laying out for each the benefits of using the schools library services, the services available and the costs involved.

Leicestershire produces an attractive folder, explaining the schools library services available and their costs and with two useful free-standing publications, recommended guidelines for libraries in schools and colleges, published as a supplement to the LEA curriculum statement and a guide to devising a policy and plan for the school library resource centre.

Sheffield also publishes a set of standards and guidelines for libraries and learning resource areas within schools, which is supplemented by information about reviewing journals, children's book publishers, bookclubs and national events.

Cambridgeshire produces a range of publications for schools and is heavily involved in training to promote the role of the library in schools, considering strategic and business planning and information skills development and in new initiatives in schools, including superhighways in education.

Suffolk publish *B cubed: beg, borrow or buy*, a recommended list of new books for schools.

Gwynedd produces a structured, attractive loose leaf handbook of library services to schools, in Welsh and English.

Publicity and promotion

Publicity and promotion were dealt with in the previous chapter. Responses from library authorities to the survey question on the importance of promotion and publicity range from: 'We are lucky to have an extremely talented team working in our publicity department' (Leicestershire) to 'X is not too good on publicity'. Publicity packs, leaflets, posters, as well as local media coverage for special events, particularly holiday activities, are fairly standard forms of publicity, although the quality of these varies enormously from authority to authority.

The response to The Library Association's *Library power* campaign during 1995 was impressive, with events all over the country and libraries taking advantage of the attractive publicity materials available through the campaign. It helped to raise the profile of children's library services nationally and was seen as a valuable promotional activity. Some of the specific activities organized locally included: a children's festival in **Berkshire**; a library mastermind devised by the schools library service in **Dorset**, with an inter-school final; **East Sussex** schools library service with a 'Beowulf in a barn' project, with the LEA County Archivist; a marathon storytelling at **Enfield**; a 'design a library mascot' competition in **Hereford and Worcester**; storytellers from different cultures in **Kent**; events in **Kirklees** over six months and including Storytellers Theatre company enacting *Wind in the willows* or *The water babies*, a treasure hunt and CD-ROM package demonstrations; a storython in a major city shopping centre in **Leeds**; a family reading group launched in **Norfolk**; **Nottinghamshire** Schools library service ran two highly successful competitions; **Redbridge** organized a photography competition and 'library of the future' competition; **Westminster** ran thematic events over four months, including science, media, poetry, and power of the past. All of these emphasize that centrally-focused promotional activities can be very valuable in stimulating action and providing a common framework for planning and promotion. One of the results of the *Library power* campaign was a checklist for parents and carers, to encourage concerned individuals to carry out their own local mini-survey of the library services for children and to take appropriate action if they don't get a good deal.

SPECIALIST LIBRARY SERVICES

Despite the economic climate and political complexities within which libraries are currently operating and many of the constraints previously mentioned, some highly professional library work with children is being undertaken. In addition to the quality management initiatives and strategic policy developments explored above, there are new initiatives, new services, splendid promotions to children, parents, carers, teachers and excellent and widespread storytelling and holiday activities. Some exciting examples of recent innovative specialist services and initiatives are explored below. It is impossible to do much beyond offering a 'taster' of these.

The Centre for the Child

Birmingham Library Services Centre for the Child in the City claims to be a state of the art library and resource centre for children and young people in the 21st century and a focus for the city as a 'child-friendly city'. Offering a unique opportunity to 'invest in the future of Birmingham's children', the **Centre for the Child in the City**:

- is a place in the heart of the city centre which highlights the importance of the child, which welcomes the child and which is for the child;
- brings together a wide range of facilities and resources to meet the diverse needs of children and young people;

- celebrates books and reading for pleasure;
- helps parents support the early reading and writing skills of their children;
- responds to the information needs of parents and carers;
- welcomes and provides for children with disabilities;
- enables children to be confident independent learners;
- provides a gateway to a range of other services for children in the City and their parents and carers.

In addition to the more conventional teenage, fiction and non-fiction areas, the Centre for the Child has a number of more unusual designated areas. These include:

- a **baby and toddler area**, specially designed with families in mind, with a broad range of books and other resources, including board books, feely books, ABC and counting books and simple stories for sharing; with a wide selection of toys and play equipment to support the developmental needs of very young children and provide a fun and child friendly environment; a programme of stimulating and enjoyable activities for children and their carers to encourage a love of books and reading for pleasure.
- **Literacy resources area**, which includes books and information for parents to help them support early literacy, including support for follow-up work for those involved in the Reading Recovery Programmes in schools.
- **Disability resource area**, which offers a range of facilities for children and young people and their parents and carers, giving greater access to library services, books, stories and information, including a wide range of equipment from state of the art computers to hand-held magnifiers, reading machines and induction loop systems, equipment to encourage independent learning, a range of information and storybooks for children with disabilities including tactile books, books in Braille, books in sign language, audio and video facilities.
- **Childcare information bureau**, an initiative which has corporate support from a number of City Council Departments as well as Birmingham Training and Enterprise Council (TEC). It includes a range of information resources covering childcare in its widest sense, a childcare enquiry and advice service with a telephone help line, advice service to employers on services to improve childcare information, networking out to the local communities to improve the level of childcare information.
- **Parent and child** facilities, including toilets, baby changing area and feeding room, with units at able-bodied and wheelchair height.

The Principal Officer, Children, Youth and Education chairs a Children's Services Working Group which brings together key people working with children across the city, covering play, sport, community development, museums and arts, and libraries feature highly in this approach.

Teenage

Bradford Xchange is the teenage library within Bradford's Central Library. Opened in 1985 it was originally planned to cater for the needs of young people using the library as a social meeting place. Xchange members have to be aged 13 to join but membership is free. Members can borrow books and cassettes. In addition to loan facilities there are television, computer and games, board games and popular periodicals, including pop culture magazines. A growing proportion of the music cassettes are bought to appeal to Asian young people. The atmosphere is informal. Xchange does not have specialist staffing but it is seen as important that staff working there have a rapport with young people. They are encouraged to build a good relationship with the teenagers and consult them on matters to do with planning the library and selection of stock.

A number of other authorities have launched new teenage initiatives recently. These include **Humberside, Kensington and Chelsea,** and **Hertfordshire** with their teenage information service.

Mobile libraries

Cynon Valley family bookbus is a specialist children's mobile service which visits targeted areas without branch libraries where there are particularly low levels of literacy and non-availability of books at home among the child population. The last HMI report on Penwaun Junior School referred to the bookbus as a 'valuable asset' in the context of fostering the development of pupils' reading skills and their enjoyment of reading. Plans are in hand to expand this service during 1995/6, particularly as there is no local schools library service.

Birmingham has a designated mobile, *Words on wheels*: the under fives mobile, an innovative promotional vehicle designed primarily to make links with parents and carers of very young children. It has an exhibition collection of the very best books for babies and young children, and a wide range of information for parents and carers. It visits health centres, shopping centres, mother and toddler groups and family fun days, mainly in the inner city.

Early years initiatives

Bookstart was a project initiated by the Book Trust's Children's Book Foundation working in cooperation with the children's team of Birmingham library services, the health visitors of South Birmingham health authority and Birmingham University School of Education. The project was underpinned by the belief in reading's centrality to learning and by the importance of sharing books with very young children. Nurses and doctors, antenatal clinics and health centres have traditionally provided information about nutrition and physical well-being of infants but have paid scant attention to the importance of informing parents about talking and reading to their babies. Bookstart sought to rectify such omissions, by encouraging parents to share books with their babies and to establish the foundations of early literacy and later learning. It aimed to provide resources to support and encourage parents, to begin to empower them to affect their children's developments in listening, speaking and reading. The sharing of books is a source of pleasure and satisfaction to infants and adults and positive early experiences lead to success in literacy and schooling.

The pilot project gave Bookstart packs free of charge to 300 parents/carers of nine-month-old babies in three areas of Birmingham, chosen to produce a cross-section of ethnic and socio-economic groups. The packs contained an introductory letter in English, Urdu or Punjabi, a book, a poetry card, an invitation to join the local library, booklists, a poster, information about local bookshops and book-related organizations. The results of the subsequent survey showed a very positive increase in sharing books with babies, more family reading generally, more babies enrolled in libraries, more book purchase and membership of book clubs (Wade and Moore, 1993).

Sunderland Libraries Bookstart Project was awarded £4,000 in the Holt Jackson Community Initiative Awards in 1995, for the way it is tackling early literacy by getting books to babies. The Bookstart team works with health visitors operating in the City Challenge area of the city where there is high unemployment. The team identifies nine-month-old babies and offers each family a free 'goodie-bag' containing a carefully-chosen book, booklist, action rhyme card and a library joining card. The chair of the judging panel believes that Bookstart 'encourages parents to play a major role in developing their children's skills in listening and speaking and reading.' The judges were impressed by the determination of the mothers to do better for their babies. While some parents have been surprised by how babies respond so positively to books, many have now made their babies members of the local library, and some have also joined themselves (YBT News, 1995).

Other Bookstart projects have been started in **Lichfield** (Staffordshire), **Walsall** and **Croydon**. Croydon, as part of its *Library power* activities organized an under-5s festival in May 1995, called 'snap it up' which had an impressive programme of multicultural storytelling, music, puppets, craft and drama in the borough's 13 children's libraries. Part of the promotion was to find the youngest baby enrolled in a library over a two-week period with the simple aim of getting the message across to parents that 'we welcome babies and that it is never too early to start the book habit' (McElwee, 1995). **Croydon** publish a very attractive leaflet entitled *It's amazing what's inside Croydon libraries for under 5s.*

Hampshire's Early Years Initiative provided the library service with an opportunity to reassess and develop this aspect of its services. Market research was undertaken among users and non-users to assess the levels of service provided and general awareness of early years provision. New links with health centres include provision of attractively boxed collections of books to promote reading and library use. A specially designed Early Years pack with free books, leaflets and information is provided to parents joining the library with their young child (under 18 months old) and to mothers at Health Clinics when their baby has a regular check-up. As well as market research, a policy document has been draw up, staff training undertaken and a number of publicity materials created. Linking with other Council departments is reported to have been of mutual benefit and the support of children's publishers was greatly appreciated.

Other initiatives in brief

Enfield are funding with the Home Office a new project, 'promoting literacy through libraries', which aims to improve literacy skills of children from Bangladeshi, Turkish, African-Caribbean and refugee groups in 3–8 age group.

Essex are extending their services to children with special needs through a subscription to Clearvision material, increased spending on tactile, large print and other special needs materials and improved provision of ethnic minority mother tongue material.

Sheffield have now held six annual children's book awards. The 1994 award had 40 local schools and 2,000 children participating in reading the books and selecting the winners. The final results are published in an attractive annotated list of award winners, with information on the authors themselves.

Lambeth have received funding during 1995/6 for a new project concerned with learning for people with learning difficulties to create opportunities for this group of all ages who enjoy literature through reading, listening and active involvement in events and activities. During autumn 1995, work was undertaken with children under five years old on storytelling.

Suffolk's Learning in Libraries programme, initiated in 1993, has been a major force in shaping the future direction of the library service and influencing other work, for example the planning of new libraries, the selection of library books and materials, and the provision and use of study space. It has been influential in developing new and on-going policy and practice and is seen as particularly important for the focus it has placed on *educational* public library services. It is made up of an extensive and growing range of projects, including: *Homework collections*, with carefully selected stock for homework use in libraries and for short, overnight loans; *CD-ROM in libraries* which are used heavily by children particularly to support homework; *Open Learning Centres* and *Project Collections* to support schools and the most recent, *Archives For All*, which comprises local studies material, together with microfilm and microfiche or original archive source material relating to the immediate local area.

Southwark set up homework collections beginning in 1993, with a grant from the Leisure Committee. Apart from non-fiction stock, the library bought multimedia computers, with a range of CD-ROMs suitable for supporting children's study. A further grant has allowed a multimedia machine to be placed in each of the children's sections in the borough and a new initiative specifically to support GCSE materials (*Library Association record*, 1995).

Planning

The most comprehensive coverage of planning and design of libraries for children, which includes examples of plans for recent new children's libraries, for example Croydon and the Centre for the Child, is Michael Dewe's *Planning and designing libraries for children and young people* (Dewe, 1995). It looks at the space requirements of children and young people, whether as pupils in schools or as users of public libraries in the community. It covers space as a resource, planning, standards and guidelines, policy and practical issues and furniture and equipment. The concentration, and most of the case studies, take a UK perspective but this provides a valuable toolbook for anyone concerned with maximizing available space and ensuring an efficient planning and implementation process. The stance taken by the book is that the librarian *must* be proactive:

> As fads, tastes, staff, library goals, and library priorities change, children's facilities must be restructured to fit these new situations, and it is the children's librarian's responsibility to effect such changes. . . By showing enterprise and preparedness, the schools' or children's librarian has a better chance of getting what is required and avoids being in the position of merely responding to the initiative and plans of others. (Dewe, 1995, p.43)

This total involvement of the librarian is best summed up in Dewe's quote from Arlene Kaspik:

> A building programme involves a great deal of analyzing, estimating, conversing, debating, conferring, writing and rewriting . . . It's exhilerating and exhausting . . . Some of the most critical problems are philosophical ones tackled at the very beginning of a building programme. (Dewe, 1995, p.48)

ORGANIZATIONAL STRUCTURES

Chapter 4 looked at the different structures within which library services might operate at local authority level, either within leisure service directorates, education directorates, libraries and arts or independent library departments (White, 1993). There is no overall pattern and it is fair to say that the remaining uncertainties about local government reorganization, the creation of unitary authorities and how they will affect various authorities are making the picture even more confused.

Just as there are no common structures, the staffing structures with respect to children's library services vary enormously, too. There is no general pattern, even within county, metropolitan or London authorities. An in-depth study of library authorities to assess why in some of them there are virtually no designated posts for children's specialists, while others have managed to retain a healthy number of specialist posts, would be fascinating. Whether it is to do with the historical profile and status of children's library services, local leadership, local politics, central government policies affecting different areas of the country unevenly or a combination of all of these remains unclear. As will be seen in some of the snapshot pictures given below, the picture is confusing. The examples are divided into county authorities and metropolitan and London boroughs. Particular issues concerned with management structures and economic stringency are highlighted. Information was collected during 1995.[1, 2]

County authorities

Following restructuring in 1995, **Leicestershire** has a Service Adviser for Children's Library Services. The county is broken into six areas, each of which has a senior librarian responsible for the coordination of activities in the area. Each senior librarian spends some time on actual service delivery within the area, including library work with children and young people, varying within the range 50–75%. Approximately 20 team librarians in the areas carry some responsibility for work with children and young people, but the time each has to spend on such work varies greatly. Since 1992, there have been posts funded via Section 11 (Home Office) funding: one storyteller post and 5 assistant librarians for work with ethnic minority communities, across adult and children's library services. The Service Adviser has no line management responsibility for the senior librarians who report directly to the area librarians.

Hertfordshire's Schools Library Service and Children's Service is led by an Assistant Head of Service: Communication and Young People's Services, who spends about 20% of time on children's work. The service is managed by six team leaders who lead a team of children's librarians or assistant librarians with responsibility for children's work in each region. These teams vary from three to six people plus the team leader.

In **Nottinghamshire**, the Principal Libraries Officer (Client Services) spends approximately 20% of his remit related to children's public library service, with 40% to the schools library service. This post is part of the library service's senior management team. In addition, the Senior Librarian (Children's Services) post is based at headquarters and is totally children's public library related. Its broad remit is the overall development, promotion and monitoring of children's library services countywide. The other children's posts are all field service based in the county's eight districts, each of which has a full time District Children's Coordinator, with Nottingham, the largest district, having three area Children's Coordinators. Support for children's work is drawn from other staff (at all levels) but these are the only specialist children's public library posts in the system.

Hampshire is divided into eight divisions each managed by a divisional librarian, deputy and divisional specialists for bibliographic, children's and information Services. Children's Services are coordinated on a countywide basis by the Assistant County Librarian, responsible for children's, schools and community services, who liaises with divisional librarians on matters of policy. Within divisions, the coordination of children's services is the responsibility of divisional children's librarians. In addition, there are special responsibility posts for children's work in all major libraries (30 in total). There is a separate School Library Service funded by the Education Department, which is run by the county library service and managed by the Assistant County Librarian. The service remains centrally funded at present which means that every LEA school in the county receives a comprehensive service. Most Grant Maintained schools have also bought into the service. The service is organized in eight divisions with an area schools librarian responsible for 100 schools.

Somerset Schools Library Service (Resources 4 learning) is completely separate from the children's library service. The county is divided into seven areas, three of which have children's services coordinators. The other four have the second-tier area librarians as the official link post for children's services.

Cornwall has two children's services librarians in the public library service. These posts cover four districts, two for each post, 18 libraries and 4 mobile libraries. Both posts also cover large geographical areas. It has been envisaged that a further post could be created to cover the other third of the county but the economic situation has not allowed this to happen. Cornwall has the problem of being a county with large areas of rural population, in providing access to resources that are the entitlement of every child. A major effect of the economic situation has been the reversal of advances in the educational services. Cornwall had reached the point of having ten professional librarians within their 31 secondary schools with the hope of increasing that provision to all schools. With educational cutbacks this number has been reduced to two specific posts and one shared public/school post. This has had a detrimental effect on the support and accessibility of resources available to children at secondary level. It also places a greater onus of support on to the single secondary school librarian who has to provide the only professional input and support to those schools buying into the service. Staffing remains a cause for concern, with one primary librarian trying to support the needs of 267 primary schools. In a county like Cornwall, where for many children their school library is their only accessible resource, this must cause increasing concern.

Staffordshire's Assistant County Librarian: Young People's Services retains responsibility for both children's and schools services in the county and is a member of the Libraries Policy Group, the senior management team. This post is involved in strategic planning and advising on young people's services, and may be consulted by districts on a 'consultancy' basis. The Principal Librarian: Young People's Services has a deputising role, and a more direct responsibility for the schools library service. The public library service is organized on a district basis, with eight districts corresponding to district council areas plus Stoke-on-Trent (which becomes a unitary authority in 1997). Each district has a community librarian who has a leading role in children's services and has line management responsibility to the district librarian.

Dyfed says that 'services to children through public libraries in Dyfed are suffering simply because there are no designated children's librarians to do the work. Schools Library Service staff are heavily committed in schools and spend a great deal of time in schools working closely with teachers and LEA staff.'

Cambridgeshire, while having a forward-thinking schools library service, has had no children's and young people's specialists within the public library service for a number of years and no one with responsibility within senior management. *Investing in children* has inspired a rethink, although what this might mean is as yet unclear.

Powys restructured in 1993 to create three functional departments, as opposed to having an area structure. Education, Schools and Children's Services is one department. This has a Principal Librarian, a Curriculum Support Librarian/Children's Librarian (Public Libraries), two school librarians, two senior library assistants, a clerical assistant and graphics/resources assistant. Powys are relaunching the Schools Library Service to primary schools through two mobiles called The Book Runner, which will aim to 'take reading on the road' to the pupils in this very rural county and aim to reach all children who could not otherwise visit a branch library. The children's librarian looks after the needs of the branches and works closely with the area support and branch librarians.

Essex is divided into three administrative groups, each with a group headquarters in a major library and three roughly equal areas surrounding it. Professional staff are grouped together in teams, based at area headquarters, from which they service the smaller libraries in their area. As well as the general duties linked to the geographical base, each librarian is allocated to a 'matrix', the expected split of time being 40:60 respectively.

Each matrix has a county head of service, based in one of the group headquarters. Librarians in area teams work only on professional matters. Operational work is dealt with by library managers. Areas are headed by an operational manager, which means that line management for professional staff goes through an operational post. Matrix leads therefore, can only manage through advice, consultation and persuasion as their professional staff are line-managed by area teams. Members of the children's services matrix are responsible for the delivery of a high profile public library service for children and young people. They each coordinate the services to about 11 libraries. Children's librarians are required to liaise with a wide-ranging client group. The county library services focus on the needs of the child while recognizing the importance of parents, carers and community agencies in ensuring that children have access to library services. Children's librarians are expected to play an active role in the liaison with relevant community groups and agencies. The children's services matrix currently has 22.5 FTE posts. The schools library service has been a completely separate business unit since 1993, with its own Head of service.

Metropolitan authorities

In **Kirklees**, the children's services are overseen by BOOKS+ (materials, support and advice for schools, libraries, playgroups and everyone involved with children) which provides a schools library service as well as advice, stock revision and activities in public libraries. Only one public library (Huddersfield) has a children's librarian (part-time). BOOKS+ has a manager (principal children's librarian) who is a member of the libraries management team), eight professional staff and one support staff supervisor.

Liverpool's Coordinator for Services to Young People heads the Services to Young People team and has city-wide responsibility, reporting to the Community Libraries Manager. In the team there are five children's librarians and two assistant librarians. Four of the children's librarians plus one assistant are based in the community libraries division with a responsibility for a number of libraries (26 in all) and reports to one of two area managers (who in turn report to the community libraries manager). The other children's librarian plus one assistant, with additional clerical support, are based in the Central Junior Library and report to the Central Library Manager. **Liverpool** libraries, with a bordering authority, **Knowsley**, have recently been awarded DNH/BLR&DD funding for a feasibility study into the establishment of a joint schools library service to operate within the two authorities: a project a number of newer authorities will be looking to with some interest.

The most notable difference in **Bradford's** library service to children is the division between education and public libraries. The education library service is part of a different Council directorate and works entirely independently of the public library. There is one full-time children's librarian, with responsibility for children's services and Xchange, the teenage library. Other members of the young people's liaison group have children's work as only a proportion of their job descriptions.

Stockport has no specialist children's librarians in the public libraries, although the Head of Services to Children does chair a cross hierarchical team of staff (including non-professional staff) who are interested in children's work. This children's services team attempts to take a strategic approach rather than 'fire-fighting' and has the following remit:

- to act as a forum for the exchange of information concerning children's services across the Borough;
- to coordinate borough-wide programmes of children's activities;
- to keep under review borough-wide children's initiatives;
- to act as a 'sounding board' on matters relating to children's library services and make proposals for service development;
- to make recommendations on staff training in the area of children's services, and assist with implementation where appropriate;
- to publicize children's services within and outside the library service.

The team organizes events such as the Summer Fun and Book Month. In the absence of specialist staff, this seems a very positive approach.

London Boroughs

Lambeth has a long record of innovative work with children and young people and has always placed a heavy emphasis on the needs of those most neglected and/or disadvantaged in social, educational, political and economic terms. The library service is organized into three geographical areas, each of which has an area librarian, two senior librarians and a number of team librarians. All librarians are appointed to generic posts but one of the senior librarians and approximately half of the number of team librarians in each area are designated young people's services contacts which means they have extra responsibility for young people's stock and services. A distinction is not drawn between 'professional' and 'non-professional' staff. For many years, Lambeth library service has appointed people without library qualifications to librarians' posts because:

> our experience has shown that there are many people who have the necessary abilities and qualities but have no formal qualifications. We run an extensive training programme which enables all librarians new to the Service to develop the skills and knowledge that we feel are essential to the kind of community librarianship we practise here in Lambeth.

Since restructuring of the library service in July 1994, **Bexley** youth services have become part of the community library services along with the mobile library and services to the housebound under the supervision of the community library services manager. Within this team there is a Senior Children's Librarian with clerical support equivalent to one full time person. This post has responsibility for the coordination of children's work and stock in the 13 branch libraries and for the provision of a limited support service to schools. The branch libraries are divided into three geographical areas and the main library in each area has a full-time professional children's librarian on their establishment. Children's work in the other branches is carried out by the customer services manager with guidance from the senior children's librarian.

Croydon's Head of Children's Services is a senior member of the Libraries Service. Her main role is the management, coordination and development of an effective and efficient library service to children and young people throughout the borough. Of the 13 branch libraries, ten have designated children's librarians and the remaining three have library managers who also have responsibility for children's work in their branch. It is the policy of the borough to appoint librarians to these three posts who have a strong background in children's work as roughly 50% of their time will be spent on work with children. The new central children's library has two-and-a-half children's librarians and one full-time library assistant plus auxiliary assistant support to allow the librarian's work to be 'professional'.

Despite several recent reorganizations, **Islington** still maintains a children's librarian in each branch library, plus a principal librarian with responsibility for services to young people. However, none of these posts spends all of its time on children's work: the children's librarians in the branches also act as deputy branch librarians and children's work is only approximately 40% of the principal librarian's job.

In contrast, **Ealing** has no children's librarians in specific posts. Professional librarians are expected to fulfil several functions within their workplace, including work with children. Ealing does have an innovative childrens' special interest group which was set up, with the back-up of a deputy librarian, about five years ago to counteract the lack of children's librarians. Each library division sends a representative to group meetings which are held approximately every six weeks, when staffing levels at branches permit. The respondent notes that staffing levels for dealing with the public generally are becoming increasingly lower. There is no one on the libraries management team with responsibility for work with children and young people, so there is no one to coordinate any changes and developments.

Brent is unusual in that it does not have a children's library service structure. Brent also no longer has a schools library service or central posts. There is only one designated children's librarian, at the largest branch library in Willesden Green. Responsibility for delivering service rests with each of the six contractor business unit directors, while responsibility for commissioning services rests with the commissioning manager (libraries).

Hammersmith and Fulham has been subject to a declining budget for a number of years with the concomitant reduction in activity in policy development. In July 1995, the authority was beginning the process of reviewing the library service structure and implementing further substantial cuts. The effects of this situation has been to depress the status of a number of service areas including services to children. The library service is qoted as being 'underfunded and overstretched'.

Redbridge has a Senior Children's and Schools Librarian plus a deputy, (although the latter post is 90% schools), and nine branch or mobile children's librarians (i.e. at all full time branches and central library).

The Royal Borough of **Kensington and Chelsea** is a small borough with six service points and one mobile library. There is a Schools Library Service with three staff, which receives funding direct from local schools. The Youth Services Librarian spends 70% of her time coordinating children's work through the public libraries and reporting directly to the head of public services. The other 30% is spent as deputy for the Chelsea area librarian, which includes coordinating all professional activity in the area and managing three senior librarians. There are four children's librarians who with the youth services librarian form the nucleus of the children's team. Professional staff are encouraged to participate in all aspects of library work and in almost every branch all professional staff do some children's enquiry work.

The new unitary authorities

Following local government reorganization, new structures are pending in a number of local authorities. After reorganization in **Derbyshire**, Derby will be a unitary authority separate from the rest of the county. At present, Derbyshire's Schools Library Service is in Derby and this will lead to either a partnership approach or the need for the city to 'buy in' to the county. A tough time is anticipated with 'tenacity' being the keyword!

North Yorkshire becomes a unitary authority in April 1996. Libraries are part of the leisure department in York and part of the education cluster in North Yorkshire. The previous county was split into seven groups, each group led by a group librarian and supported by a special services librarian who covered work with children and young people in the public library (school library services are separate), special needs and the educational role of the library. The latter covered all library users, not just children. There was also a Principal Librarian: Special Services who had an advisory and coordinating role, but no line management responsibility for the special services librarian.

From 1 April 1996, **Avon** is split into four all-purpose authorities in place of one county and six districts. The major problems for the public library service are the loss of various economies of scale, the need to set up new structures and premises, and the difficulty of continuing to fund the services in Bristol, which are of regional importance, out of a much smaller budget. For the schools library service, the big question of LGR is whether it will be possible to continue to serve schools in the four authorities through some sort of joint arrangement. Dividing the existing service into four would not be practical, and would result in much higher costs and charges: a problem other restructured authorities will inevitably face, too. Prior to April 1996, the library service in Avon was part of the community resources department, which included youth and community work, and grants to community organizations.

A similar break-up of the complete authority is happening in **Cleveland** which ceases to exist after 1 April 1996 and be replaced by four new unitary authorities.

General comments on structures

The above snapshots highlight the enormous diversity of structures and in particular the considerable differences in 'professional' posts, full-time, part-time and non-existent in different parts of the country, regardless, it appears, of type of authority, whether county, metropolitan or London borough. Inevitably, one must ask what this means in terms of the quality of service children are getting, depending on where they happen to live, and note the problems in many of the more rural areas, where the only access for children to books and information will be via their school libraries.

A number of respondents bemoan the lack of representation of children's library services on the senior management team. Increasingly in some areas, due to cutbacks and failure to replace specialist posts, the public libraries are looking to the professional staff of the schools library service to provide support with developing children's services. However, this is increasingly difficult as schools library services become more and more specialized in terms of the support they need to provide to teachers. The service is also fundamentally different from public library services to children. It might be helpful to see a wider acknowledgment of the differences and the increased pressures that schools library services are now operating under, while noting one of the key recommendations in *Investing in children* (Department of National Heritage, 1995) to integrate services at a strategic level.

One authority which anticipated one of the main recommendations of *Investing in children* is **North Tyneside** which has developed an integrated teamwork approach to work with children and young people. Until 1992, North Tyneside had parallel arms of the library service delivering quite separately to children via schools and via the public library. There had been informal liaison between these sections but each service was separately funded and resourced. Inevitably there was duplication of effort and resources, and a growing conviction that the needs of children could be met more effectively through an integrated approach. Following a major restructuring of the entire council in late 1992, the children's and young people's (CYP) service came into being in early 1993. Jan Clements, CYP team manager, writing in the *Library Association record*, emphasized that the new service is more cohesive and cost-effective, with a common aim of enhancing learning opportunities, supporting the development of reading and information skills and fostering enjoyment of books. The CYP team of a manager, four librarians and three library assistants work as a closely knit specialist team who share their specialist knowledge and enthusiasm with library colleagues at all levels. They work on a 'patch' approach, based on four geographical regions, with each of the four librarians coordinating service delivery to children and young people within their patch, linking the local libraries with preschool groups, schools and others (Clements, 1995).

One of the dangers inherent in structures where specialist posts are increasingly rare is isolation from fellow specialists, allied to a natural tendency to concentrate on routine and maintenance tasks such as Enquiry desks, stock maintenance and display/promotion, all important tasks, but leaving little scope for outreach or strategic developmental work. In some areas there is a distinct feeling among children's specialists that there is a loss of community presence. In many authorities, such posts will be filled by fairly inexperienced library school leavers, who may have little or no experience of public libraries or children's library work. As one authority says: 'It is the developmental work which provides the opportunities for growth of individual and team experience and effectiveness.'

CONCLUSION

As can be seen above, there are some very dedicated, very committed children's librarians and staff concerned with children's library work and the child, battling to keep a wide range of activities going because they want children to have access to books and the enjoyment and knowledge that wide, voracious reading brings. They believe that all children have the right to reach their full potential and that the library has a part to play in this, as part of the future well-being of society. There are, increasingly, some very good examples of current practice with regard to policy and strategic documents, promotional activities and innovative services.

Notes

1 I would like to thank colleagues in the 65 local authorities who responded to my letter requesting information about their current library service to children and young people, and in particular requesting information about local responses to the Department of National Heritage Report *Investing in children*. Where confidentiality was requested, I have respected this. Other information is taken from the first issue of *ASCEL newsletter* (ASCEL 1995).

2   A full list of library authorities and the names and addresses of the principal children's and education librarians can be found in the *ASCEL directory 1995/6* (Westminster Libraries, Schools Library Service, 62 Shirland Road, London W9 2EH).

REFERENCES

American Library Association (1988), *Information power: guidelines for school library media programs*. Chicago and London, American Library Association and Association for Educational Communications and Technology.

ASCEL (1995), *ASCEL newsletter*. 1, 1995, Christine Hall (ed.) (Westminster Libraries, Schools Library Service, 62 Shirland Road, London W9 2EH).

Clements, J. (1995), 'Ending duplication: children's services', *Library Association record*, **97** (4), April 1995.

The Department of National Heritage (1995), *Investing in children: the future of library services for children and young people*. London, Library and Information Services Council (England) Working Party on Library Services for Children and Young People. London, HMSO.

Dewe, M. (1995), *Planning and designing libraries for children and young people*. London, Library Association Publishing.

Everall, A. (1995), 'The child at the centre', *Library Association record*, **97** (4), April 1995.

Fine, A. (1993), 'Dear Mr Peach. . .', *Books for keeps*, no. 83, November 1993, 23.

Library Association (1991), *Children and young people: Library Association guidelines for public library services*. London, Library Association Publishing.

Library Association (1993), *A charter for public libraries*. London, The Library Association.

Library Association (1995), *Model statement of standards*. London, The Library Association.

Library Association. School Library Information Pack, regularly updated.

Library Association Record (1995), 'Homework pays off . . .', *Library Association record*, **97** (4), April 1995.

Library power (1995), Press release and publicity pack from the Library Association, including a regular newsletter during 1995.

Office of Arts and Libraries (1984), *School libraries: the foundations of the curriculum*. Report of the Library and Information Services Council's Working Party on School Library Services. Library Information Series no. 13. London, HMSO.

McElwee, G. (1995), 'Babies need books: under 5s need libraries', *Under five contact*, June 1995.

School Libraries Group (1995), *School libraries and school library services: key issues and concerns*. Library Association, unpublished, December 1995.

Wade, B. and Moore, M. (1993), *Bookstart in Birmingham: a description and evaluation of an exploratory British project to encourage sharing books with babies*. Book Trust Report no. 2, Book Trust.

Walsh, J. Paton (1993), 'Dear Mr Peach . . .', *Books for keeps*, no. 83, November 1993, 23.

White, J. (1993), *Frogs or chameleons: the public library service and the public librarian: a research report investigating the status of public libraries and the careers of public librarians in England*. London, The Library Association.

YBT News (1995), 'Libraries to the fore in Holt Jackson Awards', *Young book trust news*, Autumn 1995.

10

Education and training

Judith Elkin

As the useful lifespan of knowledge gained in an initial degree or professional course declines, the need for continuing education becomes more urgent. Education and training must become a continuous lifelong process to keep abreast of change. (Watkins, Drury and Preddy, 1993, p.97)

INTRODUCTION

This chapter explores ways in which the specific educational and training needs for specialisms in schools and children's librarianship and literature are catered for within Library and Information Studies (LIS) professional education. It looks at how these specialist needs are balanced against the often conflicting demands for a generic education offering the 'core' skills needed by all information professionals. The chapter concentrates on the current situation, following a study of all UK LIS schools and departments. This study identified specialist modules and electives and opportunities for students to pursue specialist interests within courses, assignments and placements. An attempt is made to see where specialist modules might be provided for practitioners as part of a programme of continuing professional development.

BACKGROUND

Library and information work has changed rapidly in recent years, with the strategic and operational value of good information provision recognized by a wide range of employers, many in new sectors of the market. We live in an age of increasing complexity with regard to the range and quantity of information available. Information handling and information management have become recognized as crucial for survival in an increasing diversity of markets: health; financial; legal information; software development; publishing; multimedia; research; information-broking and information consultancy. In addition, the traditional areas of the academic, public and government library sectors have widened in terms of their definition of service delivery.

Within this context, the role of the professional librarian as handler and manager of information; as trainer of others to use information effectively and efficiently; as evaluator of quality of information and information provision; as carer for user needs, becomes critical. This is a role which will become more central as we head towards the next century, but a role which will be constantly changing. It will need flexible, adaptable individuals who can manage change innovatively, imaginatively and proactively, recognizing new opportunities and grasping new challenges. This will require well-educated professionals, constantly developing through a varied programme of continuing professional and personal development.

Professional LIS education

To accommodate such diversity, professional Library and Information Studies (LIS) education has also diversified against a background of significant economic, political and technological change. The recent changes in higher education and the effect these have had on first professional education, have been well rehearsed, both in this work and elsewhere. (Wood and Elkin, 1993; Elkin, 1995) However, it is worth looking at the current state of higher education in the UK before assessing how this affects professional education and, more specifically, how specialist needs are catered for.

Higher education

Initial professional LIS education now takes place entirely within the university sector, with Information and Library Studies courses offered at 17 universities in the UK. Each university has powers to develop its own courses and award its own degrees and postgraduate awards. Some institutions no longer have a separate school or department of LIS. 'Work groups' or 'sections' concerned with LIS continue within a broader grouping of disciplines, often in computing or business environments. These have an enormous variety of names, none actually called 'Library School' although this remains a useful generic title. They will be referred to as LIS departments regardless of their specific titles.

Core Studies

- The LIS departments aim to provide generic courses which emphasize the principles, theories and skills which are common to all occupational sub-groups, and which make students aware of the range of environments in which libraries and information services can be found.
- The basic core elements are taught in most courses: information retrieval, information sources and services, management, communication and research methodology and basic information-handling skills.
- All students need to be computer-literate, able to cope with changing technologies and the demands of the market place beyond 1995. A study commissioned in 1993 for the Higher Education Funding Council's Libraries' Review Group IT sub-committee demonstrated how UK LIS schools are delivering the requisite IT skills (Wilson, 1993, p.303).

- Electronic information and networks are seen as basic areas of study in all courses.
- Potential employers expect students to have skills in IT, in analysis, synthesis and repackaging, as well as high quality management and personal transferable skills, allied to the ability to communicate effectively through a range of media.

Student profiles

- The profile of UK LIS schools and departments has changed, with greater emphasis on postgraduate and higher degree work, with full-time undergraduate numbers remaining fairly static.
- There are more research students and a greater emphasis on academic staff being involved in research and publications.
- There are more mature, non-standard access and part-time students, all bringing different perspectives to the learning process.

Patterns of delivery

- Changes in teaching and learning, with a much greater emphasis on student-centred study, credit accumulation and modular degrees, and more emphasis on continuous assessment, have led to a much more flexible approach to education with considerably more choice for the individual student.
- With pressure on universities to recruit more students and with no extra teaching staff, group sizes have inevitably increased. Viable teaching groups have to be maintained.
- A number of universities offer modular degrees which encourage students to select modules from any course within either a distinct area or faculty or from across the university. There has sometimes been criticism of the lack of cohesion of such programmes, particularly from a professional standpoint, but the tendency to offer students flexibility and choice remains a priority in many universities.

Continuing professional development

- First professional courses increasingly aim to provide a grounding which needs to be built upon later, through continuing professional education and development.
- Modular courses allow relatively easy access and updating opportunities for practitioners.
- Currently, LIS departments appear unable, for a variety of reasons, to offer many opportunities for short courses, outside the award-bearing programmes.

The above framework is the one in which all departments of LIS in the UK now largely operate. Their primary aim is to produce newly qualified professionals who can move confidently into their first post. With the diversification of the LIS profession, students have an ever-broadening range of job and career opportunities, with an increasing proportion outside the 'traditional' LIS markets. There are also growing opportunities for students to use information skills in an emerging range of new occupations. The departments cannot realistically prepare first professional students for any specific job or even for a lifetime in an unchanging profession.

LIS CURRICULUM: CORE OR SPECIALIST?

The majority of courses have a relatively similar core of studies which all students will follow. The 'core' studies are taken to be information retrieval and storage; management/human resource management/information management; information society; information resources and services; research methods; communication methods; Information Technology (IT) and electronic networks. The terminology may differ from department to department. The weighting given to various core studies and the actual content may vary. There will be differences between undergraduate and postgraduate programmes. But it is essentially this common core which is deemed to be central to the initial education of all information professionals and which is constantly revised and updated in line with technological and professional developments.

What flexibility and choice students have beyond this core will vary from course to course. A variety of specialized options and electives can be found, e.g. in business information, health information, schools librarianship, work with young people, public librarianship, academic librarianship, though the number and range of these has changed over the years, in response to both the changes in higher education highlighted above and the change in the employment market:

> As 'core' studies increased, the range of specialisms decreased. Cutbacks in higher education exacerbated this: optional courses were either discontinued or only ran if sufficiently in demand from students. This erosion of specialisms concerns members of the profession who feel that their particular area of interest is no longer being taught. (Wood and Elkin, 1993, pp.29–30)

As Professor John Feather has said:

> We are . . . seeking to produce well-educated generalists with a broad understanding of librarianship and associated activities. In recent years this has led us to emphasise skills of management, and also to teach students the understanding and use of the technology which all librarians need in their work . . . The alternative to the loss of specialisms is to sacrifice the knowledge and skills which lie at the core of professional practice. (Feather, 1992, p.449)

One of the major barriers to any department offering a taught specialist module is the need to guarantee attracting a minimum of 10–15 students (and rising). This is increasingly difficult to guarantee and reinforces the need for interested students to take every opportunity to study within their chosen field, wherever individual assignments allow. As Professor Joan Day states: 'It is uneconomical and impractical for everyone to be offering the range of specialisms . . . Students who do have a specialist interest, e.g. music, have ample opportunity to apply this within the generic course' (Day, 1994).

CHILDREN AND SCHOOLS

We shall now turn more specifically to the opportunities to study topics related to children and schools librarianship and literature. A survey was carried out by the Youth Libraries Group Committee of the Library Association in 1993 to compare the current children's specialisms on offer from LIS departments with five years previously. Their findings showed little change over the five-year period but did suggest that 'the different universities were dividing into two camps – those that are gearing themselves to the needs of special libraries and information science and those that continue to teach public librarianship. The teaching of children's librarianship and literature is part of this wider debate' (Saunders, 1993).

This is a somewhat simplistic analysis but the rest of the report does reinforce this author's finding that modularization of courses and flexibility of delivery has enabled a better coverage of children's librarianship and literature, depending on the encouragement and commitment of teaching staff. It concluded:

> It seems that there are good opportunities to study children's librarianship and litera-
> ture if a student arrives at college motivated to pursue this course of study . . . the cru-
> cial factor for all students must be the chance to find employment . . . and, as the
> opportunities for the newly qualified children's librarian decline, so this course of
> study looks less attractive. (Saunders 1993, pp.17–18)

The rest of this chapter refers to the responses obtained from UK LIS depart-
ments as part of two studies carried out by the author: one in 1993 for the Library and Information Services Council (England) (LISC (E)) to discover what opportunities existed in LIS schools to specialize in library work with children and young people (Elkin, 1993a; 1993b); the other a study of all UK LIS schools con-
ducted in 1994 to extend this survey to other specialist areas (Elkin, 1996). The original survey requested information on: existing or planned modules/courses which encompass some aspect of library work with or for children through public or school libraries; opportunities for students to use a particular interest in children's/schools librarianship to focus within a particular piece of course assessed or project work; research, continuing education and placement opportunities.[1]

The responses (13) to the original survey, largely supported in the second survey, made interesting reading and provided a much less gloomy picture than might have been expected, following the decline in *taught* specialisms (Elkin, 1994). In particular they highlighted a continued and substantial interest among many of the departments in children's and schools librarianship and literature, both in terms of staff expertise and student interest. Additionally, they emphasized the – largely still untapped – opportunities which exist for LIS schools to build on existing expertise and enthusiasms and work much more closely with practitioners and specialist groups, to enhance continuing professional development and research within the children's/schools library sector. It should be noted, as a word of caution, that courses in universities are reviewed and revised regularly (the norm being a five-year cycle). This leads, inevitably, to changes in course structures and content to meet changing market needs and student expectations and to keep at the leading edge of developments, particularly with relationship to technology and networked information.

Taught specialisms

The majority of taught modules are at undergraduate level. Both Manchester and UCE, Birmingham have pathways through the degrees, allowing a study of children's/schools librarianship. Modules at UCE include: *The child in society, Children's literature, Libraries in an academic environment*; at Manchester: *Children's literature; Management of libraries for children and young people*; *Post compulsory education*. Aberystwyth offer a number of modules: *School libraries and learning resources; Focus on the child: literature and libraries; After Alice: children's literature* in full-time and distance learning mode.

Other examples of undergraduate taught modules are offered by several other departments. These are: Loughborough with *Childhood and children's literature*; Robert Gordon's with *Management of children's and popular reading*; *Published media (children and young people), Published media (educational)*; North London with *Children, learning and the media*; Leeds with *Information services for young people; Libraries in education*; Newcastle with *Current trends in children's literature*; *Management of school libraries/resource centres*; Brighton with *Librarianship and information centre management*; Liverpool with *Library services to young people*.

Fewer taught options are available in the intensive postgraduate/courses, but four schools do offer some: *The management of learning resources; Literature and libraries for young people* at Aberystwyth; *Children's literature* at Loughborough; *Children's literature; Management of education resource centres* at Newcastle; *Children's libraries and literature; Schools librarianship* at UCE in Birmingham.

All of the above have assessment schemes related to the module and a range of innovative assignments are set. The reading diary and learning review used at UCE, Birmingham has been outlined recently (Denham, 1994).

Focused projects

All LIS departments allow students to develop or enhance specialisms through the flexible approach to course work in core modules and electives/ optional modules: student-centred assignments allow considerable flexibility for students to choose topics to study in depth within the framework of the specific module or course. This means that students may choose schools or children's libraries or literature as a focus for more general assessed course work or for their major dissertation.

Dissertations

The majority of LIS undergraduate courses contain a substantial dissertation element, varying between 10–18,000 words. Choice of topic is broad and may be work-based, placement-based or free-standing. Provided the topic meets the requirements and rigour of the individual course and subject tutor, then students have considerable freedom to explore areas of particular personal interest.

In practice, this is a popular opportunity. For example, at Newcastle, 18 out of 58 undergraduate projects completed in June 1993 were on topics relating to children. Similarly, at Aberystwyth, 17 of their first qualification masters and 6 undergraduate dissertations in 1992/93 were in the field of young people's librarianship and literature. At UCE, all second year undergraduate students studying the Child in society module (36 in 1995; 35 in 1994) carried out a small-scale observation of children's reading in six local primary schools and analysed their findings for their assignment.

A number of departments report that dissertations are often of such a high quality and potential value to the community that they are edited within the department and offered for publication.

Research opportunities

Masters and postgraduate diploma students similarly have considerable freedom in their choice of topics for dissertations, with a number of courses insisting on a research proposal as part of the assessment, perhaps following a research methodology course (Robert Gordon's; UCE). The majority of masters dissertations are between 15,000 and 20,000 words.

Again student interest often leads them to select topics for dissertations or research areas for MPhil and PhD in this area. Examples are: Morality and personal responsibility in adolescent children's literature; Sexism in children's picture books; School library media centres in Kuwait; Performance criteria for school libraries; Sex education information in the national curriculum; The impact of recent curriculum developments on libraries in independent schools in Scotland; Information skills in Scottish education: Bridging the gap between school and higher education.

Each year at Loughborough, two or three good masters students undertake research in the field (currently three on children's literature and school librarianship) and doctoral students do so regularly.

Even the departments which profess not to offer any expertise or specialism in this area will have a number of students following masters or MPhil dissertations related to children and young people, because of the nature of the clientele they attract.

Contextualizing courses

A number of LIS schools have contextualizing and awareness-raising courses, particularly at undergraduate level, looking at the role of libraries and information in society. These allow all students, as part of their core studies, to understand the role of many different types of library and information units. Many of these inevitably contain some consideration of the role of the child in society and the value of libraries and information in the development of the child. A few examples may illustrate this point:

- Brighton's undergraduate Library Typology module takes the form of a sequence of presentations from professionals working in a variety of library environments, e.g. special needs, picture, music, school, academic, public, archive, film, map, newspaper, commercial libraries.
- Manchester's second year part-time postgraduate students undertake a series of case studies examining technical and other changes affecting libraries, such as information technologies, income generation, contracting out, new library and information needs: cases are chosen to reflect current professional concerns and frequently relate to events and changes taking place in the student's own organization. This is a fairly common approach elsewhere, too, particularly in part-time undergraduate and postgraduate education, where the majority of students are in full-time employment and linking assignments to the work place is appropriate for the student and the employer and allows for pursuit of specialist interests.
- Manchester's full and part-time postgraduate/masters in Information and Library Studies allows a study of the information needs of a user community, where students select one community from a small range, usually academic, public, young people.
- Sheffield's Libraries Information and Society II module allows masters students to choose to study either an academic, public or special libraries pathway.
- UCE's current undergraduate course allows students to select modules from four pathways: Public libraries; Libraries in education; Business information; Information management. All pathways have foundation

courses giving a broad introduction to the sector. The undergraduate course at Manchester similarly allows students to follow one of four pathways: Public libraries; Information management; Children and young people's librarianship; Business world.

Placement opportunities

Placements, short or long term, taken before or during courses, also offer students the opportunity to specialize. Placements in the area of school and children's libraries tend to be popular, if available, in most areas, although this varies from department to department, depending on geographical location, timing, length and whether or not the placements are paid or unpaid. Only UCE, Birmingham has a compulsory long (full-time nine-month) paid placement in their undergraduate programme, although Loughborough has an optional 12-month placement; students successfully completing the latter are awarded a Diploma in Professional Studies, in addition to their BA (Hons) degree. UCE, though, has had virtually no placements in public libraries, largely due to the current political and financial situation in the public sector. However, school library placements have been forthcoming, with eight placements in school libraries in 1992 (four of which have led to the establishment of permanent full-time posts) and a further eight placements in 1993 and 1994, two in 1995 and six in 1996.

Other departments with shorter unpaid placements often need to rely heavily on local employers. Inevitably the range of opportunities depends on the profile of local employment. A research study is underway at UCE to study the value of short and long placements. (Chivers, 1994, 1995a, 1995b). Loughborough, with 6-week vacation placements finds that this is easier in children's libraries than school libraries. Aberystwyth, with 3-week placements for first qualification masters and 2 periods of 4 weeks for undergraduates, has no serious problems in finding fieldwork placments in schools or public libraries, but feels that placements are getting tighter.

Liverpool finds that the demand for placements has been in areas where there is a clear career structure (public libraries, FE/HE, civil service, business and industry) with no interest in school library placements, whereas at North London and Newcastle, school library and children's library placements are very popular.

Research opportunities

There is still considerable individual research being undertaken by academic staff, and a common feeling among respondents that there is potential for much more research, particularly in those schools which have been committed to this area for many years. There is a wealth of research expertise built up over many years waiting to be tapped. The area noted as being particularly poorly served in research terms is children's literature/librarianship.

Aberystwyth has had external funding for research into the provision and use of AV material for young people in public libraries; development of a Welsh language database and thesaurus for NERIS; and bibliography of twentieth century Welsh language books for children, but also notes that funding is very difficult to obtain.

Other respondents bemoan the lack of funding for research, for academic staff, practitioners interested in pursuing a research topic and full-time research students.

Continuing professional development

As the useful lifespan of knowledge gained in an initial degree or professional course declines, the need for continuing education becomes more urgent. Education and training must become a continuous lifelong process to keep abreast of change. In addition to their vocational skills, professionals need managerial skills to survive an increasingly commercial environment, and cross-functional skills to enable them to negotiate and communicate with other professionals. (Watkins, Drury and Preddy, 1993, p.97)

Professionals are expected to have the expertise appropriate to their professional roles. In a rapidly changing environment, professional knowledge is becoming increasingly complex and specialized so that individuals need constant updating to keep in touch with their area of specialization . . . At the same time they have to develop a whole range of managerial skills which include: business skills, to manage resources effectively and to understand the basic principles of marketing, information technology and finance; interpersonal skills to work effectively in groups and to liaise with a wide range of clients; applied intellectual skills to make appropriate decisions in a fast changing environment; self-management and entrepreneurial skills to achieve results through individual initiative. (Watkins, Drury and Preddy, 1993, p.59)

The recent Follett report on academic libraries in the UK has highlighted the need for ongoing training and development, particularly with respect to technological developments:

Whatever the proportion of the libraries' spending on staff, their effectiveness is central to the functions of a successful library . . . if the full potential of the investment [in IT] . . . is to be realized, it must be accompanied by investment in awareness and training . . . failure to provide staff with adequate training and deploy them effectively represents one of the single most important constraints on change and development in library and information provision, and can seriously undermine its effectiveness. (Follett, 1993, p.68)

The statement above can be broadened away from the purely IT context to cover many aspects of librarianship and information work. It highlights the need for professionals in all sectors to keep abreast of political, economic and social change as well as technological, as a major part of their own professional and personal development. At the same time it emphasizes the need for institutions to maximize the value of staff, through training and awareness, to achieve best value for money.

The report for the Department of National Heritage, *Investing in children: the future of library services for children and young people*, highlights the need for in-service training and particularly emphasizes:

> The major under-developed area in which LIS schools could usefully join with practitioners is that of continuing professional development. Whilst some of the courses run by specialist professional groups are well-received, there is overall a lack of structure and consistent quality that belies the very strong professional commitment we have observed among children's and education librarians. A partnership between practitioners and LIS schools with interest and experience in this sector could assess needs and examine mechanisms for promoting a more structured, high quality continuing professional development programme targeted at those already working with, or interested in working with, children and young people. (Department of National Heritage, 1995, p.23)

> Every library authority should have a strategy for specialist training of staff engaged in work with children and young people. (Department of National Heritage, 1995, p.29)

The report also draws attention to the needs of school libraries, implicitly calling for further and adequate training of librarians and adding:

> . . . the need for teachers to receive some basic training in library and information skills if they are to pass these to their pupils, and so encourage and enable them to make full use of the services available through school and public libraries . . . Evidence suggests that the whole issue of effective provision, use and management of learning resources is largely ignored at the initial teacher-training stage, as are information handling skills (Department of National Heritage, 1995, p.viii).

The Library Association has been increasingly concerned through the Continuing Professional Development (CPD) framework to help members see the importance of on-going development and is seeking to encourage more members to structure their development and also to seek chartership and fellowship (Library Association, 1994). Short courses, conferences, professional briefings and seminars are organized through the LA Continuing Education Department and by individual Library Association branches and groups. Similarly, the Institute of Information Scientists organize regular conferences, meetings and seminars. These are reinforced by commercial organizations such as TFPL (Task Force Pro Libra), Aslib (Association for Information Management), etc.

There is, however, a growing concern that, within the framework of a better skilled workforce, one-off, one-day, stand-alone courses may be seen as of only limited value; they may be useful for upgrading and revising specific skills, but insufficient for the high quality professional development which is increasingly required and evidenced by recent reports (Follett, DNH (LISC(E)), DNH Review).

In the past, many of the LIS departments offered short course programmes but financial constraints have led to their no longer being viewed as cost-effective, particularly in areas where there is only a limited local market. UCE, Birmingham has run short courses on IT for schools, such as introducing CD-ROMS and has offered within the last year in-service courses on topics such as children's literature, popular fiction, school library management, reference sources, business information.

But, in reality the present priorities in LIS departments are to deliver award-bearing courses, at undergraduate, postgraduate and research levels and to carry out research and publish. Although this may appear not to support continuing professional development, the very nature of modular courses increasingly opens up opportunities for individuals to study modules from taught courses as part of their continuing professional development. What is being offered in existing taught course programmes, because of its currency and fitness for the market, is clearly appropriate for individuals wishing to enhance existing qualifications, upgrade specific skills, rethink in the light of current research or to change career direction.

Newcastle emphasizes this opportunity and reports that IT based modules, including online services, have proved particularly popular. It adds that taught modules or units also form the basis for workshops and short courses or tailored training packages: this has proved particularly successful in the records management area. North London states that all modules are open to anyone with an interest in the subject and finds that many practitioners use these as updating mechanisms or as part of formal CPD programmes. UCE, Birmingham has begun to market taught modules for updating and recent research carried out for PICKUP has demonstrated a considerable demand for these (Denham, 1995). Popular modules to date have been *Children's literature*, *Popular fiction* and *Information networks*. Brighton notes that it is about to embark on consideration of delivery mechanisms and content of its part-time MA: Information studies, with the particular intention of addressing its CPD market. Robert Gordon's reports little local demand for CPD but states that all modules are open to day release students for updating.

Leeds states that all existing modules are available to practitioners as associate students. Although this has not been widely publicized, it has found that the online module has been successful. Its revised MA librarianship, aimed at librarians in middle management posts, is currently being relaunched, with an investigation of the local demand for post-professional education. Similarly at Liverpool, associate students may register for individual modules as part of a CPD programme, leading to a certificate of professional development.

The increasing concentration in all departments on a research base and research culture has widened research opportunities, part-time or full-time, at MA, MSc, MPhil and PhD levels. For many individuals, research degrees, perhaps studied part-time, are seen as an ideal way of enhancing professional and personal development while achieving a higher degree. Sheffield offers CPD largely through MA in library and information management which provides an opportunity for those who already have a qualification and are experienced in LIS work to study for a higher degree through coursework and dissertation. UCE, Birmingham offers a similar opportunity through its MA/MSc information and library studies research entry route. This allows LIS postgraduate diploma and degree holders, associates and fellows of the Library Association and professionals with considerable professional experience to study for masters through dissertation only, following production of a professional portfolio.

Increasingly, modular courses and credit accumulation allow much more flexible access to continuing professional development, either for free-standing modules or leading to a higher degree, for example at UNL through the structure of the undergraduate degree, which is totally modular and UNN where all full-time and part-time courses have an access route which enables them to be offered as continuing education units.

Aberystwyth has attracted funding to embark on initiatives to provide quality training for librarians and others in the field of young people's and school's librarianship. The programme has included on-site courses and workshops, four short courses on IT in school libraries, and information skills teaching during 1992/93. Funding has now dried up and continuation will be difficult. In addition, it offers a module on Schools and young people's librarianship, to those pursuing a masters by distance learning. Twenty-two students have opted for this during the last three years.

CONCLUSION

There is little prospect that the general pattern at first professional level will change significantly, with respect to specialist options. Evidence above suggests that, although there are now *few* specialist modules on offer, there are some and the opportunity for students at undergraduate, postgraduate, masters and doctorate level to undertake projects and research in some aspects of children's/schools librarianship or children's literature is considerable and expanding. However, the still largely untapped and under-exploited areas, in terms of collaboration, are probably through opportunities for research and continuing education.

Too much on-going professional development within the area of work with children and young people has been piecemeal, unstructured and not always of the best quality. Subsequently, the picture presented to the profession and to the outside world, has often been low grade and unprofessional. This belies one of the most professionally committed groups. A partnership between LIS schools and practitioners is required to assess research needs within the sector and look at mechanisms for promoting a more structured, high quality professional continuing education programme targeted at those already working with or interested in working with children and young people.

Full list of names of LIS departments/schools in the UK

Aberystwyth: Department of Information and Library Studies, University of Wales, Aberystwyth

Brighton: Department of Library and Information Studies, University of Brighton

City: Department of Information Science, City University, London

Leeds: School of Information and Management, Leeds Metropolitan University

Liverpool: Information Management, Liverpool Business School, Liverpool John Moores University

Loughborough: Department of Information and Library Studies, Loughborough University of Technology

Manchester: Department of Library and Information Studies, Manchester Metropolitan University

Newcastle upon Tyne: Department of Information and Library Management, University of Northumbria at Newcastle

North London: School of Information and Communication Studies, University of North London

Queen Margaret College: Department of Communication and Information Studies, Queen Margaret College, Edinburgh

Queen's University: Information Management Division, Queen's University, Belfast

Robert Gordon: School of Information and Media, The Robert Gordon University, Aberdeen

Sheffield: Department of Information Studies, University of Sheffield

Strathclyde: Department of Information Science, University of Strathclyde

TVU: Centre for Information Management, Thames Valley University, London

UCE, Birmingham: School of Information Studies, University of Central England, Birmingham

UCL: School of Library, Archive and Information Studies, University College, London

(BAILER, 1995/6)

Notes

1 I would like to thank all colleagues in the departments and schools of librarianship and information studies for their invaluable help in trying to make sense of the range of core and specialist modules and electives currently on offer.

REFERENCES

BAILER (1995/6), *Directory of courses in library and information studies in the U.K. 1995/1996*, British Association for Information and Library Education and Research, Department of Information Science, City University, Northampton Square, London ECIV OHB.

Chivers, B. (1994), *The value of LIS school work placements: a report of a placement coordinators workshop*. London, British Library Research and Development Department, 1994.

Chivers, B. (1995a), *The value of LIS school work placements: final report*. London, British Library Research and Development Department. BLR&DD Report no. 6222.

Chivers, B. (1995b), *Work placement on library and information studies first degrees in UK universities: suggestions for good practice*. London, British Library Board. Research dissemination guidelines. BLR&DD Report no. 6222.

Day, J. (1994), Communication from Professor Joan Day, Head of the Department of Information and Library Management, University of Northumbria at Newcastle.

Denham, D. (1995), *Information handling skills market research: a feasibility study of the marketing of masters modules from the Faculty of Computing and Information Studies. Enterprise Unit, University of Central England*. Internal document, May 1995.

Denham, D. (1994), 'Children's literature: a reflective approach to learning', *International review of children's literature and librarianship*, 9 (2), 1994, 88–103.

Department of National Heritage (1995), *Investing in children: the future of library services for children and young people*. Library and Information Services Council (England) Working Party on Library Services for Children and Young People. Library Information Series No. 22. The Department of National Heritage, HMSO, 1995, 23–5.

Elkin, J. C. (1993a), *Library services to children: opening the national debate*, paper presented at LA seminar, Hadley Wood, 1993.

Elkin, J. C. (1993b), *Education and training in library and information work with children and young people*, commissioned report on behalf of BAILER Heads of Departments and Schools to LISC Working Party on Library Services for Children and Young People, September 1993.

Elkin, J. C. (1994), 'Children's modules', *Library Association record*, 96 (1), January 1994, 33.

Elkin, J. C. (1995), 'The role of LIS schools and departments in continuing professional development', *Librarian career development*, 2 (4), 1994, 19–24.

Elkin, J. C. 'Specialist Provision in LIS education', chapter in *LIS education in the UK*. Mansell, 1996, in press.

Feather, J. (1992), 'Schools are aiming for well-educated generalists', letter in the *Library Association record*, **94** (7), July 1992.

Follett (1993) *Joint Funding Councils' Libraries Review Group: report for HEFCE, SHEFC, HEFCW and Deni*. HEFCE, Northavon House, Coldharbour Lane, Bristol, BS 16 1QD.

Saunders, L. (1993), 'Youth Library Group Library School Survey 1993', *Youth library review*, **17**, Spring 1994, 17–18.

UCE (1994), Survey by the School of Information Studies, UCE, Birmingham to elicit feedback about proposed undergraduate course developments from practitioners across various information and library sectors. Unpublished.

Watkins, J., Drury, L. and Preddy, D. (1993), *From evolution to revolution: the pressures on professional life in the 1990s*. Bristol, University of Bristol.

Wilson, T. D. (1993), 'Information technology in the curriculum: a review of the Departments of Information Studies and Librarianship, in *Libraries and IT: working papers of the Information Technology Sub-committee of the HEFCs' Libraries Review*. Bath, UKOLN.

Wood, K. (1992), Reply to letter from R. Turbet. *Library Association record*, **94** (6), June 1992, 376.

Wood, K. and Elkin, J. C. (1993), 'They are the very module . . .', *Library Association record*, **95** (1), January 1993, 29–30.

11

Finale

It is evident from previous chapters that children's librarianship is undergoing significant change. What the future holds is uncertain. In the interests of the child, the future has to involve synergy of libraries, literacy and learning. This chapter draws together the changes and speculates on what the future holds.

Public Libraries

A study of public library services in the UK during the 1990s shows that they are:

- reeling under the effect of national government policies which are cutting back the power of local government. The result has been huge cuts in expenditure on stock, services and staff, endless internal restructuring to manage change and an inward focus on fighting, or preparing for, local government reorganization;
- anticipating local government reorganization which in many areas of the country will result in smaller unitary authorities and may have a crucial effect on the ability of individual authorities to provide a 'full and comprehensive' service and provide the networks required for cooperation;
- facing an increasing demand for services across the board and for specialist services, particularly for an ageing population, while being forced to reduce opening hours in libraries: in the last ten years, the number of libraries open for 60 hours or more per week has dropped from 119 in 1980 to 46 in 1995;
- struggling with inadequate funding for school libraries alongside increased demands for resources to support the National Curriculum;
- coping with Local Management of Schools which has thrown school library services into crisis and led to the total demise of some;
- beginning to recognize that electronic and optical media and networked communication are leading to an information revolution that will have profound results on future developments and the changing information needs of the 21st century, but with budgets inadequate to meet the infrastructure and hardware needs and a workforce poorly prepared and largely untrained;
- having to report nationally on performance measures developed by the Audit Commission;
- meeting the needs of the Children Act 1989 which requires local authorities to make provision for the social, cultural and recreational activities of

children and young people and ensure that children, parents and their carers have access to information.

In 1995 library supporters were encouraged by the fact that the Department of National Heritage seemed to be focusing on libraries, with four major reports, including the first review of the public library system for 50 years. But they are now concerned that these will simply gather dust, and that the chance to put libraries on a healthier footing will not be grasped: 'It is seen as deeply ironical that the public library review takes such a positive, forward looking approach while the government presides over a situation where library provision is very patchy, and many authorities are having to cut opening hours, cut staff, and even shut libraries' (Library Association, 1995).

Children's libraries

A study more specifically of library services to children in the UK during the 1990s shows:

- huge variation in standards from local authority to local authority, some with no obvious focus on library work with children, other than through the schools library service;
- enormous implications for library provision, children's and teachers' needs and the whole children's book world, following changes brought about by the Education Reform Act of 1988;
- the demands of the original National Curriculum and the more recent revisions to the National Curriculum, following the Dearing Review, have had considerable effects on publishing, bookselling and library supply;
- considerable growth in parental and government concern for standards of reading and ensuing pressure on public libraries to provide support materials –
- BUT not matched by general recognition that libraries are part of that debate or acknowledgment that a broad range of reading materials and access to libraries are of critical importance for children, from their earliest years;
- little awareness of the role of children's librarians as having expertise in the field of early literacy and learning, information skills development, information management;
- little research which demonstrates the value of libraries in the child's development;
- a decline in children's professional posts, allied to a lack of recognition of children's librarianship as requiring high level professional ability and knowledge;

- a demise in the *role* of children's specialists, increasingly replaced by generalists, leading to:
- a decline in professional knowledge of children's books, and subsequent reduction in libraries of advise and help to children in their choice of reading materials and to parents and carers about the value of books;
- a decline in the study of children's, schools, public librarianship in the Library Schools;
- little structured training or continuing professional development at anything other than very basic levels;
- little attempt to anticipate the information revolution in terms of changing attitudes, awareness and training; it is unclear how well the nation's children (and their carers, parents, teachers) are being prepared for this revolution: the prospect of an increase in the information rich/information poor split is potentially destructive;
- increased emphasis on funding for technology in schools, leading to improved access to information via the latest technology in schools but not generally matched by increased funding or access through public libraries, exacerbates the former point;
- increased fragmentation of local authorities, following the local government review of the counties, allied to the lack of statutory obligations for library services to children, leads to increasing disparity of services and to the role of the specialist children's librarian (if they still exist) being under increasing scrutiny, particularly in the new, smaller authorities;
- the demise of inner city partnership funding and the redistribution of central government money away from the inner cities has a disproportionate effect on library services to children: the proportion of the population who are under 16 is generally higher in the inner city areas;
- the quality of services to children is not recognized in any league tables drawn up as a result of the Audit Commission's performance measures: measures relating specifically to children's services are excluded.

School libraries

All of the above impact on school libraries, too. While school libraries appear to be undergoing a positive reappraisal in the light of recent curricular development, e.g. National Curriculum, GNVQ's etc, and a growing feeling that the National Curriculum is undeliverable without good school library resource centres, there is a lack of reliable data to confirm this. A study of school libraries shows that:

- the role of the librarian in the school as an education professional is not widely recognized within the education world (from schools to the DFEE);

- the librarian's distinct curricular role as coordinator of both resource requirements and of the development of information skills is underestimated;
- the role of the library as an agent of curriculum delivery is still far from understood in many schools and LEAs;
- while the overall importance of National Targets for Education and Training (NETTs) as part of the government's overall educational policy is recognized by OFSTED, the role of the school library and librarian is insufficiently recognized in supporting young people seeking accreditation;
- the quality or existence of library provision in schools is largely hit and miss;
- new schools are still being planned and built without libraries.

Schools library services

A study of schools library services, in addition, shows:

- lack of statutory basis, outside Northern Ireland;
- lack of commonly accepted definition of what a schools library service is;
- lack of awareness among policy makers, at national and local level, of the existence of school library services;
- damaging effect on many schools library services of the delegation of budgets to schools;
- school library services will be further affected by local government reorganization and the effect of both disaggregation into newly formed authorities and the reduced size of constituencies with the subsequent need to divide assets between the newly created authorities. Whether schools library services are wholly or partially delegated or already successfully adapted to delegation, the result is likely to produce considerable uncertainty;
- new chief officers need to be persuaded early on to incorporate the schools library services into their authority's organizational plan.

Investing in children (Department of National Heritage, 1995) highlighted the vital role of libraries in the development of the child and the future economic health of the nation. It made some strong and sensible recommendations about children's libraries, and inevitably, the link with school libraries and school library services. It has been welcomed in the specialist professional arena. However, it has barely touched the wider professional or educational scene or political thinking and has had little impact in publishing or bookselling circles.

Happily, though, one of the recommendations of *Investing in children* has already been implemented, with the launch of ASCEL (The Association of Senior Children's and Education Librarians) in October 1995. ASCEL brings together three formerly disparate groups of senior librarians who have managerial responsibility for providing library services to children and young people through public and education libraries in England and Wales. It aims to be a 'proactive forum to stimulate developments and respond to initiatives so that quality services for children and young people . . . are offered to all.' It is hoped that many of the concerns expressed above, as well as the recommendations from *Investing in children* will be addressed as a matter of some urgency by this now united body, essential at a time when library services of all kinds are under threat.

Professional education

All of the above affects general LIS professional education, too. As the market changes, LIS courses change to meet market needs. Within the context of specialist professional education for children's or schools' librarians, there is little prospect that the general pattern at first professional level will change significantly, with respect to specialist options. Evidence suggests that, although there are now few specialist modules on offer, there *are* some and the opportunity for students at both undergraduate, postgraduate, masters and doctorate level to undertake projects and research in some aspects of children's/ schools librarianship or children's literature is considerable and expanding. However, the still largely untapped and under-exploited areas are probably through opportunities for research and continuing education.

As *Investing in children* stated:

> There is a lack of hard evidence, drawn from well-conducted research, to demonstrate unequivocally that reading and library use make significant impacts on the personal, economic and educational achievemnt of children and young people, enabling the individual to make valuable and life-long contributions to society; that there are positive and wide-reaching benefits arising from the constructive use of leisure time in reading. (Department of National Heritage, 1995, p.16)

Clearly, a longitudinal study of the benefits of reading to children as they grow up, is needed, along the lines of the Bookstart research, but with children being tracked at various stages of their development. Hard evidence to support warm feelings about the value of libraries in the development of the child is, as yet, unavailable.

A partnership between interested LIS schools and practitioners, perhaps through ASCEL, is required to assess research needs within the sector and look at mechanisms for promoting a more structured, high quality professional continuing education programme targeted at those already working with or interested in working with children and young people.

Publishing and bookselling

A study of the current state of children's publishing and bookselling shows:

- a decline in public sector bookfunds, in schools and public libraries, at one time the mainstay of children's book publishing;
- a decline in schools library services;
- the far-reaching effects of the National Curriculum and Local Management of Schools;
- the potentially damaging effects, on publishing and library supply, of the ending of the Net Book Agreement

have all had significant effects on children's and educational book publishing. This has led to a decline in:

- hardback sales;
- opportunities for new authors;
- availability of backlists;
- heavy concentration on National Curriculum titles;
- the demise of a number of small publishers;
- the potential demise of a number of small booksellers and library suppliers.

This has been, in part compensated, as far as the publishers are concerned, by:

- a growth in paperback sales to public and school libraries;
- a growth in direct sales to schools, cutting out booksellers and library suppliers;
- a growth in bookfairs and mail order direct to children in school and at home.

Some of this is good news, some of it is bad news. But, with a few notable exceptions, there is little acknowledgment, among publishers, of the role of librarians, school or public, in advising or helping children in their choice of reading materials. This is a role publishers think that *they* have taken on. This decline in specialist knowledge of children's books among children's librarians is a potential worry, particularly in the volatile market and framework for libraries highlighted above. As one publisher of children's books stated: 'More and more, alas, I feel that libraries are rather static ways of getting books to children.'

General issues

The major issues, then, are concerned with the effect of government cutbacks, local government reorganization and political thinking on public libraries for children; the effect of educational change on public and school libraries and school library services; the implications of both on professional librarianship, education and training and publishing. There are also related issues such as the management of the relationship between the children's library and schools library services, the possible impact of externalization or contracting out.

There is inevitably a danger, however, of creating a 'feel bad' factor by emphasizing the problems facing children's and schools library services. It is as important to highlight good practice and the benefits that both can provide as it is to report on reductions in service or closures. Local government reorganization can provide *opportunities* as well as problems and it is entirely possible that continuing and newly formed authorities will take the opportunity to create and implement strategies for the coordinated delivery of children's and schools library services, as recommended in *Investing in children*.

A future role for the public library?

What of the future? The present, as outlined above, is uncertain, but clearly if literacy and access to information remain important, the availability of libraries also remains crucial, albeit in a changed role. The editors believe that libraries of all kinds and in whatever form will continue to exist. They believe that in any context, the role of the librarian as handler and manager of information; as trainer of others to use information effectively and efficiently; as evaluator of quality of information and information provision; as carer for user needs, will remain critical. It will need flexible, adaptable individuals who can manage change innovatively, imaginatively and proactively, recognizing new opportunities and grasping new challenges. This will require well-educated professionals, constantly developing through a varied programme of continuing professional and personal development.

They also believe that whatever happens in technological terms, reading and the book will remain significant. The book will retain all of the benefits it has over technology, seen probably most clearly in books for children. Electronic information still requires a sophisticated ability to read. Literacies will broaden to include visual and technological literacies. But **reading will remain the key**. Surfing the Internet is fine for the whizz kids but effective and efficient use of information networks will require **information navigators**, **information facilitators**: the librarians of the future.

What will the role of the public library be in the future? Will it survive? If so, in what form?

- Purely for leisure reading, the Mills and Boon and Point Horrors of the future?
- Purely as regional/grand information centres of the future (à la *Public library review*)?
- No local public libraries – networked information direct to the home?
- Purely to serve the business community?
- As educators of the future, following the demise of the universities?
- Will school libraries be the growth area?

Two senior education and children's librarians are adamant about a future role for libraries for children:

> If I had just one prime issue with which we had to be concerned, it would be literacy and the need for a literate citizenry. This would be a major political issue for every librarian, and the case and potential have never been greater . . . Whatever happens in the future – to technology, to education, to libraries – we have to be quite clear about the role and purpose of children's libraries. They must not be a low priority item on anyone's agenda and the politicians' and public's understanding of our services must be paramount. (Parker, 1992, p.86)

> Children's services are both too important to leave to the specialists and too important not to have a high quality core of specialist knowledge and experience. (Kempster, 1992a, p.522)

> The lure of information and allowing people to make informed choices about their lives is only half the story. What about imagination? What about ideas? In equal part, information and imagination are what public libraries should be about for a balanced enrichment of a local community. (Kempster, 1992b, p.5)

The Comedia Report was realistic about the environment within which public libraries will have to operate:

> Whilst the book will not disappear and will remain popular in all kinds of way, its relative position in relation to other media will change. The book, in fact, is in many cases an inferior and cumbersome tool for finding out what you want . . . Media literacy and computer literacy are now increasingly seen as necessary in a world in which people are bombarded with images and information – largely on air and on screen – throughout their waking hours. The ability to interpret, judge and understand the processes and meaning of the media environment are seen as essential. The ability to log on and operate computers . . . is today possibly as important as the ability to write with paper and pen. (Comedia, 1993, pp.69–70)

The role of IT and the need for a coherent IT structure is clearly a vital part of planning for the future of library services for children and young people. Access to the vast information resources of libraries will increasingly need to be from where children and young people are, i.e. schools, clinics, youth clubs and home via IT connections into libraries. This is fundamental to enabling the nation to have full and equal access to information in the future. Both the government and local authorities will have to acknowledge their need for investment in these areas.

The future of education

The future direction of education is clearly an issue, too, and will affect the role of libraries, both public and school.

Education 2000, a charitable foundation established in 1983, believes that the world is changing so radically and so rapidly that the education system needs to be completely overhauled in response: 'learning has to become a total environmental process. We can't leave it to the schools alone.' In *Learning makes sense: re-creating education for a changing future*, Director John Abbott lays out very clearly and very persuasively what this should mean and suggests that libraries as learning centres have to be pivotal in this new world view.

> Learning and schooling are not synonymous. Schools have a vital role in starting a dynamic process by which pupils are progressively weaned from their earlier dependence on teachers and institutions. They should be given the confidence to manage their own learning, to co-operate with colleagues and to use a range of resources and learning situations. But such skills, practices and attitudes cannot be taught solely in the classroom, nor can they be developed solely by teachers. Schooling in the future must involve both learning in school and learning through a variety of community experiences. Young people require a 'new learning environment', made up partly of formal schooling and partly of informal learning opportunities, so that they receive the support not only of teachers but of other adults. (Abbott, 1994, p.5)

Education 2000 emphasizes that education is for learning:

> The future belongs to those who know how to learn . . . how to learn whatever we need to know, alone or together with others; to participate confidently in a complex and rapidly changing world; to exercise autonomy with care and responsibility . . . in order to live an enriched, satisfying and productive life in the future. (Abbott, 1994, p.2)

> Real learning gets to the heart of what it means to be human . . . Through learning we recreate ourselves. Through learning we become able to do something we were never able to do. Through learning we perceive the world and our relationship to it. Through learning we extend our capacity to create, to be part of the generative process of life. There is within us a deep hunger for this type of learning. (Senge, 1990)

> It is critical that every child has so to learn how to learn that each develops a range of skills which can be applied with confidence to changing and unfamilar situations at any time in their lives. (Abbott, 1994, p.3)

For these editors, the role of libraries in that learning process is of the utmost importance both now and in the future.

REFERENCES

Abbott, J. (1994), *Learning makes sense: re-creating education for a changing future*. Letchworth, Education 2000.

Aslib (1995), *Review of the public library services in England and Wales: for the Department of National Heritage*. London, Aslib (The Association for Information Management).

Comedia (1993), *Borrowed time?: the future of public libraries in the UK*. London, Comedia.

Comedia Working Papers (1993), *Key themes and issues of the study*. The future of public libraries working paper 1. London, Comedia.

Department of National Heritage (1994), *Schools library services and financial delegation to schools: a report to the Department of National Heritage by Coopers & Lybrand*. The Department of National Heritage. Library and Information Series, no. 21.

Department of National Heritage (1995), *Investing in children: the future of library services for children and young people*. Library and Information Services Council (England) Working Party on Library Services for Children and Young People. London, HMSO.

Greenhalgh, E. and Worpole, K. (1995), *Libraries in a world of cultural change*. London, UCL Press.

Kempster, G. (1992a), 'Tomorrow's politicians need libraries now', in *Library Association record*, **94** (8), August 1992, 522–3.

Kempster, G. (1992b), 'Kids' stuff?: the future of library services', *Youth library review*, **13**, Spring 1992, 5–7.

Library Association (1995), Fundamental questions about the future of public libraries. Press release from the Library Association.

Parker, A. (1992), *International review of children's literature and librarianship*, **7** (2), 1992, 75–88.

School Libraries Group (1995), *School libraries and school library services: key issues and concerns*, Library Association, unpublished, December 1995.

Senge, P. (1990), *The fifth discipline*. New York: Doubleday Century.

Youth Libraries Group (1995), *Key issues and concerns 1995*, draft document, unpublished.

12

Postscript: Organizations associated with children's librarianship

Keith Barker

Throughout this book, reference has been made to a wide range of professional and non-professional organizations who have, as a common aim, the desire to support the literacy needs of children and young people. Some of these bodies are primarily concerned with the library profession; others support children's literature, reading, and the information needs of the child. In this respect they work with librarians but also with teachers, educationalists, parents and other adults concerned with young people.

The aim of this postscript is to offer a personal overview of the work of some of the bodies previously mentioned, giving some flavour of the qualities of each organization, furnishing further insights into their contribution to children's librarianship, and addressing a number of issues concerned with cooperation.

It would appear on the surface that nothing could be more straightforward than the cooperation of a number of organizations representing the needs of children and young people in their choice of reading material and their access to libraries. They are, after all, striving to achieve the same goal: to bring the highest standards to their client group. Surely it would not be impossible for these groups to work closely together? However, nothing could be further from the truth. A number of attempts have been made over the years to find some common ground for these various organizations and to provide some type of overarching structure. These attempts, although encouraged enthusiastically by the groups concerned, have failed to come to fruition. Why should this be so? One reason is that practically all groups connected with children and young people are surviving on the charitable goodwill of their members rather than on any constructive funding or even equal goodwill from any government. This is no doubt a reflection of the low esteem with which children are held by public fund providers, and the inadequate and uncertain funding which they attract, for organizations involved in this field have an unfortunate habit of disappearing. All these bodies do exist, although in various shades of healthiness.

Our examination will begin with those organizations connected with the UK Library Association. The Association itself has been a great supporter of library and literacy rights for children and young people, and as we know, has targeted many of its campaigns such as Library Power towards the needs of that group. It has also been instrumental in publishing guidelines both for public libraries and for school libraries (described in Chapter 3). While these have not been as widely adopted as was originally hoped, they do at least give some indication of the ideal towards which local authorities and schools should be working.

In 1994 The Library Association established a number of interest area committees to support the work of its Council. The Youth Libraries Sectoral Committee consists of representatives from three Library Association groups, the Youth Libraries Group, Schools Libraries Group and Education Libraries Group. Each member of The Library Association is eligible to become a member of any number of groups as long as they pay for this privilege.

The Youth Libraries Group (YLG) has a long and distinguished history as far as such organizations go. It has roots in the Association of Children's Librarians, established by Eileen Colwell in 1937. According to Robert Leeson, The Library Association looked on this as a sort of Communist plot. Nevertheless the small but growing band of children's librarians, those 'sympathetic and good-tempered' ladies the professional journals advertised for, were pioneers of change. They were learning, teaching each other and restoring to the children's book world some of the moral fibre it had lost (Leeson, 1985).

This spirit is still evident in YLG, although tempered with a realization of the world modern children inhabit. It is organized into a grouping of 11 branches representing the whole of the UK. Each branch has its own autonomy and will run courses and literary events for the membership of its own area. In addition, the central core committee, at which all branches are represented, organizes an annual conference which is attended by anyone interested in children's library work. It also has a healthy publications programme, publishing both monographs and sets of photographic posters. One of its major ventures is the selection of the winners of the Carnegie and Kate Greenaway medals annually. The administration of these highly prestigious awards is carried out by the Library Association and since 1991 the publicity for them has benefited enormously from the sponsorship of the Birmingham-based Peters Library Service. Indeed many branches use the services of library suppliers in planning and hosting their courses. This is an example of the ways two dissimilar organizations, with a common aim, have benefited each other through working together.

As well as its twice yearly journal, *Youth library review*, which contains, articles, reports from the YLG branches, news items, reviews and correspondence, a supplementary *Newsletter* was launched in 1996. This appears in summer and winter, complementing the news sections in the spring and autumn issues of *Youth library review*, and is distributed to local branches. The YLG is often consulted both by the Library Association and by outside organizations, particularly the media, on matters concerning literature and library provision for children and young people.

The School Libraries Group (SLG) of the Library Association is a more recent organization but it has quickly established itself as a spokesperson for the turbulent world of education. SLG is not organized regionally apart from in a few areas but it still makes a distinct impression nationally, mainly through its annual conference. Professional librarians in schools have taken a severe knocking in recent years both through the introduction of Local Management of Schools (LMS) and particularly through the dismemberment of school library services as a result of local government reorganization. It remains to be seen if the impending local government reorganization will be the final nail in the coffin for many school library services. However, the SLG will no doubt be fighting all along the way for this not to happen. In this respect, it will be helped by such organizations as CENTRAL, a voluntary organization set up to fight the savage cuts in libraries and which is discussed below.

The organization most often confused with SLG is the School Library Association (SLA). Founded in 1937, the SLA has a very distinct role which distinguishes it from the Library Association groups. It was established to further the cause of libraries in schools rather than those administered by school library services. Consequently the main body of its membership comprises teacher- librarians rather than professionally qualified librarians. The Association still sees itself as an organization whose main aim is to support the lone librarian in a school who is inevitably going to be a teacher and who has, among other responsibilities, the task of running the library. However, it will remain an organization consulted by and involved with professional librarians.

Unlike the Library Association groups, it has a main office staffed on an office-hours basis as well as a committee consisting of professionals who take on SLA responsibilities in their spare time. A very healthy publications programme has been established which is indicative of the fact that it employs a publications officer and a publications secretary. One major series which has been published is its set of guidelines to various aspects of school libraries: these are short, pithy introductions to practical aspects of a teacher-librarian's work. The Association also publishes a quarterly journal, *The school librarian*, which is highly regarded and whose review coverage is more extensive than any comparable British journal. As well as an annual conference, it also runs a series of training days which are administered centrally through the SLA office.

The regional organization of the SLA is carried out through its network of branches which covers most of the UK; these branches have their own events, both evening and day events. The main contact SLA has with the Library Association groups and with other relevant organizations is through half-yearly meetings where common concerns are discussed and where the organizations relate events and publications which are of interest to each other.

One of the organizations which attends this meeting is the recently formed Association of Children's, Schools and Education Librarians (ASCEL). This has been formed from three previous groups, AMDECL which had a membership from metropolitan district authorities, SOCCEL which covered county libraries and YELL which consisted of London librarians. The membership of these groups consisted of the heads of children's library services, some of whom are more involved with council committee work than with the daily administration of children's libraries. This makes for a very different viewpoint from the membership of the previous groups already mentioned. ASCEL is not responsible to any official body and so therefore has more ability to be critical of organizations like The Library Association. However, this lack of official status means that it is less likely to be consulted by government and other bodies. The Association does produce a valuable *Newsletter* which collates information about current developments in children's librarianship nationally and within authorities. As it has only recently been formed, it is too early to say whether ASCEL is going to be more effective than its predecessors in gaining recognition.

In a similar way, the independent group, CENTRAL (Children's Education Needs Teaching Resources and Libraries) is able to make statements and protests without being responsible to a particular official body. CENTRAL was set up by the children's writer Mary Hoffman as a national campaign to save school libraries in the UK. She has successfully gained the support of a large number of organizations, perhaps because her campaign has a specific purpose in mind rather than just being vaguely about children and reading. It is a pressure group which is determined that school library services shall not be completely destroyed by local authority cuts, and hopefully other groups will continue to support it.

Those, then, are the groups specifically concerned with libraries for children and young people. However, there is also a variety of other organizations concerned with promoting children's books, each with its own agenda. The most influential organization concerned with children and their reading should be Young Book Trust (YBT) but for a number of reasons it has been less than influential in the past in determining policy and influencing significant organizations. YBT is part of Book Trust, the organization established as the National Book League. It has had a chequered history. Set up in 1988 as the Children's Book Foundation and to a great flurry of high hopes, it had three directors in as many years until Wendy Cooling gave the organization some stability and vision. In the early 1990s, the Book Trust found itself in financial difficulties and decided to reorganize the structure of the Foundation with the loss of the Director. Hopefully with a new name, the YBT, which firmly establishes it as an integral part of Book Trust and with a dynamic new director, Lindsey Fraser, the successor to the Foundation should begin to make a greater impression on the book world.

What did the Children's Book Foundation achieve? It continued some of the work which had been undertaken with children's books before its establishment, including Children's Book Week. This is still highly successful in libraries although a certain razzmatazz some years (travelling trains and roadshows) hardly gave it the publicity it sometimes (rather naïvely in many cases) craved. Until recently, the annual Children's Books of the Year was selected and exhibited through the auspices of the Foundation, continuing through the work of Julia Eccleshare, the impetus established by such doyennes of the children's book world as Elaine Moss and Naomi Lewis.

One of the most valuable aspects of its work has been the provision of an information service both through personal enquiries and through its increasingly wide range of book lists provided by the Trust's librarian. The Trust has also for some years initiated a scheme whereby institutions can subscribe to Bookfax. This is an extremely useful and regularly updated folder containing all types of information about children's books. In this way the Trust has acted as an unofficial central body coordinating information about children and their reading. The recent successful bid for National Lottery funding means that this database will be able to expand significantly in future years.

Another achievement was the Bookstart project (Cooling, 1992), now successfully trialled in a number of areas of the UK and administered through children's libraries. This is a scheme whereby at nine months, each child in the area is given a pack containing a book, information about reading (often in community languages) and an introduction to their local library. Research is still being carried out on the early recipients of the first Bookstart packs but indications are that it has been successful in establishing reading with families who might not normally be expected to consider it as a viable option. In 1995 Sunderland Libraries received the Library Association/Holt Jackson communities initiative award for its contribution to the Bookstart project.

Despite these obvious successes, YBT and its predecessor have received a substantial amount of criticism. The major problem is that it inevitably has to try to be all things to all people. Publishers, many of whom are asked to pay an annual subscription to support the Trust, feel that it should be taking more of a lead in integrating the work of the many organizations connected with children and reading. They often compare it to its counterparts in Australia and the USA where a great deal more publicity is generated about children's book events, including national television coverage. Librarians and teachers look to YBT for advice and support on a number of areas and because of the limited resources the Trust has, sometimes find those areas poorly represented. The Trust itself is keen to promote itself to parents, often appearing at exhibitions where it can talk directly to parents and provide book lists and advice for a group which often feels isolated and unaware. All these aspects are highly commendable but if many arts organizations work on a shoestring, YBT has to work on an even smaller shoestring while it tries to successfully satisfy the demands of all these disparate groups. Much of the Trust's money is obtained through donations or through the Arts Council, itself an organization where the literature department is poorly funded, and therefore is not able to staff an organization which could provide all the possible facilities. Its director is based in Scotland and its staff of four (who also provide an excellent library service in Book Trust's Wandsworth home) are divided between London and Edinburgh. If large projects like the Bookstart are contemplated, sponsorship has to be sought from a wealthy outside body. At one time the suggestion was made that the Children's Book Foundation (as it then was) should act as a clearing house for information provided by all the various children's book organizations: however, a great deal more financial assistance would have to be provided if that were ever to become reality.

One of the major problems of the children's book world is that it has no national body which can speak to, for example, government departments in an authoritative way. An expectation of the Arts Council of England is that it should have the power to do this. However, the literature department of the Council is small and it is given a miniscule proportion of the budget with which to service the literature needs of the whole community. Since 1991 it has run a very successful biennial children's literature summer school at Westminster College, Oxford in conjunction with W H Smith (Beeson, 1993 and 1995). This venture apart, the Arts Council does not have a major commitment to children's books other than through the occasional support of research projects (Lonsdale and Everitt, 1996) and the provision of its regional offices which have often worked with local regions on large projects. Often, however, the amount of provision given to such proposals depends very much on the interests of the regional officers. The Well Worth Reading project began with this collaboration.

The lack of a central organization specifically concerned with children's reading means that there are a number of groups, each with its own specialist interest, which often work in isolation from each other. The Publishers Association has a group of children's publishers as a specialist body. This group has worked with other organizations, for example the Youth Libraries Group, in ensuring closer links. However, as publishers do not have to belong to the Association, there are inevitably gaps, such as the lack of a major player like Walker Books, which mean that coverage is not as comprehensive as it might be.

The children's group of the Booksellers Association is a more comprehensive and powerful body, particularly with regard to its specialist children's booksellers but obviously has its own agenda and its own viewpoint, which may well clash with the less commercial interests of other organizations. There is also in existence a group called the Children's Book Circle which is a body of individuals who pay an annual fee and which holds regular, London-based meetings. However, because of its locality it is dominated by publishers, so that librarians, teachers or even individuals just interested in children's books feel that they are acting as disseminators of information to the publishing profession rather than initiating well-balanced debate.

Away from trade or arts organizations, there are a number of groups involved in work with children's reading whose role adds a different dimension to the field. One of the most significant of these is the Federation of Children's Book Groups (Bates, 1994). This was established 30 years ago by Anne Wood who felt there were large numbers of parents who wanted to know more about children's books but who felt they were unqualified to join any other organizations. The Federation has therefore relied on the voluntary support of interested parents for the whole of its existence. This has both advantages and disadvantages. The major advantage is that the parents who want to become involved in such an organization are keen and interested and willing to give up much spare time for a cause about which they have deep feelings. They are also non-partisan and are listened to by institutions who would feel professional organizations have a vested interest in any campaign. The disadvantages are that, as with any such organization, those who do become active in it tend to be articulate, white and middle class and quite often professionals already involved with children, such as teachers and librarians. A core group (groups are normally organized around a particular locality) will rise or fall according to the commitment of its members some of whom may have been part of the Federation for some time and indeed may themselves no longer be parents of young people under 16. Nevertheless, this should not detract from much of the good work the Federation does. Its annual awards are the biggest to be judged primarily by children and has, through sponsorship, managed to raise their profile quite significantly. It also holds an annual conference and an annual National Tell A Story Week. Through its branches, it regularly holds author and illustrator events and is instrumental in getting children and creators of their books together. It produces a journal, in 1995 re-launched and re-christened *Carousel*, which provides an alternative way of looking at books. Its approach is direct and unfussy and any children's librarian would do well to attract the sort of enthusiasm the Federation inspires in their locality.

A variety of other organizations exist whose work is either mainly or partially concerned with children's reading matter, many of which are more linked to the world of education. There are two major literacy organizations, the National Literacy Association originally called 99x99 because its aim was to get 99 per cent of the world reading by 1999, and the National Literacy Trust which was set up by Sir Simon Hornby shortly before he retired as Chief Executive of W H Smith.

Obviously the briefs of these two organizations are wider than just children's books, although this is bound to be an aspect of their work. Organizations connected specifically with reading include the United Kingdom Reading Association (UKRA) and the National Association for the Teaching of English (NATE). These are both mainly teacher-orientated. The Reading and Language Information Centre which is attached to Reading University has a tradition of being a great support mainly to teachers who are interested in all aspects of reading but in recent years has taken on a wider remit. It has an extensive publications programme of pamphlets many of which will be of interest to other professionals interested in children's literature and it offers an advisory service as well as providing a reference library of publications concerned with reading.

Of the other teacher organizations, the National Association for Special Educational Needs (NASEN) is notable for including in its annual awards a recent one for a children's book which shows children with special needs in a positive way.

One organization which is also concerned with children with special needs is the National Library for the Handicapped Child (NLHC) and its Reach Resource Centre (Spiers, 1996). This is, as its name suggests, a reference library containing all types of material intended to be used by children with special needs. It can be visited by anyone interested in seeing what type of material exists for these special requirements. Much of the material is imported and often demonstrates the lack of resources available in the UK to those searching for books and other formats suitable for the 20% of the child population designated by the government as having special needs. The NLHC also works closely with other agencies and, having a clearly defined focus, often finds itself able to provide the type of inter-organizational cooperation which should be the ideal of similar groups. It has produced booklists and other material, including a number of attractive posters, which help to promote its philosophy. However, like many of the organizations discussed in this chapter, the NLHC is a voluntary organization which depends on funding for its survival. Its future is constantly under threat. It was set up under the auspices of the Enid Blyton Trust because Imogen Smallwood, Blyton's daughter, who had contracted polio as a child, was particularly involved in the project. However, in 1995 the Trust found itself unable to support the annual funding it had provided since the mid-1980s and so the NLHC has had to seek funding elsewhere.

Two international organizations have representatives from the UK, although one of them, IBBY (The International Board on Books for Young People), has had problems in the past finding support, both moral and financial. IBBY was founded in 1953 with the express object of linking national organizations internationally. It holds an annual congress where its 60 member countries discuss similarities and differences in their aim at bringing children and quality books together. It produces a quarterly journal, *Bookbird*, and also is responsible for the annual Hans Christian Andersen Award for a writer and an illustrator (although few British people have won this). The UK was a fairly active member of IBBY until the late 1980s when the group foundered both because of a lack of support for the committee members who were doing their best to keep the organization afloat and because of another major feature, funding. The annual subscription to IBBY is estimated on the basis of the number of children's titles published in that country. As the UK's annual figure is now around 7000 titles (more even than the USA), the subscription is £3000 per year.

However, there has been an upsurge of interest in reviving the IBBY British section mainly due to the enthusiasm of the writer Alison Leonard who attended an IBBY Congress and was shocked to find little representation from the UK. The new IBBY section is obviously keen to get as many interested parties involved as possible and has already established a regular pattern of meetings and conferences. Hopefully this new impetus will take the UK into the midst of the international scene and make it less insular-looking.

The International Federation of Library Associations (IFLA) also has an interest in work with children's libraries under the blanket of its school libraries section and its public libraries section. The latter is currently involved in producing a set of guidelines for children's and young people's libraries, although with the very great differences in provision throughout the world this can be a difficult operation. The UK has a place on this group through the auspices of The Library Association; in recent years this has been organized both through the Schools Library Group and the Youth Libraries Group which also made a financial contribution for attendance at the annual conference.

That, then, is the present. What of the future? It can be seen from the above that there is an enormous amount of enthusiasm and goodwill available for the aspect of library provision, with a wide variety of individuals giving up much spare time for a cause in which they sincerely believe. However, it can also be seen that many of the organizations for which they are working so keenly are foundering due to lack of financial resources. There can be no vision for the future if any organization lives so precariously each year. Unfortunately, children and books are neither very glamorous subjects, except when a political party is trying to score points. There is some duplication going on in all these organizations, which a coordinating body could bring together while still helping to leave the various groups with their individuality. Efforts to bring these organizations together have foundered, usually through a lack of financial resources. A proposed conference was cancelled after it was felt the conference theme would have to be so broad to attract all the disparate groups that it would end up by being attractive to none of them. Perhaps the answer for greater cooperation will lie in electronic communication. There already exist on the Internet a number of American groups connected with children's reading and children's libraries (Armstrong, 1996); surely a UK equivalent will soon be on its way. Unfortunately this will take away much of the personal contact which is an important part of what already exists. However, it will help to provide the type of cooperation which all these groups have been seeking for some time.

REFERENCES

Armstrong, C. (1990), 'Threads from the Web: Internet sites for YLR readers', *Youth library review*, 21, Spring, 44–5.

Bates, S. (1994), 'The Federation of Children's Book Groups and Libraries', *Youth library review*, 18, Autumn 25–6.

Beeson, L. (1993), 'Ways into reading – quality and diversity in children's literature', *Youth library review*, 16, Autumn, 11–14.

Beeson, L. (1995), 'A letter to Alex', *Youth library review*, 20, Autumn, 14–21.

Cooling, W. (1992), 'Bookstart: a project to encourage parents to share books with their babies', *Youth library review*, 14, Autumn, 20–1.

Lonsdale, R. and Everitt, J. (1996), 'Breaking down the barriers: the provision of modern foreign language material to young people in public libraries in the UK', *Journal of librarianship and information science*, 28 (2), June, 71–81.

Leeson, R. (1985), *Reading and righting*. London, Collins.

Spiers, D. (1996), 'Reach Resource Centre', *Youth library review*, 21, Spring, 29–30.

ORGANIZATIONS DISCUSSED

Arts Council
14 Great Peter Street
London SW1P 3NQ

ASCEL
c/o Steve Hird
Maltby Library HQ
High Street
Maltby
Rotherham
South Yorkshire S66 8LA

Book Trust
45 East Hill
Wandsworth
London SW18 2QZ

Booksellers Association
Minster House
272 Vauxhall Bridge Road
London SW1V 1BA

CENTRAL
28 Crouch Hall Road
London N8 8HJ

Children's Book Circle
c/o Anne Marley
Children's and Schools' Services
Hampshire County Library
81 North Walls
Winchester SO23 8BY

Federation of Children's Book
Groups
c/o Alison Dick
6 Bryce Place
Currie
Mid Lothian EH14 5LR

IBBY
c/o Children's Literature Research Centre
Downshire House
Roehampton Lane
London SW15 4HT

IFLA
c/o The Library Association
7 Ridgmount Street
London WC1E 7AE

NASEN
4/5 Amber Business Village
Amington
Tamworth
Staffs B77 4RP

NATE
50 Broadfield Road
Broadfield Business Centre
Sheffield S8 0XJ

National Library for the Handicapped
  Child
Reach Resource Centre
Wellington House
Wellington Road
Wokingham
Berkshire RG40 2AG

National Literacy Association
5 Airspeed Road
Priory Industrial Park
Christchurch
Dorset BH23 4HD

National Literacy Trust
1A Grosvenor Gardens
London SW1W 0BD

Publishers Association Children's
Group
19 Bedford Square
London WC1B 3HJ

Reading and Language
Information Centre
Bulmershe Court
Earley
Reading RG6 1HYS

School Libraries Group
c/o The Library Association
7 Ridgmount Street
London WC1E 7AE

School Library Association
Liden Library
Barrington Close
Liden
Swindon
Wiltshire SN3 6HF

UKRA
Warrington Road CP School
Naylor Road
Widnes
Cheshire WA8 0BP

Young Book Trust (see Book
Trust)

Youth Libraries Group
c/o The Library Association
7 Ridgmount Street
London WC1E 7AE

Index